Praise for P

No one is better placed than Au   ist
Neil Chenoweth to cast a sceptica   ey
corporate scene, connecting the d₀   ne
reader to connect even more; [*Packer's Lunch*] is an exegesis of major
importance, analysing with equal care power, greed and influence.

Sydney Morning Herald

[Chenoweth] does much more . . . than simply make sense of the
tangled transactions and furtive finances of his protagonists, the book's
great achievement being its ability to weave its disparate strands into a
broader narrative that takes in the political and cultural spheres as well
as the corporate. This is a book about the shifting sands of the power
structure within Australian society.

Australian Book Review

Chenoweth has performed for us . . . a literary pillorying where he,
happy man, gets to throw all the ordure and the rotten vegies. It is deeply
cathartic and satisfying.

Australian Financial Review Magazine

A brilliant exposition of business at the top end of town.

The Launceston Examiner

Neil Chenoweth

PACKER'S LUNCH

A rollicking tale of Swiss bank accounts and money-making adventurers in the roaring '90s

ALLEN&UNWIN

First published in 2006
This edition published in 2007

Allen & Unwin
83 Alexander Street
Crows Nest NSW 2065
Australia
Phone: (61 2) 8425 0100
Fax: (61 2) 9906 2218
Email: info@allenandunwin.com
Web: www.allenandunwin.com

National Library of Australia
Cataloguing-in-Publication entry:

Chenoweth, Neil.
    Packer's lunch.

    Includes index.
    ISBN 978 1 74175 323 3 (pbk.).

    1. Packer, Kerry, 1937-2005. 2. Kennedy, Trevor.
    3. Richardson, Graham, 1949- . 4. Rivkin, Rene, 1944-2005.
    5. Capitalism and mass media - Australia. 6. Capitalists and
    financiers - Australia - Biography. 7. Stockbrokers -
    Australia - Biography. 8. Australia - Economic conditions -
    1990-2001. 9. Australia - Economic conditions - 2001- .
    I. Title.

332.60994

Typeset in 12/15pt Granjon by Midland Typesetters, Australia
Printed and bound in Australia by Griffin Press

10 9 8 7 6 5 4 3 2

Contents

Part five: The rise of the suits

Part six: A change of cutlery

Acknowledgements

This book is a story about networks. Its focus is not the activities of the Packer family. Rather, it is about the people who from time to time have managed to find a seat at the Packer table. It follows the varying fortunes of some of these dinner guests.

I am deeply grateful for the assistance and friendship of Shraga Elam, whose work has had such a dramatic effect on the way offshore trading is understood in Australia; of Ali Cromie, who mixes outstanding investigative skills with a rare generosity of spirit; and Andrew Main, Colleen Ryan and Rosemarie Graffagnini at the *Australian Financial Review*.

Deborah Light started me on this book by lending me her copy of *Corporate Cannibals*, which I have cunningly managed to avoid returning. I'm in the debt of my publisher and editor at the *AFR*, Michael Gill and Glenn Burge. My thanks also to Tony Byrne, Richard Coleman, Philip Cornford, Alan Deans, Fiona Buffini, Angus Grigg, Roger Johnstone, Kate McClymont, Julie Macken, Karen Maley, Anne Noonan, Bill Pheasant, Jeni Porter, Jimmy Tsimikas and Brook Turner as well as the many others who spoke to me off the record.

At Allen & Unwin it was a pleasure to work with Richard Walsh, Patrick Gallagher and Alex Nahlous. My thanks to my agent, the estimable John F. Thornton, who, in the event that he lived in Penzance, would clearly be a pirate. My family has been a continual support for me, in particular my wife Joëlle.

For my parents
Joan Brooks the 'plain-speaking woman'
and Norm Chenoweth, whose Thai name was Dr Loud Laugh.

Everything about her was at once vigorous and exquisite, at once strong and fine. He had a confused sense that she must have cost a great deal to make, that a great many dull and ugly people must, in some mysterious way, have been sacrificed to make her.

Edith Wharton
The House of Mirth, 1905

Lunch (ln), sb. 1 Obs. exc. Dial. Also 5 lonche. [App. Onomatopoeic. Cf DUNCH sb.] *The sound made by the fall of a soft heavy body* . . . She heard a lunch, bud she thoht it was th' childer plaayin'.

OXFORD ENGLISH DICTIONARY

Oh, better far to live and die
Under the brave black flag I fly,
Than play a sanctimonious part
With a pirate head and a pirate heart.
Away to the cheating world go you,
Where pirates all are well-to-do;
But I'll be true to the song I sing,
And live and die a Pirate King.

W.S. Gilbert and A. Sullivan
Pirates of Penzance, 1880

Introduction

November 2003

There are moments in every man's life when circumstances turn against him. Adversity faces him on every side, even his own friends look at him askance and he must take matters into his own hands to strike out boldly in new directions. Moments, in short, when he has no other course but to book into a thoroughly expensive luxury hotel. As Trevor Kennedy flew into Heathrow airport in November 2003, he was facing one of those moments. In the early hours of Saturday morning, London is a cheerless desert for the lone wayfarer. Friendless, fatigued and forlorn, Kennedy made the best of it and headed for a friendly haven. He took himself to Piccadilly and booked into the Ritz.

For just on a century, the Ritz has been a beacon for weary travellers. It offers quiet elegance, historical glamour and an uptown address. Since the renovations in the late 1990s, its superior suites have offered an even more disgraceful level of opulence and comfort. A deluxe hotel room is a wondrous thing. It offers reassurance, entertainment, refreshment and rather a lot of soft furnishings. The interior designers had done their work with such steely determination that whatever disaster, mayhem or carnage may unfold in the room, it will always be against a backdrop of good taste and a fine colour scheme.

Kennedy, always one to mind his pennies, appears to have settled for a basic room, a 'Superior Single' in Ritz-speak—which still says a lot, even though the Ritz saves its best work for the 'Super King' and 'Deluxe King'. The Ritz claims no two of its rooms are alike, which only goes to show how many different things you can do with blue, yellow, peach and pink. The details are important, because there must surely be some hint in the decor to explain the debacle that followed. As Kennedy was shown up to his room on 1 November, he was hours away from doing something desperately silly. That's the downside of hotel rooms, which they never mention in the brochure. For all their comfort, they're hellishly dangerous. It's a truth about hotels that anxious mothers and head porters have known for millennia. Peril lurks among the bath towels, disaster beckons from the clothes' cabinet. We will not speak of the bar fridge. Strange and dire things happen in hotel rooms, and the further you are from home, the more dangerous life in one can become. It's not a physical danger. It's just that alone in a hotel room many people feel an overpowering urge to be . . . indiscreet. They do things which the next morning they wish they hadn't.

To be fair, Kennedy had a grave disadvantage when facing personal catastrophe: he was a former media executive. Worse than that, he was a former journalist. It's a measure of the man, though, that he had surmounted these natural disabilities to become, at sixty-one years of age, a pillar of Sydney society. Everybody liked Trevor. He had a larrikin charm and a bullish vitality, tempered with a rather inept and endearing manner when he was trying to please, which carried him over many hurdles. It was also rather comforting that Trevor was no oil painting. He had the balding head and heavy glasses that go with a caricature of a chartered accountant, which he wasn't. Under stress he had a habit of patting down his remaining hair at the back, as if to ensure his head had not fallen off. But behind the appearance, Trevor Kennedy was smart, and he was decisive. In his forties he had run Kerry Packer's media and investment empire for six years. He had survived an acrimonious split from Packer in 1991, and in a town where Packer's network often decided who succeeded and who failed, he had thereafter rebuilt his contacts and his life and made his fortune.

In the course of reinventing himself, Kennedy had become the quintessential Sydney success story of the 1990s. He was everything a senior member of Sydney society's A-list should be: a seamless combination of money, power and presence. Kennedy moved effortlessly in so many worlds. He had extensive political contacts. He sat on the board of Qantas. As chairman of Oil Search he effectively controlled most of the oil and gas resources of Papua New Guinea. When he was a hot prospect to head the ABC in 2002, even the prime minister was rooting for Trevor. Kennedy knew everyone. But as it turned out, not everyone really knew Trevor. Which is how he came to be booking into the Ritz at a godforsaken time on a Saturday morning in late 2003.

Two days before, on Thursday 30 October, Kennnedy had picked up a copy of the newspaper on which he had worked more than thirty years ago, the *Australian Financial Review*, to find details of his Swiss bank accounts splashed across the front page. A year before, he had written to the Zurich District Attorney's office about these accounts. Israeli journalist Shraga Elam had obtained copies of his letters, which were now plastered across the *Financial Review*. It was all there: his careful descriptions of how he kept no records of his Swiss bank dealings in Australia, his multiple accounts, and his horror that the information would be revealed to Australian authorities: 'This would be catastrophic for me and totally unjust.'

The revelations continued on the Friday as the *Financial Review* published further damning material about secret share trading by Kennedy's friend Rene Rivkin. The trading was the key to a corporate whodunnit called Offset Alpine—a tangled story of a printing press, a fire, an insurance payout and a multimillion-dollar money trail that led to Zurich. Mixed in with that was another, darker tale about the murder of a Sydney model.

As a solid press phalanx gathered outside both men's houses, Kennedy made his move. He booked a flight to London, slipped past the press cordon around his home and headed for the airport. Late on the Friday afternoon a *Daily Telegraph* journalist spotted him in the departure lounge at Mascot. Kennedy was on his way to Zurich . . . via London. It would add six hours of flying time to his journey, but it would ensure anonymity. He would stay Saturday night at the Ritz, then fly to Switzerland on Sunday or Monday. As passport control at Zurich does not stamp passports on internal European flights, his passport would show only that he arrived in Britain. On Monday morning he would walk the few streets from his hotel in Zurich to the offices of his Swiss lawyer, Benno Hafner, on Genferstrasse. Kennedy had left instructions with his secretary in Sydney to work out the meeting time.

The first piece of bad news for Kennedy when he got to the Ritz was that Hafner couldn't see him on Monday because he wouldn't be there. Hafner was in Geneva and was then travelling on to Paris. Tuesday was the earliest he could meet Kennedy. Until then Kennedy had nowhere to go, and nothing to do but wait. He was tired, jetlagged and anxious, and stranded at the Ritz for three days. Back in Australia, the *Financial Review* had published a third instalment of the story, including copies of cheques, share-trading ledgers and bank statements from a Swiss account operated by Labor Party powerbroker Graham Richardson. The *Financial Review* kept referring to other names in the documents.

This is the point where hotel decor becomes an issue. It's one thing for the weary traveller to hang up his boots gratefully for the night at the local hostelry. It's another thing when there is nowhere else to go. Kennedy had business that kept him occupied through Saturday, but then there was Saturday night, then Sunday, and all Monday. He would not fly to Zurich until Tuesday morning. There he was, stuck in a tastefully decorated box for seventy-two hours. Disoriented by jetlag. Nowhere to go, doing the little things you do in a strange hotel room: trying the television, turning off the television, checking the bar fridge, looking through the complimentary toiletries, calling room service. And all the time thinking about the crisis that had brought him here.

He had made it quite clear to the Zurich DA's office the previous year, when he was interviewed as part of an investigation into embezzlement by an executive at Bank Leumi le-Israel, that he thought it was terribly unfair he should be dragged into the affair. He had done nothing wrong. He was the victim of an embezzlement. It was Bank Leumi's fault for not overseeing their people as they should. 'Why do I have to be the victim of their incompetence?' he had said. He would repeat it unhappily two weeks after the *Financial Review* story in 2003, when he resigned all his public directorships, including his board seats at Qantas and Oil Search, giving up nearly half a million dollars in director fees: 'I believe I have done nothing unlawful,' he said.

The worst thing was, Kennedy had no copies of his Swiss correspondence in Australia—'I kept absolutely no records,' he told the DA—so he could not even be sure whether the quotes in the *Financial Review* were right or wrong. The Offset Alpine affair had unfolded more than eight years before, after which anyone's memory would grow fuzzy. While no one knows what was going through Kennedy's mind in the hotel room, it had to be a mixture of anger, indignation, and something close to panic.

There is a certain inevitability in the sequence of events that followed. As he was looking and pacing, Kennedy found himself at one of the handsome Georgian writing desks that grace each room of the Ritz. They are really quite comfortable and very amenable to writing. What could be more natural than to take up the handy pen lying there, and to scribble down some rough notes on the pad of Ritz notepaper about what happened in the Offset Alpine saga, so as to get it straight in his own mind? Kennedy the journalist was taking over. He grew up living with the written word. Writing is the apologetic of the modern celebrity. I exist, therefore I write and am written about. And that fierce obsession to impress his own order upon the world, to take control of the story, kept him going for a page of dot points until he ran short of inspiration and returned to brooding.

At least that's how I see it. I had been trying for weeks to puzzle out the inner psyche of Trevor John Kennedy. Along the way the *Financial Review* team had given him a codename. It was a pathetic attempt at secrecy, to keep the details of our investigation secret in that most public of spaces, the middle of a major newsroom. Trevor Kennedy we called Kevin—Big Kev. Rene Rivkin was Ralph. No one ever found a repeatable nickname for Graham Richardson. He was referred to as the Other Guy, or He Who Must Not Be Named. Or just Richo.

Some of Kennedy's jottings were cryptic; others hard to read. There was a name and also a telephone number. Later, Kennedy would tell the Australian Federal Court that his dominant purpose in making the notes was to ask legal advice from Hafner—a claim which the Court of Appeal rejected. Whatever the reason for writing, when Kennedy checked out of the Ritz on Tuesday 4 November he ripped the page out and took it with him. Then, like the seasoned traveller he was, he slipped the notepad with the Ritz letterhead into his bag as well. He flew to Zurich in the fever dream of international travel and wrote another page of dot points on Hotel Florhof notepaper. Those days were 'just a blur in my mind,' he said later. While he would remember making the notes, he had no idea when he did it.

Back in Sydney, the Australian Securities and Investments Commission had launched an investigation into the *Financial Review* revelations. After negotiations with editor Glenn Burge, ASIC subpoenaed me under Section 19 of the *ASIC Act* to give sworn evidence in a private examination on Thursday 6 November. The orders required me to produce the Swiss documents obtained by Shraga Elam, which were the basis of the *Financial Review* stories. In later conversations ASIC officers asked for home and office addresses for Rivkin, Richardson and Kennedy. It was clear the next step would be search warrants. 'You don't have to be Einstein to work that out,' Justice Roger Gyles commented later in the Federal Court. Kennedy flew back into Sydney on Monday 10 November. Three days later, at 7.25 on Thursday morning, the Australian Federal Police appeared at his home. The visit would have been perfectly straightforward—as it was in other searches taking place across the city at the Rivkin and Richardson homes, their offices and Rivkin's luxury boat, the *Dajoshadita*—except that Trevor and Christina Kennedy didn't answer the door.

The three Federal Police officers despatched to the house in Elamang Avenue, Kirribilli, rang the bell for ten minutes without result. In subsequent witness statements they said that eventually they concluded no one was home and called their office to arrange for a private locksmith to open the door. This meant further delays, calling in state police to supervise. The rest of the search team, who had been waiting discreetly around the corner, now emerged. For the next hour, nine Federal Police and ASIC officers milled about in front of the house while they waited for reinforcements and the locksmith. It turned out the locksmith would not be needed, for Trevor and Christina were inside. Trevor had called his law firm, Atanaskovic Hartnell. Lance Sachs, a mergers and acquisitions partner who had never met Kennedy but who happened to be free and in at work early, was despatched in a taxi to Elamang Avenue to supervise the search and advise the Kennedys of their rights. Until Sachs showed up, his clients were perfectly entitled to sit quietly and wait for their lawyer. In the meantime, the police waiting outside were not aware of the Kennedys' presence.

Across Sydney, media organisations were hearing the first whispers that a major police search operation was underway. In the following hours press cordons would form outside the homes of Rivkin, Richardson and Kennedy. By that stage they must have been becoming used to it. 'From the moment [the *Financial Review* story] appeared there were television cameras, photographers, journalists stalking my house, my office, my family,' Kennedy later told ASIC officers. 'If you haven't been through one of these things, I wouldn't expect you to understand, but let me tell you, it's a hell of an experience.'

Actually, by now Rivkin, Richardson and Kennedy were no longer the main story. The rumour machine at the big end of town had moved on from the revelations about the three amigos to speculate on what other names the *Financial Review* was sitting on. There were two other big names to come out in Rivkin's Zurich network. No, it was eight. Then twelve. Sixteen. Rivkin had had fifty numbered client accounts in the 1980s, including some of the biggest names in politics.

The speculation made little difference to Trevor Kennedy. He had spent much of the previous two weeks in limbo: killing time in hotel rooms, airport departure lounges, lawyers' offices and now this final indignity beside his wife in their silent house, with the police at the door. What emotions and thoughts gripped the Kennedys during this latest interlude only they knew. To an outside observer the issue is a simpler one: how had it come to this? How had one of the most powerful figures in Australian business been reduced to such a peculiar position? What did the Swiss bank documents mean, and how had so many people come to be caught up with them?

This book follows the trail of events in the 1990s which led up to the awkward scene at the Kennedy home. It is about the rivers of power and influence which shape Australian society, and the people who navigate them. The Offset Alpine scandal was something more than a ruckus about some questionable share trading. This was about a way of life. A whole class of business figures was accustomed to operating in the world of nominee companies and blind trusts in the Bahamas, Liechtenstein, Hong Kong, Monaco, the British Virgin Islands, the Dutch Antilles and Switzerland as deftly as they plied Australia's social networks. It is the side of Australian business that no one talks about. It is not necessarily illegal or improper. But it is a world of perilous secrets, a private universe divided between winners and losers: those who dine out on the rewards and those who become part of the menu. In an age of conspicuous consumption, the richest pickings were often found on the edges of orthodox deals made by the Packer family. Even a crumb from a Packer deal could hoist a minor player many rungs up the economic food chain.

The feeding pattern in this secret world played out against a wider tapestry, as Australia came to terms with a new economic order at the turn of the millennium. The excesses of the 1980s had left the country's old institutions crumbling; the new institutions that would take their place were still forming. A wider generational transfer of power among an ageing population of Australians hung in the balance. The book begins with the incident in 1990 when Kerry Packer signalled that the party was over; a landmark moment which nonetheless provided a lifeline for shipwrecked corporate survivors of the 1980s. The story then casts back further still to sketch the origins of the three amigos and how they came to play such key roles in the networks which flowed around the Packers in the rollercoaster ride of the 1990s; a voyage from the edge of disaster to resounding triumph and back again, as it all turned bad once more; and the denouement which led to the unhappy tableau at Elamang Avenue in November 2003.

The stand-off outside Kennedy's house lasted little more than an hour. Sachs showed up in a taxi at 8.30, and after some discussion the search team was allowed into the house forty-five minutes later. An hour into the search the federal agents reached the room the family called Trevor's Den. There on the desk they found the two pages of notes that Kennedy had written in London and Zurich. The man who had told the Zurich DA 'I keep nothing in writing' had broken his own rule. The Ritz notepad, which could be expected to retain faint impressions of what had been written on the pages torn off, was also on the desk. The agents put it all in evidence bags and took them downstairs to the property search register, which Kennedy duly signed.

It would be four days later when he first claimed the notes carried legal privilege; and three months before he remembered that the two pages were written in different hotels, 700 kilometres apart. After thirteen months of court battles Kennedy's lawyers got the blank notepad back, arguing it was not covered by the terms of the search warrant, but failed to retrieve the notes themselves. In December 2004 the Federal Court of Appeal finally gave ASIC unfettered access to the two pages of notes in which Kennedy discussed his role in the Offset Alpine affair in his own hand-writing. With bullet points. They already had a copy of the computer hard drive from Kennedy's city office, which contained 12 000 references to Rivkin and several mentions of Bank Leumi officers. Now if ASIC investigators could untangle the cryptic comments in the notes, they hoped they had a smoking gun.

ONE

Back in the saddle

July–October 1990

It was always going to be a bad day, from the moment the white 7-series BMW pulled up at the gatehouse. Some quick conversation followed, then the boom rose. Too late.

Even as the security guard picked up the phone to call ahead, the Beemer with the 'KP' licence plates was through and following the driveway past the cluster of production cottages and the huge studios to pull up with its nose just outside the glass reception doors. The big man swung out and strode inside, leaving the car door ajar behind him. The Australian television industry had just entered a new era. Kerry Packer was back.

He was early. Eleven days before, on 19 July 1990, the shareholders in Bond Media, the nearly bankrupt company that owned the Nine Network, had approved a deal which wiped out most of the company's capital and gave control of Nine back to Packer, three years after he had sold it to Alan Bond. But Packer wasn't supposed to show up for another month. Or at least another week. His staff had said so. In any half-normal world Packer would still be on the polo circuit, whizzing through money in Argentina. Everyone at the Channel Nine headquarters at Willoughby was braced for the fireworks that were inevitable upon his arrival. But, please God, not yet. Not at 7.30 in the morning. The stream of

Nine executives who made their appearance at more conventional times would discover there was something worse than Kerry Packer making an unannounced visit. It was to arrive at their office and find he was already there.

The most obvious change in the three years since Packer had left was the foyer. Along with the glass doors, Bond Media chief Sam Chisholm appeared to have secured Australia's entire supply of aqua-green marble. Then there was the glass-sided lift that took executives to a new top floor, which Chisholm had decorated with all the marble left over from the foyer. It was referred to as 'The Palace', or the 'Green Latrine'.

'I can't believe all that foyer is real,' wrote television anchor and columnist Peter Luck. 'Do Laminex do that stuff?'

When Sam celebrated his fiftieth birthday the year before, Nine management had arranged to buy him a Harley-Davidson—then taken out part of the wall and the roof so they could drop the bike in on a cherry picker at the appropriate moment. That now looked a little extravagant.

For weeks, Nine had been abuzz with talk of the cost cuts Packer was going to introduce. Packer had been overseas with the polo ponies and it was left to the managing director of Packer's Consolidated Press Holdings group, Trevor Kennedy, to give the official line to the *Sydney Morning Herald*: 'It is all just gossip and speculation. I can tell you that no decisions have been made yet . . . The last thing we need, in view of the fragile state of morale, is a story getting around that those bloody madmen from Park Street are going to come charging in creating havoc.'

That was before Monday 30 July, when Kerry Packer showed up in person, after which Kennedy's assurances seemed a little beside the point.

Packer took to the task with the same steady commitment that Alaric the Goth must have shown when the road map of Italy told him he was getting close to Rome. Packer knew a lot about television—probably more than anyone else in the country. But he held no illusions about it. The story was told of Packer in the mid-1980s, sitting silently through a story conference for a soap opera, finally turning to tell the group as he left: 'If it doesn't rate, you're all fired. If it does rate, it's still a heap of shit.' Packer was a natural. He was dyslexic, which meant writing had little appeal for him. But television was a whole different category.

Sydney is a loud town. For three decades, the ninety-metre television broadcast tower at Willoughby had given whoever owned it the loudest voice in the city, and in Australia. Nine was the ultimate megaphone and the Packers had always been its rightful owners, apart from three bad years when Alan Bond had minded it for them. 'How many television stations do you own, son?' was Kerry Packer's regular rejoinder to nosey journalists and inquisitive shareholders. In a town where everyone had their own private raison d'être, the Packer family credo was simple: We own television stations, therefore we are. You may not see us, but we're with you, all day until the station identification screen comes up around 3 a.m. We'll be back with you after this commercial message.

Kerry Packer was never meant to be a mogul. His elder brother Clyde was the one groomed to be the heir. But Clyde quarrelled with their father, Sir Frank Packer, in 1971. Clyde had a lifestyle change and took to wearing a caftan—which on someone the size of the Packer men is a garment that can cover several smallish suburbs—before moving to California. Sir Frank died fifteen months later, in 1972, and Kerry bought his brother's half-share in Consolidated Press for $4 million. In the two decades since then, Kerry Packer had done three big deals. In 1982, he paid $218 million to privatise Consolidated Press Holdings. Four years later, he sold part of it, the Nine Network, to Alan Bond for $1.05 billion. As Packer put it in 1990, 'You only get an Alan Bond once in your life.'

Actually this was arguable, because the month before he had bought a coupon-inserts business in the United States called Valassis Communications on which he would make an even bigger profit. The return from those three deals—privatising Cons Press, selling Nine and buying Valassis—would eventually be worth $5 billion to Packer. But Packer's real skill was not in making money. It was in holding on to it. This is why he was so unhappy with Alan Bond.

Packer is a cash kind of guy, but when Bond bought the Nine Network in 1987, he slipped some funny money into the deal. Packer would get the last $220 million only in 1990, when a bunch of preference shares that Bond Media issued to him as part of the sale fell due to be paid out. Unfortunately, by the time 1990 came around, all three Australian commercial television networks were in desperate trouble after overspending on programming just as the advertising market collapsed. Bond Media was broke, and Alan Bond couldn't pay Packer the money he owed him.

If one thing distinguishes Kerry Packer's attitude towards money, it is his ability to imitate a limpet. However much he may spend on his own private pursuits—and his personal expenses have at times ranged between $50 million and $100 million a year—when it comes to business, the philanthropy stops at the door of the Packer compound in Bellevue Hill. Yet here was Alan Bond, with all his arms and legs still attached, owing Packer $220 million.

Packer is not one for bottling up his emotions. While he might have preferred a more immediate revenge upon Bond, in the end Packer settled for a deal to convert his $220 million debt into shares and options that gave him 60 per cent of Bond Media, which would be renamed Nine Network Australia. It would prove a stunning coup, but that didn't mean the Big Fellow was happy.

'Congratulations, gentlemen, you are now in charge of a company with no money,' Packer growled when he welcomed a 'pretty motley lot' of new directors, as he described them, on to the board in November 1990. Packer was so unexcited about Nine that he sold his options to fund managers the following year. The fund managers made a $500 million profit from the options and the new shares cut Packer's stake to 40 per cent. Even if reclaiming the Nine Network for a modest $220 million had been Packer's plan all along—a line that would become part of the Packer myth—he showed every sign of wanting to have his money back as well. This set up a simple dynamic for every encounter that Packer had on that first day back at Nine on 30 July. He had lost $220 million, and every person he met at Willoughby was responsible. He wanted his money back. All of it. Preferably from each of them.

The first intimation Nine's head of current affairs, Ian Frykberg, had that the world had changed came when he turned a corner and saw Packer advancing on him. Packer poked him in the stomach and growled, 'Hey, pudgy, why don't you lose some weight?' At least that was the gist. Then he was gone, sailing down the corridor as other desperate executives racked their brains for ways—any way—to cope with the stress of confronting a deeply unhappy Kerry Francis Bullmore Packer.

Wonderful stories emerged of the desperate days that followed. The more excitable members of staff recalled that when Packer first appeared he was about eight metres tall. More conservative observers suggested his height was no more than 6.5 metres. In the first hours some fool of an accountant told Packer that Nine's drinking bill was running at more than $10 000 a month. Rather than congratulating the Nine crew on their superior taste and character in refusing to drink anything cheap or that came in cardboard, Packer took draconian steps. He broke the ghastly news to the troops at a late-morning meeting: Nine would be going dry. From now on, no alcohol would be allowed on the premises. A mail boy was despatched with a trolley and two security guards to search out and remove all the booze from the fridges.

In that dark hour the noble minds that fill the senior ranks of the television industry had their finest moment. Adversity brings out the best in us. The steady clinking noise of the approaching trolley triggered extraordinary undercover manoeuvres as Nine executives struggled to hide bottles in the boots of their cars.

For the soft-hearted, sensitive types who run television networks, this was an admirable, disinterested gesture—a Hollywood-style rescue operation somewhere between *The Scarlet Pimpernel* and *Free Willy*. At least it seemed that way after the second or third bottle. Stalked by the world's largest teetotaller, not all the booze made it to freedom. During a tour of one section at Nine, Kerry Packer is said to have stormed into a recently vacated room to find a fine bottle of white sitting alone on the table. It was probably a chardonnay, quite likely rather a good one, although no one had the chance to find out after Packer supposedly picked up the bottle and hurled it across the room towards the sink.

The most brutal casualty was lunch. Henceforth, Packer ordered, one hour was the most that any executive could take to restore the tissues. Willoughby went into shock. On some outings, it could take longer than that just travelling to and from the rest-aurant. Nine was a culture that lunched not wisely but too well. It was Nine's chief executive Sam Chisholm who had decreed, 'Losers have meetings, winners have parties.' But *everyone* had lunch. Chisholm himself—once described as the greatest luncher in Sydney's history—had been a formative influence on Sydney's restaurant scene. His patronage had helped elevate Darcy's, Imperial Peking and Tre Scalini into the city's hottest lunching spots, before he insisted on similar quality cuisine for the Channel Nine boardroom.

'Sam was a social animal—he didn't have to have a reason to lunch,' Graham Richardson later told David Dale. 'He spent an extraordinary amount of Kerry Packer's money, which Kerry didn't mind because Sam got results. You always started with Cristal [champagne that is, at $300 a bottle], and then the best whites and reds.'

From a legendary luncher like Richardson this was praise indeed. Admittedly, not everyone at Nine ventured as far as Chisholm. Media people always seem to gravitate to Chinese restaurants, maybe as a subconscious reminder of all those nights having to eat takeaway food. But lavish corporate hospitality had become part of the Nine culture—and part of Sydney's culture as well. And now Packer was raging around Willoughby like the Spirit of Anti-Lunch itself. Inevitably, Packer's trajectory through Nine brought him up against the chief luncher.

Sam Chisholm had run the Nine Network since the mid-1970s. The power he wielded in Sydney society reflected not merely his position at Nine but also his skills as a superb networker. As a raconteur he had the uncanny ability to put his finger on just the spot where someone else is ridiculous. Like his celebrated disdain in the late 1990s for the managing director of Telstra—he wasn't really called Ziggy Switkowski, Sam would claim gravely, he was John Smith but the poor fellow was just so boring that he made up a funny name so at least he would have one interesting thing about him.

The story was so Sam, so full of *brio* for a man whose parents christened him Hewlings. That would be the plural of Hewling. Suggesting many Hewlings, perhaps a pack of Hewlings. It's an easy name to forget. Whoever filled in the company forms for directors for the Channel Nine group in the late 1980s put him down in company after company as Samuel Howlings Chisholm. On a slow news day in 1995, I duly reported this fact in the *Australian Financial Review*'s 'Rear Window' column. Fairfax cartoonist Rod Clement drew a picture of two wolfmen baying at the moon while holding a baby over their heads. The caption read, 'The birth of Samuel Howlings Chisholm is celebrated in the traditional family manner'. I realised the mistake the next day and briefly considered running a correction. A further search of company records revealed that an alternative misspelling of the name was Samuel Mewlings Chisholm.

Middle names. Now there's a thing. John Atanaskovic, one of Sydney's most respected corporate lawyers, would probably kill for a middle name like Hewlings. Instead he is saddled with Ljubomir. Television interviewer Jana Wendt has been called many things—the Perfumed Steamroller, the Smiling Assassin—but rarely her middle name and her mother's favourite, Bohumila. Like Hewlings, this one also doesn't get a lot of airplay, but it is helpful to remember that in the theme song of *The Lion King*, which begins 'In the jungle / The mighty jungle / The lion sleeps tonight', the chorus in the background is chanting, 'Bohumila, Bohumila'. There's a sad music in the names Ljubomir and Bohumila, a whole tragic opera waiting to be written.

Four weeks after Packer appeared at Willoughby, Chisholm was gone, taking up a job offer from Rupert Murdoch to fix his troubled Sky satellite television business in Britain. Bohumila announced Sam's departure on *A Current Affair*. Two days before Chisholm resigned, Packer sacked forty-seven staff. It was 'the end of a golden era', *60 Minutes* executive producer Peter Meakin said as he packed up. 'Kerry's let everyone know he's back, and good on him. We're all back at boarding school. Now he can stop climbing the mast and doing King Kong impressions.'

Five weeks later, on 3 October, another seventy staff at Nine were retrenched, along with thirty-one from its satellite racing channel Sky Television. And then, four days after that, everything was turned upside down when Kerry Packer died on horseback during a polo game.

Just past 3 p.m. on Sunday 7 October, three minutes into the first chukka at Warwick Farm racecourse, Packer clutched his chest and pitched forward on his horse. It was a classic drop-dead heart attack. A fatal arrhythmia had disrupted the timing mechanism for his heart muscles, triggering acute ventricular failure. And just like that, the most powerful man in Australia was dying.

Accounts of the frenzied moments that followed had a strange, slow-motion quality. James Packer, in his position at goal defence, saw his father slump down and rode towards him. The ambulance officers on the sideline were reacting, too slowly, to the shouts for help. Kerry Packer hung there unconscious on the horse, his arms locked tight in a death grip around its neck. Three minutes without oxygen and brain damage begins, so the question was how fast could the paramedics get across there and begin heart massage.

The adrenalin started to surge through James Packer as he began to realise what he was facing. In those seconds, as he reached his father and tried to unlock the motionless arms and get the body down off the horse, the future hung in the balance. James Packer was not ready to step into his father's shoes. He didn't know it but the Packers had their own financial crisis building just over the horizon, and it would hit them in the middle of the following year, 1991.

This was the turning point, this moment on the horse. Not just for the House of Packer, but for the future of Australian business, for politics, for media—indirectly for the culture itself. Everything that Packer would do in the next decade—and not just Packer, but the networks and social ecosystems that fed off the Packer money mine—was about to fall to nothing on this field.

It wasn't only Packer, it was a generation of business idols that was facing annihilation. Rupert Murdoch's empire was in crisis. Three days earlier, News Corporation's new finance director, David DeVoe, had told the group's bankers in London that News could not meet its debt repayments. Robert Holmes à Court had died three weeks before. Westpac would put the Lowy family's Ten Network into receivership within days, the Fairfax group would go into receivership a month later. The Seven Network had been in receivership for a year and its former owner, Qintex boss Christopher Skase, was already giving hints in Majorca that he was feeling a little chesty when Australian authorities raised the subject of him coming home. Larry Adler had died two years before, leaving his son Rodney to cope with his inheritance, FAI Insurances, which was arguably next to insolvent. Warren Anderson was sliding towards crisis. Laurie Connell was facing court in Western Australia over the Rothwell collapse, John Spalvins would not be able to save Adelaide Steamship, Brian Yuill was facing charges over looting the Spedley group, Bruce Judge was long gone from Ariadne, while Alan Bond was fighting off the banks with the resourcefulness of a human eel. There were also the mortally wounded politicians like John Cain in Victoria and Brian Burke in Western Australia, the crippled building societies and friendly societies, and the state banks—the State Bank of Victoria, Tricontinental, and the State Bank of South Australia. And then there were the major banks . . .

While he had given no outward sign, Packer had been experiencing heart problems for months. It was only a matter of time before the big attack came along. The truth is, when he descended on Channel Nine in July he was a dead man walking. But then, so was everybody else in town. Every 1980s entrepreneur in the country was struggling to survive what had become a form of economic genocide, a sort of socio-economic house-cleaning. It was the end of the generation that came to power too early.

Something profound happened to Australia in the 1970s and 1980s that changed the way we live. It began with the Vietnam War. For more than two decades, Australia's prosperity had been guarded by an international agreement signed at Bretton Woods in England in 1946, which fixed the world's major currencies to the gold standard. International money flows were restricted and the West enjoyed low interest rates and low inflation. But Vietnam was an expensive war for the United States. Richard Nixon financed it by printing money. That set off inflation and forced the US to devalue the greenback. That adjustment spelt the end for the Bretton Woods agreement and broke the interlocking monetary system that had guided the West since World War II. It would take decades for the full effects to work through but, without fixed currencies, the whole world now supped from the same soup bowl. You could no longer quarantine a local economy or arbitrarily set a currency rate—at least not for long—without triggering a flight of capital. In the new world order, interest rates could no longer be fixed. The world was on a treadmill that kept pushing the effects of economic deregulation and rationalisation through each national economy.

Coupled with the oil shock of 1973, that meant a decade and a half of high inflation. The effects on Australia's class structure were profound. Put simply, if you were rich in 1970 and did not remake your fortune in the next two decades, by 1990 you were no longer rich. Over that period, inflation rose 300 per cent. But upmarket housing prices—comparing the same eastern Sydney suburbs from Rushcutters Bay to Vaucluse across twenty years—rose by up to 1500 per cent. If you take out the effect of inflation, then in real terms the increase in property values, including renovation and rebuilding, was up to 500 per cent. It wasn't just the top end of town that was affected, this was a society-wide change. In 1970, people didn't talk about property prices at dinner parties. Actually it's hard to imagine what they would have talked about because two decades later they talked of nothing else.

These were tough years for the Establishment, which had controlled Australian society for so long. Old networks of influence and interlocking directorships and club memberships were heavily tied to the traditional property model. The housing booms and busts proved lethal for the state banks and the finance companies and finally for the Big Four banks, on whose boards so many Establishment figures sat. The Establishment was in retreat, which was just fine for the one group that did very well out of this reorganisation.

Australia has always had a divide between the mainstream business establishment and the adventurers and wide boys. Traditionally the latter has been a marginal group associated with mining stocks and minor property bubbles in a low-inflation, low-interest rate environment. They were mavericks, but they were containable. Economic deregulation and asset inflation now posed an exceptional opportunity for this group. They despised the hidebound Establishment. By the early 1980s, the mavericks had the flexibility and now the credit facilities to take charge. And they did. Bond and Skase and Holmes à Court and John Elliott and Judge and Yuill and Anderson and Connell and Spalvins and Larry Adler became the central players. Part of it was an age thing. Most of them were in their forties, born in the period from 1937 to 1946, the last cohort before the Baby Boomers arrived nine months after the end of World War II. They were twenty years younger than their Establishment rivals. They didn't just challenge the Establishment—they wanted to buy it. And then it was all over.

After the 1987 Stock-market Crash, almost every entrepreneur in Australia was living on borrowed time. The crippling high interest rates and credit squeeze that Treasurer Paul Keating introduced to kill off inflation, and the deep recession it triggered, did the rest ('It's a slowdown we had to have, which turned into a recession'). But it wasn't just the big fish that were caught. The 1980s boom had created an entire infrastructure, an ecosystem of minor players who fed off the action—the facilitators, the technical specialists, those who did the warehouse deals, who advised, who did the trades—the journeymen of the asset boom. They too were sinking with no patrons and no oxygen line.

That was why Kerry Packer was so important. He was the last great whale. His lucky sale of Nine to Bond meant he was the only major player who was cashed up when the Crash came. As a result, for the next decade he would be the biggest mobile source of capital in Australia. With all the 1980s entrepreneurs beached high and dry, Packer was the only major player still swimming. Now he seemed to be dying.

The epic story of the polo field rescue was plastered over the next day's newspapers: the resuscitation gear that was on hand, which came to be called Packer Whackers; the ambulance trip to St Vincent's Hospital; the helicopter flight to pick up Victor Chang, Packer's surgeon. 'He wanted to shake my hand, though I don't think he liked seeing me,' Dr Chang said later.

By Monday Packer was sitting up in bed, barking instructions and signing documents. Professor Bob Baxt at the Trade Practices Commission wanted a word with him about the latest round of media intrigue, concerning the future of Nine's rivals, Seven and Ten. It was business as usual. Australia's king of television had barely missed a beat.

Packer's recovery would have enormous repercussions in the 1990s for Australia and particularly for Sydney, a town that is run by insiders. To sift through many of the headline events of the decade—from politics to casinos, from rugby league to telecommunications, along with every conceivable arm of the media industry—is to wonder at the decisive impact that one man's life can have on a culture. A more subtle measure may be gained by surveying the ranks of Australia's wealthy, measuring how many fortunes were achieved, to lesser or greater effect, by proximity to Packer. A multitude of alternative futures branched out from that moment when Packer suffered his heart attack on the polo pony. And yet the question of what might have happened in the end is immaterial. The episode on the horse was merely a sideshow in the larger drama. If you are looking for a pivotal moment in 1990 which showed the nature of the decade which would follow, I think you need to look at the day Packer returned to Channel Nine. I think it's the lunch thing. It is the moment when Packer pronounced, more clearly than any other, that the wild times of the 1980s were over and would not return. The business rules had changed for everyone, not just for the power players and wheelers and dealers. The 1990s would be a decade where the networkers, the friends, the lunch partners and the school alumni fought a rearguard action against the economic change that was engulfing them. What that meant for the network of players who floated around the Packers may be seen best through the careers of three men—Rene Rivkin, Graham Richardson and Trevor Kennedy—who had played such key roles in forging the network, and who had been largely mute figures in 1990 in the drama surrounding Packer. They were victims of the times as much as anybody. The 1990s would prove to be a marvellous escape act. To understand just how marvellous it was, one must first consider what they were escaping from.

PART ONE

The three amigos

RUTH: One moment! Let me tell you who they are.
       They are no members of the common throng;
       They are all noblemen who have gone wrong.

                                    Pirates of Penzance

TWO

Mixing with money

If Kerry Packer's heart attack had convinced him of one thing, it was that he needed to speed up the in-house training program he had already begun to prepare his son James for the day he would take over the family business. James would be mentored in the following years by a succession of Consolidated Press executives, notably Al Dunlap and Brian Powers. In the meantime, James's education had been in the hands of Packer's old friend, Rene Rivkin.

'So one day I get a phone call—"I'm sending my fucking son over and I want you to lose him some fucking money on the stock market so he understands the fucking value of the fucking dollar,"' Rene Rivkin told Andrew Denton later. It turned out that Rivkin, that old legend of the bourse, had a couple of dubious investment ideas that would prove the very thing. He had a wealth of experience to share.

For more than three decades, Rene Rivkin was the best-known figure in the Australian stock market. The tributes his friends paid to him after his tragic death in May 2005 reflected a man who, by dint of sheer personality and out-of-the-box charm, had made himself an Australian legend. Rivkin had a razor wit and a brand of outrageous repartee that was awfully difficult not to like.

However his legacy was flawed and his darker side, which had intermittently peeped out of hiding throughout his career, did finally reveal itself. If his rise to fame had been over the top, so too was his fall. The public disgrace that marred his last two years was no doubt exacerbated by his bipolar condition, his chronic over-consumption of Prozac and brain surgery, and he had to endure huge media coverage of his weekend detention sentence and ongoing investigations by regulators. Today, for all those who regard him as a hero or victim, there are others who see him as a villain. In fact, none of these labels gives credit to the man. His was a complex character, which is not so surprising in view of the history that shaped him.

Rene Rivkin had an unconventional childhood. His father, Walter, was born in Georgia in 1917, a week before the Bolshevik revolution. As civil war gripped the country, Walter's parents joined a stream of White Russians who fled to China. They settled in Shanghai, only to find that China too was facing waves of social upheaval. Shanghai was under occupation by the Japanese when Rene was born in 1944. By this time, Walter was in his late twenties and a successful trader, married to Rachel, who was born in Japan. Their well-to-do lifestyle, which revolved around the expatriate community at the Jewish Rec-reational Club, provided a buffer that left Rene and his younger brother Leonard oblivious to the wider events around them. Rene was barely a toddler when the Japanese surrendered. He was almost five years old when Mao Zedong's communist army overran Shanghai, and seven when his father finally closed down their house, dismissed their twelve servants and moved the family to Sydney. While he never talked publicly about it, the links Rivkin forged with old China hands, such as Bart and Ronald Doff, celebrity real estate agents of Sydney's eastern suburbs who were born in 1947 in Tientsin, would last a lifetime. Walter prospered in Australia by turning his hand to property development and building flats in eastern Sydney before investing in mining companies. But it was nothing like the style of living the family had enjoyed in China.

Rene went to Sydney Boys High where he ended up sharing a desk with a young English boy called Bruce Corlett. He and Rene had been together 'pretty much every day since then', Corlett told journalist Ali Cromie, who taped a remarkable series of interviews with Rivkin's friends and associates in 1998, in the days when his friends still talked publicly about him. Corlett was as unlike Rene as it was possible to be, but he would stick with Rivkin through a lifetime of violent mood swings. It was 'a very special relationship' according to Rodney Adler, who was close to both men for more than a decade when he ran FAI Insurances. 'Bruce is a man of great detail, very conservative, very proper,' Adler told Cromie. 'He's a very good sounding board for Rene. He has a very good stabilising effect on Rene.' This was a fair description, Corlett conceded to Cromie. 'I can only assume that is why we talk as often as we do.'

'Bruce is as straight down the line as Rene is weird, they make a fairly odd couple in that sense ... Bruce is a starchy, Royal Sydney Golf Club character, quite unlike Rene but they are good buddies and they trust each other,' said Chris Walker, who was hired to write Rivkin's biography in 1998, before Rene tired of the venture. 'Corlett reckons Rene is a great bloke, straight as a die, honest, a terrific friend. But he does say he is a difficult fellow and has burnt almost all his friends.'

Another of Rivkin's childhood friends was Robert Whyte, whose father was a paper merchant. Corlett and Rivkin went on to study law at Sydney University, where Whyte did an economics degree. Rivkin was already outrageous. Mallesons Stephen Jaques partner Graham Bates described Rivkin arriving at law classes each morning in the 1960s and parking right outside the door of the lecture hall, ignoring the parking tickets he would receive each day. Corlett made no waves, while Whyte was regarded as one of the nerdier students on campus. It was the mid-1960s and the three friends were in the middle of a social revolution to which they were oblivious. Instead they were fixed on ways to make money.

Rivkin had already made up his mind about the value of the law. 'I was always disappointed my father made me do law rather than commerce, but clearly there are times when I had to bullshit my way through,' Rivkin later told Elle McFeast. 'The school of life has been great, making money you don't need a commerce degree. But there are times when you sit with business management and you definitely need bullshit.'

Whyte went on to work as a merchant banker with Schroders in London. Corlett stayed with the law for two years after he and Rivkin graduated in 1967, before moving into commerce. But Rene already had the trading bug. 'I was a fourteen-year-old kid when I received in the mail a prospectus for United Telecasters, which was Channel Ten in those days,' Rivkin said later. 'I asked my father whether I should send the fifty quid in, and I did and four weeks later I made 150 per cent profit. And being a kid who liked money, I thought, "What better way to make money?"'

The most salient part of this anecdote is that Rivkin at fourteen had the equivalent of about $1500 of pocket money in today's money to spend on a share flutter. By his own account it was a much indulged childhood in which the figure of his father, Walter, loomed very large. The contrast was between the chubby and indulged child who didn't like sport, and the athletic and tempestuous father who had once been a boxing champion in Shanghai. 'I didn't like my father,' Rivkin would say later. 'I . . . I loved him, I think, but probably because I had to, because one's supposed to love one's father, but I didn't like him. I adored him for the first twenty years . . . We were absolutely inseparable until [I was] twenty, or twenty-two, and after I became successful in my own right and, therefore, he appeared to lose control over me, I think that's where the problem arose.'

The break appears to have coincided with Rene taking articles as a clerk at a city law firm. He said later his mother was so concerned about the distances he had to walk delivering documents she would spend days circling the block in a car, ready to drive him. Once he finished his articles in 1969, he moved into work at a stockbroking office, J and J Norths.

A Norths partner, Michael Hobbs, took Rivkin with him as a junior partner when he left the firm soon after to start his own broking operation. It was spectacularly bad timing. The glamour mining stock Minsec collapsed in 1970, the market dived and, after trading for two months, Hobbs and Rivkin split. Rene was left with the company. Undeterred by the crashing mineral stocks, Rivkin became the laughing stock of the market in August 1970 when at the ripe age of twenty-six he paid a record $82 000 for a seat on the Sydney Stock Exchange. Actually, it was probably Walter who paid the $82 000 as Hobbs & Partners reopened its doors as Hobbs Rivkin & Partners in September 1970, and Rivkin started plying his father's friends for work. Rene Rivkin's secret life began almost immediately.

'We had almost no clients,' Rivkin later testified in Zurich, by which he meant no clients except his father's friends. 'But then there was a float. We deposited the proceeds from the float at Bank Leumi in Zurich.' By 'we' Rivkin meant himself, his father, a mining partner of Walter's who was also financing Rivkin, and a fourth investor he did not name. From then on, the Rivkins were a Swiss banking family, with separate accounts for father and son. Walter Rivkin appears to have treated it merely as a tax dodge. 'My father was a very conservative investor, the exact opposite of myself,' Rivkin said. 'I knew that he only had bonds in his account.' Walter had correspondence from Bank Leumi sent to his sister-in-law, Pauline Tribe, Rene testified: 'He believed that was an adequate security measure.'

It was in 1970 that Rene met Gayle Perkins, a twenty-year-old from Brisbane who at one point had been going out with his brother, Leonard. Rene 'was quite different from anyone I'd ever met before,' Gayle told *Australian Story* in 2004. 'He wasn't attractive, but he was definitely a very intelligent, interesting person. But he felt he had to be a success to be anyone, and I knew that.' They married two years later, and by 1979 they had four children—Damien, Jordan and twins Shannon and Dion (a fifth child, Tara, was born in 1986). But these years were overshadowed by personal tragedy. Leonard had drowned in the surf at Bali at Christmas 1978—Rene later described it to Andrew Denton as a drug overdose. 'That death was incredibly traumatic for the family,' Gayle told *Australian Story*. Rene spent the next three years crying each morning in his shower, she said.

Despite the turbulence in his private life, Rene Rivkin had become a player in the economic upheavals that unfolded in Australia in the 1970s. At times he would be rich, at other times he would be like a polar explorer scrambling for dear life as the ice pack split and disintegrated beneath his feet. The fabric of power and wealth that had underwritten Australia in the 1950s and '60s was cracking. Rivkin was young, clever and not very scrupulous. As the old networks of the Establishment began their long, withering decline, Rivkin finally found himself winning the sort of professional and social respect that he had never received through his childhood and university years. There was a whole new breed of player out there.

Stephen Tsung and Andrew Lakos joined Rivkin at the new broking firm, which became just Rivkin & Partners. But the young venture did not survive the 1973 oil shock and the worldwide recession it triggered. The All Ordinaries Index dipped below 200 as property group Mainline crashed. Cambridge Credit teetered for a time on the edge of the abyss before it too fell. Rivkin & Partners closed its doors in 1974.

'Rivkin handled it badly,' a friend said later. 'He had an episode of depression and wanted to leave the country.' But he rallied and headed back to the bourse, setting up a new venture, Rivkin and Co, with Brent Potts and Willie West. This effort was far more successful. It was during this period that Rivkin's contact book (back in the days before God created the BlackBerry) became the most extensive in town. 'There is no doubt if you mix in the right circles, *vis a vis* making money, not having fun, you will learn a hell of a lot,' Rivkin observed later. 'In the 1980s I made sure I mixed with Kerry Packer.'

Rivkin was having a fine old time. In 1979, he and Potts joined with Brian Yuill of Spedley Securities to take control of a garment company called Bisley Clothing. The future of menswear, they told shareholders, lay in 'commodities, futures and money market broking and general investment'. Rivkin had his first brush with regulators when Bisley bought 23 per cent of Country Broadcasting Services, which made him the leading television mogul in Orange and Dubbo, with all the glamour that conjures up. However, Rivkin had not bothered to obtain the government approval he needed at that time to take such a large stake. He told the Administrative Appeals Tribunal that he had looked at the *Broadcasting and Television Act 1942* before buying the shares, but 'without much comprehension' because it was a difficult Act to follow. Justice McGregor thought it was 'unwise (though perhaps commercially advantageous)' for Rivkin to skip any legal advice before he bought the shares. 'His evidence does not persuade me that he really believed Bisley's transactions [were legal],' McGregor ruled.

Eight years later in the NSW Supreme Court, Justice Rogers would give Rivkin another reality check in a case he brought against a former employee, Tim Allen, over a $96 000 loss from a failed share placement. Rogers described Rivkin as someone who 'paints with a broad brush', 'an aggressive man, insistent on his rights, and what he conceives to be his rights.' He is 'extremely impatient of detail and has a tendency to proceed with some lack of concern for the rights of others. This no doubt makes him a success as a stockbroker, but it also means his recollection of details is vague in the extreme.'

Rivkin had his favourite people. 'In my day Rivkin used to have what we called his "pet monkeys",' Andrew Lakos told Cromie.

'He always had someone he favoured. These were mainly the stock exchange operators on the trading floor. He had a very close relationship with these operators because he spent his time on the trading floor and directed them on what to do. Every now and then he favoured one more than the other two.'

As Tim Allen had discovered, Rivkin could also go off people. As another Rivkin associate put it: 'He drops people left, right and centre. He would drop them like a tonne of bricks if they came between him and his money. There were people in his office who may have made a mistake, and Rene was totally unforgiving. He thinks he could bullshit them or buy them off with money . . . You have to blame somebody, it was never his fault.'

With Bisley needing a new chief executive in 1981, Rivkin turned to Bruce Corlett to run it for him. It ended unhappily. 'Rene is a very hard task master,' said Lakos. 'He was hard on Bruce, and Bruce resigned and said to Rene, "I want to be friends with you again."'

In the early 1980s, the economy went pear-shaped again and Rivkin's partnership with Brent Potts fell apart. Up to then, Lakos noted, 'They were the best of buddies, they lived in each other's pockets, their wives went shopping together, they went on picnics and boating together.' According to Rivkin, the trigger for their falling out in mid-1983 was his refusal to include Potts's name in the title of the firm. 'By the time I was prepared to let him have his name in the title it was too late. Our relationship was beyond repair,' he said in an address to students in 1997. In contrast, Rivkin told his biographer, Chris Walker, that Potts had concluded that Rene was losing his marbles.

In fact, Rivkin had been diagnosed with bipolar disorder, a condition characterised by alternating periods of euphoria and depression. Rivkin retired to London, where life only got worse. 'I spent six months in bed crying—not overtly—because I had just had a nervous breakdown,' he said later. 'Fortunately I was rescued by an old school friend of mine whom I had employed at various times in my career, and he offered me to start a stockbroking firm with the Hongkong and Shanghai Bank, and that became known as Rivkin James Capel and that went on to become a very successful firm.' Bruce Corlett, now with HSBC's local arm, Wardleys Australia, had bailed his old school friend out.

The three years from the day Rivkin James Capel opened its doors in October 1984 were the apex of Rivkin's career as a broker. In the wild melee of takeovers launched by Alan Bond, John Elliott, Robert Holmes à Court, Larry Adler, John Spalvins, Christopher Skase, Lee Ming Tee and so many other entrepreneurs, Rivkin was a key player. He was king of the stock exchange trading floor, whether he was buying up lines of stock for raiders, or taking advantage of the special situations that takeover bids created. 'I was playing with my money, the others were playing with the principal's money,' he said. He loved what he called the one-cent option, buying shares in a takeover target one cent above bid price. He was gambling that the bidder would have to raise the price. If he didn't, he sold into the bid and lost the one cent.

'He is a special situations man because he is part of the network,' Andrew Lakos told Ali Cromic. 'Rene is probably the best connected man in this country.' Lakos, who died in early 2005, ran the back office for Rivkin James Capel. Rivkin masterminded the takeover of Castlemaine Tooheys for Alan Bond in 1986. That same year Rivkin bought half of John Singleton Advertising, which went on to run the Labor Party's successful 1987 federal election. Rivkin was mixing socially with senior Labor figures like Graham Richardson, Laurie Brereton, Bob Hawke and Paul Keating. He had also become a close friend of Kerry Packer—so close that when Rivkin moved to London in 1983, Packer secretly bought Cararra, Rivkin's mansion on Rose Bay Avenue in Bellevue Hill, for $3 million. When Rivkin returned to Sydney six months later, Packer agreeably sold the house back to his friend for $3.3 million.

In July 1985, Rivkin invested three quarters of a million dollars in a little oil exploration company called Oilmet NL, which became his investment vehicle. Seventeen months later, the market value of Oilmet shares had jumped from $2 million to $151 million, and Rivkin was very, very rich. 'It's such a wonderful feeling. A wonderful, successful feeling that you have won,' Rivkin said of his trading successes.

These were the days of ostentatious wealth. Rivkin had a huge rambling apartment in St James in London, together with a house-keeper and chauffeur. He kept a stretch Rolls Royce, one of the first off the production line in 1986, which he would park flam-boyantly outside the office of his genteel British partner James Capel, much to the annoyance of Capel chief executive, Peter Quinnan. Then there was the Rivkin air wing—a $4 million Lear jet, a Cessna and a Falcon F20 corporate jet worth $3.5 million. The F20 was a neat twin-engine job that took ten passengers. He used the jets to ferry guests to his Christmas party on Hamilton Island in 1986, a two-day affair that cost $250 000; to fetch them to his forty-fifth birthday party in Sydney in 1989; and to ferry himself and friends like Robert Whyte around the country while he inflicted endless games of backgammon on them.

In 1987, *Australian Business* magazine named Rivkin 'Stock-broker of the Year'. His friends couldn't say enough about his generosity and character. 'He's a really straight shooter, and a generous bloke both publicly and privately, he's hugely intelligent and very entertaining and I'm proud to have him as a friend,' Trevor Kennedy said of Rivkin in 1998.

'No one has ever been robbed, conned or cheated by him,' Graham Richardson said of Rivkin in 1997. 'Charities have bene-fited by untold millions although no one of us will ever know by absolutely how much. He is a man of honour, intellect, generosity, humour and, above all that, knowledge.'

In September 1987, Rivkin went to hospital for surgery to remove a benign brain tumour. He was incapacitated for five weeks, returning to work on 20 October just in time to see the world as he knew it fall apart in the share Crash. It was the end of the party for all the entrepreneurs, including Rivkin. His company, Oilmet, which had peaked at $1.95, now saw its share price drop to 16 cents. Before the Crash, Rivkin's fortune had been estimated at $40–$50 million, much of it based on his now faltering Oilmet shares. But Rivkin had lost more than paper money. While he had been away, the stock exchange had switched to a computer trading system and closed the trading floor. The skills that had made Rivkin so formidable on the trading floor in the 1970s and 1980s were now redundant. 'When [Rene] was trading on the floor, he could judge situations and players very well,' said Adler. 'Now it is screen trading . . . Rene's whole occupation, as he knew it and liked it, has changed. It would depress anybody but it certainly depresses Rene.'

Even before the Crash, Rivkin's partner in the broking business, James Capel, had been in a state of near panic about the chaos that characterised the broker's back office, which handled the paperwork for the share trading. Close to fifty Rivkin clients were identified only by account numbers, which began at 1000 and worked up. Each had credit balances between $10 and $15 000. While there were no clues as to who the clients were, Rivkin was in the habit of withdrawing several thousand dollars in cash from some of the accounts on days when he had lunch with several high-profile Australian figures.

After the Crash, Rivkin James Capel had $11 million in debt. James Capel now discovered that the broker owned more than fourteen million Oilmet shares in various nominee accounts. Rivkin claimed he had bought them for foreign clients but these clients now declined to pay for them. At the height of the boom the shares had been worth $21 million. Now they were worth a tenth of that sum. James Capel had little legal recourse. Unlike Tim Allen, Rivkin was not going to be forced to pay for the losses. Capel's London management bit the bullet and bought Rivkin out in December 1987 for what Lakos told Cromie was more than $12 million. That appears to have included the artwork that Rivkin had bought for the business and part of the air wing.

Capel had fallen victim to Rivkin's secret life, an alternative world that existed side by side with his public face. It had been there since he became a broker, from the day he opened his first Swiss bank account with his father in 1970. Walter, who had lived through two revolutions and a world war, took no risks and invested his money at Bank Leumi le-Israel in bonds. For Rene, a Swiss bank account offered far more than just a bolthole for money. It was the opportunity to be a masked player, to take actions that had no recourse back to himself. He could warehouse shares for other people, he could conduct insider trading without fear of detection, he could manipulate share prices and he could ignore the disclosure and takeover rules that were there to protect other investors. In short, he could do whatever he wanted. He was invisible. When the Australian Tax Office investigated Rivkin in 1981, he simply closed his old Leumi account and opened a new one called Stilton. (At the height of his art-buying phase, Rivkin was naming his accounts after painters—Withers, Signac and Streeton—before adopting a pastoral theme with accounts like Stilton and Cheshire: Swiss banking from the dairy.)

With the encouragement of Otto Wolff, the private client advisor at Bank Leumi, he had used the Swiss accounts to take positions in Australian stocks—buying shares as a broker and booking them to nominee companies in the name of Bank Leumi. Rivkin's offshore buying explained in part why Oilmet's share price had soared so high. Oilmet's records for the week before the Crash show that Rivkin had parked seventeen million Oilmet shares in Australian nominee companies that would later be linked to Swiss accounts. After Rivkin's departure Rivkin James Capel appears to have been stuck with half of these. It wasn't just Leumi. By the mid-1980s Rivkin had also linked up with Alexander Fundulus (also known as Axel), the client manager for EBC

Zurich, a Swiss finance company associated with Bank August Roth. By the late 1980s Fundulus was coming to Australia every six months to trawl for clients. Rivkin used EBC for his racier trading. So did his estranged partner, Brent Potts, and more than a hundred other Australian business figures. It was a cottage industry bubbling below the public face of the Australian share market.

It went beyond share trading. For Rivkin it was a way of life, hiding behind the names of other people, both in Australia and offshore. It could work the other way, too. Rivkin would say he owned something, like his boat, *Dajoshadita*, in the 1990s, but it was actually owned by a company, in this case one registered in the British Virgin Islands. Everyone knew that Rivkin owned a Falcon F20 jet, but it was actually owned by Simdock Pty Ltd, a company ostensibly owned by two Rivkin employees. A string of people who worked for him ended up nominally holding assets that in reality belonged to Rivkin.

'Having businesses in the names of others is a good way of avoiding liability,' a long-time Rivkin associate said. 'You pretend it's you but it's not really you ... What he does is limit his risk to the amount of equity investment. So somebody carries the can. It's his name, his hype, a little bit of his seed money but most of the risk—the downside risk, not the upside risk—goes to someone else. Rene has always been good at taking the margin. This is just another form of it.'

In April 1988, four months after splitting with James Capel, Rivkin bought another small broking business, Bridge Son & Shepherd. But the wild days of the 1980s share boom were over. The share market would go sideways for the next six years and Rivkin's fortunes subsided, along with those of his public company, Oilmet. By 1990, Rivkin was in serious trouble. He had bet wrongly that the Japanese share market was about to crash. Instead it kept on rising. The bet was in the form of futures contracts on the Singapore Mercantile Exchange, which were tied to the future level of the Nikkei 225 stock index in Tokyo. 'I've only had one bad year in my life and that was when I shorted the Tokyo market at 36 000 index points and I lost a lot of money because I covered at 39 500 points because I couldn't stand the pain,' Rivkin told an investment seminar in 1997. 'Six to nine months later that Japanese market collapsed so really I got it right.'

Rivkin lost close to $10 million on this play. The broking business was losing money. Oilmet was next to moribund. The position was even worse in Zurich, where his accounts were millions of dollars in the red and Bank Leumi was making a margin call.

And now Kerry Packer wanted Rene to help his son James lose a little money.

THREE
Leaving Albany

In the early months of 1991, after duly consulting his financial advisor and mentor, Rene Rivkin, James Packer decided to put a little money into a hot prospect on the speculative end of the market ... which meant investing several hundred thousand dollars in Rivkin's struggling investment company, Oilmet. Rivkin, after all, was one of his father's closest friends. Kerry Packer's right-hand man, Trevor Kennedy, oversaw the purchase of another two million Oilmet shares by the family holding company, Consolidated Custodians. It wasn't enough to get Rivkin out of trouble or to turn around the Oilmet share price, but it was nice to have the Packer name on the share register. The golden circle of mateship guided the House of Packer and its satellites. Kerry Packer's world spanned the gamut of social and political circles in Australia. Packer's name opened all doors. To understand that world, you must consider one of the men who played a major role in shaping it, the worldly wise former editor whose earlier staff remember him fondly as 'Our Trev'.

Trevor John Kennedy, two years older than Rivkin, grew up as a good Catholic boy in modest circumstances in Albany, Western Australia. Kennedy senior was a tailor, a vocation that seems to have had a terminal effect upon his son's dress sense. Trevor

Kennedy grew up with a succession of part-time jobs, including holding a professional fisherman's licence at thirteen. As a teenager his parents sent him to St Aquinas College in Perth, where he was a classmate of Peter Smedley, who would later earn the nickname 'Pacman' for his acquisitive ways of running Colonial Group. Growing up poor in Albany shaped Kennedy's life. His path from Aquinas would be marked by a determination to move as far away as he could, as quickly as he could, from the world of his childhood. The recurrent feature of that journey would be impatience.

The first escape attempt failed. Kennedy worked as a cadet journalist at his local paper, then went on to join the *Canberra Times*, but this ended badly. By 1964, at age twenty-two, he had sworn off journalism to return home to join his father's venture into potato farming. He lasted two years there before rescue came by way of a call from the editor of the *Australian Financial Review*, Max Walsh, whom Kennedy knew from his Canberra days. Walsh put him to work as a *Financial Review* correspondent, first in Canberra, then in London. He met a dizzying array of famous names; all of them went into the contact book, many of them as lifelong friends. 'He has met and kept a lot of friends during his life, which says a lot about a person,' an old acquaintance commented in 2004.

'I can remember Keating when he was first starting out—we have a long history,' Kennedy would say later, after he tapped the prime minister to launch Ozemail's Internet phone service in 1995. Another former West Australian, Bob Hawke, went on a fishing trip with Kennedy in the late 1960s. In the 1980s, Kennedy would give Hawke and his wife a copy of *The Journalistic Javelin*, a recently published history of the *Bulletin*. It was inscribed with easy familiarity: 'For Bob and Hazel, the best people to inhabit The Lodge ever. Cheers, Trevor Kennedy.'

Kennedy had married Christina Miller, the daughter of the legendary surgeon, Sir Douglas Miller, of St Vincent's Hospital.

Christina was blue-blood Establishment, descended on her mother's side from one of Australia's early corporate titans, Thomas Mort. While Kennedy usually wore his Catholicism and Irish heritage lightly, it could be evoked when necessary to forge useful links, as with the somewhat pious senior Millers.

After London, Kennedy became Melbourne bureau chief for the *Financial Review*. Then, in February 1971, Vic Carroll appointed him to edit a new Fairfax weekly, the *National Times*. He was twenty-eight and the high life was just beginning. A year later he was headhunted by Sir Frank Packer at Consolidated Press to edit the *Bulletin*. To sweeten the offer, Kennedy would tell friends later, Sir Frank made him a director of Australian Consolidated Press and slipped him some of that company's shares—Kennedy's first serious money.

The deal was so good that a story circulated at the time, repeated with relish by Kennedy's rivals, that Sir Frank had hired the wrong man; that he meant to hire Vic Carroll, who had been overseeing Kennedy at the *National Times*, but he got them mixed up. Nevertheless, Kennedy was able to tap into a new wave of interest in current affairs to lift the *Bulletin*'s circulation, which was languishing at 20 000 when he arrived. In this position he mentored a generation of journalists. 'He was a journalists' editor,' says one of his former staff.

Once ensconced at Consolidated Press, with superb timing, Kennedy turned his formidable charm on the forgotten member of the Packer clan, Sir Frank's hapless younger son, Kerry. With his brother Clyde favoured by his father, Kerry had been left to stooge around in nowhere jobs. In 1972, aged thirty-five, he was working as an ad rep for the *Women's Weekly* when Clyde quarrelled with his father and left Cons Press. Eighteen months later Sir Frank was dead. Clyde, now living in Los Angeles, sold his share of Cons Press for $4 million; this left Kerry Packer king of the company: chief controller of the Nine television stations in Melbourne and Sydney and of the country's biggest magazine group. As Kerry took his first tentative steps on the road that would make him Australia's first billionaire, it turned out he wasn't hapless after all.

Kennedy had been supplementing Kerry's shoestring allowance from his father with secret advances written off as expenses from the *Bulletin* and helping Kerry whoop it up on the town. Kennedy was in the box seat. 'By day, Trevor was running the magazine and, by night, he was out with Kerry Packer in the nightclubs and gaming joints of Sydney,' Carroll later told *Bulletin* reporter Adam Shand.

With the long boozy lunches and wild nights, Kennedy's contact list grew ever longer. When Labour Council secretary John Ducker's former speechwriter was looking for a job, Kennedy put Bob Carr on the *Bulletin* payroll, where he stayed until he was elected to state parliament in 1983. Kennedy also hired an aspiring Liberal called Tony Abbott. A young Malcolm Turnbull was given part-time work while doing his law degree and then, when he returned from a Rhodes Scholarship to Oxford, Kennedy put him on staff as Cons Press company secretary and later legal counsel. Kennedy's links to the emerging figures in the New South Wales Labor Right—Keating, Laurie Brereton, Leo McLeay and Graham Richardson—would shape the marriage of convenience that Kerry Packer fashioned with Labor, initially through Neville Wran and his advisor Peter Barron.

Kennedy was not all conviviality and larrikinism. 'He had another side to him,' says a former senior Consolidated Press colleague. 'He was obsessed with money.' That would not surface until later. In the meantime, he had become a regular share trader, which was how he became friends with the hottest young broker in town, Rene Rivkin. In turn, this was how Rivkin and Brent Potts became Kerry Packer's house brokers.

The subsets of friends, contacts and associates forming around Kerry Packer at this time would become a network like nothing Australia had seen. The Labor Party was in the process of an historic shift of its funding base, from relying on the unions to bankroll its election campaigns to hitting the big end of town for money. The evolving relationship with Packer would be the key to this brave new world. At the same time, Rivkin would introduce Packer to his own network. The most enduring relationship would be with Robert Whyte, who had returned to Australia in the mid-1970s to run the funds management arm of insurer QBE. He would become one of Packer's closest friends.

There was nothing extraordinary in this—politics and money have never been strangers in Sydney. What made this alliance different was that it was forged and mediated through a media organisation. Packer had come into his inheritance just as the communications revolution, which would transform economies and societies around the world, was gathering pace. In the milieu around Packer's offices in Park Street, Labor politicians were mixing with fast money and aggressive young journalists; the new breed of young entrepreneurs, besides cementing access routes to politicians, were discovering how to manage their media profiles; and journalists were forging key relationships not just with politicians, but with stockbrokers. Eventually large swathes of senior Nine management would be taking investment advice from their dear friend Rene. As Graham Richardson found, in Rene's world his very special clients never lost money. 'I have never had a losing trade. Ever,' Richardson told a Rivkin investment forum in 1997.

The most interesting figures in this new grouping of politicians, journalists and the big end of town were those who navigated their way from one camp to another. Like Bob Carr, who returned to politics to become NSW Premier. Or Peter Barron who, after helping to set up Wran's new alliance with Packer, went on to become Bob Hawke's closest advisor before becoming a lobbyist for Packer. Barron's closest friend, Graham Richardson, later charted a similar course from politics into the safe harbour of Consolidated Press, but in his case he made it into media as well . . . as did Richardson's other close friend, Rene Rivkin. In July 1990, two months before he ripped off his father's Swiss bank account to stave off his creditors, and while the Australian Stock Exchange was investigating a series of suspicious share trades he was making in Stroika, Rivkin signed on as financial reporter with his friend Ray Martin on the *Midday Show*. As the face of respectability, he would share his thoughts on screen about the latest moves in world markets. The figure at the heart of these new alliances and friendships was, of course, Trevor Kennedy.

Early on at Park Street, Kennedy's chief challenger in the court of King Kerry was *Women's Weekly* editor Ita Buttrose. That Kennedy was able to overcome the advantages that Ita's close friendship with Packer gave her is no mean tribute to Kennedy's schmoozing powers. Ita saw the writing on the wall and left before she was pushed, taking a job offer from Rupert Murdoch in 1986. That left only the cocky new head of Nine, the one-time floor wax salesman, Samuel Hewlings Chisholm as a rival. 'I'm just a heartbeat away from running this place,' Chisholm would say to Kennedy, to taunt him.

For all the jostling among courtiers, there was never any doubt who was in control at Consolidated Press. Kerry Packer was a 24-hour-a-day, mercurial, shrewd and overbearing boss. His executives and editors had a yellow phone on each of their desks to communicate among themselves; when Packer wanted to speak to them he had a special ring tone, which could be heard even when they were talking to someone else. When the 'bat phone' emitted this much feared tone, the editor had better be there, or their PA had better know exactly how to contact them quickly, or someone would be fired. Packer could be extremely generous, but he expected instant obedience.

He carried similar expectations in his encounters with merchant bankers and politicians. In 1977, when Packer was having problems finding playing grounds for the World Series Cricket—his attempt to replace the Australian Cricket Board with his own professional league—Premier Neville Wran ensured the

Sydney Cricket Ground ultimately came to the party. In 1979, Rupert Murdoch and Robert Sangster won a valuable concession to run the Pools but, when the deal was finalised, Kerry Packer's name popped up as an equal shareholder. Packer's character and operating style became the template for Cons Press management. It could be a little like working for Genghis Khan. Not that there was anything wrong with that. As Packer said of his favourite Mongol, 'He wasn't very lovable but he was bloody efficient.'

Packer kept only good people in the Mongol horde. 'You don't survive there long term unless you are a good quality executive,' a senior banker commented in 2004. But with the drinking and the partying it was a blustering, blokey culture—the Shouting and Screaming School of Management Theory. Glenn Barry, who was brought in from New York in 1979 to run Lotto Management Systems, remembers his chairman, Trevor Kennedy, as focused on the politics of the job rather than practical difficulties. When Barry discovered on his arrival that the company had ordered the wrong computer software, Kennedy told him, 'That's your fucking problem.' When Barry tried to explain the technology, he was interrupted: 'Who do you fucking well think you are, Buck fucking Rogers?'

At Cons Press, Kennedy preferred memos to him to be only one page in length. They would come back with a scrawled 'yes' or 'no' on them. More than one page and the memos went straight into the file unread, says one former colleague. Kennedy did not believe in paper trails, either. 'His nickname was Trevor the Shredder, because after a board meeting there were always documents he wanted shredded,' says Barry.

When Kennedy approached Sean Howard in 1984 about buying into the computer magazine group he had built up, Howard recalls his opening lines were: 'My name is Trevor Kennedy. I run the company that publishes the *Bulletin* and *Women's Weekly*. You may have heard of us.' He wasn't afraid to use power. And he always wanted a discount, whether he was buying rare books, or taking shares in a float. 'I think you've dropped a zero off my allocation,' he told one broker whom he'd called to complain about the shares he received in a tech stock float in the late 1990s. It may not have been meant that way, but for this broker the inference was that Kennedy, as chairman of several major companies and therefore in a position to direct future work away from him, was asking for his personal allocation to be increased ten times. 'If there was a commercial gain to be made there is no doubt he would play the cards brutally,' said a banker who worked with Kennedy. 'He was guilty of being brutally commercial. The guy had a lot of presence.'

He took no prisoners. Greg Pynt, a former merchant banker with Deutsche, told journalist Angus Grigg of the time he surprised Kennedy with his presence in a secret meeting with Merrill Lynch bankers ahead of the Oil Search merger with Orogen Oil in Cairns in 2002. 'What are you doing here, you little bastard?' Kennedy said mock seriously, before grabbing the bemused Pynt in a headlock and marching him out of the terminal and across the road. 'You've seen nothing,' Kennedy told him sternly with deadpan humour, then walked off.

It was through running Kerry Packer's affairs that Kennedy got his introduction to offshore banking. Sir Frank Packer had set up the family holding company in the Bahamas back in the 1960s and the network of Packer companies in tax havens had grown considerably since then. 'When I worked for Consolidated Press there were a lot of companies that were established in the Turks and Caicos, and Netherlands BV, Liechtenstein, Switzerland, et cetera,' Kennedy would later tell the Australian Securities and Investments Commission. That was how, at some point in the 1980s, he came to be talking to some 'smart London lawyers and accountants' about setting up a little operation of his own, called Brampton. If only he hadn't subsequently forgotten every single aspect of who set it up, who ran it, what it invested in, and where the money went, Kennedy's conversation with ASIC could have been quite interesting. But then, as he told the Zurich District Attorney, 'I have never had a particularly good memory.'

There was nothing particularly novel in this. In the fast money world of the new entrepreneurs, offshore banking was often de rigeur. When you looked closely enough at the takeover battles that transformed Australia's business landscape in the 1980s, offshore money streams and tax havens popped up in deal after deal. Not that anyone was talking about it, except at Elders, after the Elliott boys discovered the delights of Monaco. In one of the debt reshuffles that marked John Elliott's transformation of Elders IXL from a pastoral company with a nice line in jam into a multinational empire, a handful of mystery investors made a fortune from Elders bonds issued in Switzerland and held through Monaco. The lucky investors were Elders executives, but when the details came to light and charges were laid against them in the mid-1990s, only one of them was convicted. That unlucky one was Ken Jarrett, the former Sunday school teacher who confessed and testified against his former friends. The charges against the others were dismissed.

＊

Faced with slick operators like this, Australia's great families could only watch in bewilderment. In most direct fights with the entrepreneurs they were outgunned and outmanoeuvred. Fending off the new boys wasn't their only problem. For many leading families, the succession issue had become a time bomb, exacerbated as inflation placed an intolerable pressure on family fortunes.

The Fairfax family empire imploded after Warwick Fairfax's ill-fated bid in 1987 to seize the family's destiny back into its own hands with a tragic privatisation (though Warwick's stepbrothers have built a major new newspaper chain in Rural Press). But similar succession dramas were playing out across Australia.

The Gowings had transformed Sydney's best-known discount department store into a successful investment company with a sideline in retailing. But Gowing senior made a critical mistake when his eldest son joined the business in the 1970s. He decided his heir would have to work his own way up in the store from the bottom, winning promotions without any favouritism. His son finally made it to ladies underwear, a prospect he found so daunting that he threw in the towel and decamped to Queensland.

The Darling family had two branches. The elder brother, John Darling IV, was the dashing one. He was a fighter pilot who flew with the RAF during World War II, then went on to found Darling & Co, the merchant bank that became Schroders Australia. But in the 1970s he lost his way. By 1979, a failed wheat deal with Iran left him bankrupt for the second time. His younger brother Gordon was more staid. He fought in the infantry in World War II and followed a stolid corporate career on Establishment boards. Gordon's son Michael founded a financial services company that he sold in 1987 before the Crash to Clayton Robard for $170 million.

In the inevitable clashes between new money and old, the Mort family found itself one of the casualties. Thomas Mort was one of Australia's great corporate giants of the nineteenth century. The Goldsborough Mort wool stores and the statue of Mort outside the Australian Stock Exchange are just faint echoes of the way one man's vision and character transformed an economy and a country. In the 1840s, Mort, with his brothers William and Henry, revolutionised the way Australian wool was sold and marketed, then did the same thing for livestock. Mort made shrewd investments in pastoral property, railways and mining ventures and helped found two Australian institutions: the Australian Mutual Provident Society and Elders. He built a huge dry dock to turn Sydney into a major port, then pioneered the use of refrigeration to ship chilled meat to Britain. He set up the first dairy company on the south coast at Bodalla, where he had a huge estate worked by share farmers. More than this, Mort was remembered for a rare generosity of spirit, a man who understood better than most the nineteenth-century idea of the social contract. Mort offered shares in his businesses to his workers and was a major philanthropist. In 1878, he attended a funeral for an employee in blinding rain and used his umbrella to cover the grieving widow. He subsequently caught pneumonia and died a legend in his lifetime, and then left his house in his will to be the home of the Anglican archbishop.

Mort fitted within a broader stream of social conscience. While corruption in its many forms has been a recurrent theme in Sydney history, there has been a parallel tradition of the Good Family: deeply religious dynasties like the Fairfaxes who believed in the social responsibilities of wealth. It's a somewhat faint echo of this *noblesse oblige* that made Kerry Packer and Rupert Murdoch so solicitous of long-term employees, along with Packer's tradition of providing every employee with a lavish Christmas hamper each year—a very generous decision even after modern tax laws on deductibility helped reduce some of the pain.

A century after Thomas Mort's death, his descendants were not doing so well. Their active holdings had been reduced to Bodalla, the dairy company that was now run by Mort's grandchildren, Charles and Thomas Laidley Mort, both in their seventies. This sleepy company in 1987 was a natural target for a takeover bid by Sam Gazal's Panfida Limited. Gazal offered $5 million for the company but met some spirited resistance. The Morts weren't without resources. In fact, one member of the family, the husband of Charles and Thomas Mort's niece, was a major power in Sydney.

Kerry Packer's right-hand man, Trevor Kennedy, had married into the Mort family through Christina Miller. Earlier in 1987 Kennedy had strengthened his business links with his wife's family when he and Rene Rivkin invested in a travel agency business run by Kennedy's brother-in-law, Adrian Miller. At the height of the takeover battle for Bodalla, Rivkin and Kennedy helped convince HSBC, the bank that owned half of Rivkin's broking business and which was bankrolling Gazal's bid for Bodalla, to loan money to Miller's company, The Traveller's Organisation. But not all his activities favoured the Mort family.

Eventually, the opposition to Gazal's bid for Bodalla ran out of steam. The dairy business was still dependent upon share farmers, who did not own their farms but had lived on them for generations. The general feeling among them was that smarter, younger management might do wonders for the business. In the end Gazal had to raise the price to $7.3 million before the family folded their cards. But, instead of revitalising the business, Gazal embarked on a classic asset strip. In 1989, he sold off the farms, the post office and most of the town in a massive auction. Farmers who had worked for Bodalla for fifty-five years and more had their farms sold out from under them. Gazal raised $17.3 million from the sale—small beer in the heady days of the boom but enough to ensure the old community ceased to exist, at least in its former state. The surprising thing here was that it turned out that Trevor Kennedy, in addition to running Kerry Packer's empire, had been moonlighting as Sam Gazal's advisor. He was paid some $700 000 for his role in the takeover. Part of it was in the form of Horse Island, a magnificent island in the Tuross Lakes that had been part of the Bodalla estate. The title deeds show the seventy-hectare island was valued at a modest $370 000 when it was transferred to Kennedy's company, Golden Words. Four years later, Kennedy would put its value at $3 million. So at least someone did well out of the dairy business.

FOUR

The Olympian

October 1997

The evening had taken a surreal turn. The ballroom at the Regent Hotel on this balmy spring evening in 1997 seemed faintly out of sync with the rest of the universe. It wasn't a problem with the numbers. A solid crowd had shown up—worthy burghers who had decided they could live with a few more zeroes in their bank balance. A few were milling about in the hotel foyer but the rest had filed into the ballroom to take their seats. The mood was upbeat, with the amiable expectation that seizes any group of people thinking about increasing their wealth. By general consensus, the time was right to put a bit of *nouveau* back into *riche*. The punters might not be millionaires by the time they left, but they expected a good show. They were prepared—they were *determined*—to be entertained. Everything was ready. But where was Rene Rivkin?

Graham Richardson was still pressing flesh in the foyer. The veteran of thousands of political meetings looked nervous. 'Two minutes away,' an aide whispered. And then Rivkin walked through the foyer doors. Richardson broke away from his conversation, moved to greet Rivkin, and ushered him into the Regent ballroom and onto the stage under the spotlights. Then Richardson was at the microphone introducing Rivkin to the $100-a-head crowd. We had lift off.

Richardson is a great front man. Two weeks earlier, on 30 September, he had been master of ceremonies at the gala dinner at the Intercontinental for Bob Carr's fiftieth birthday. As he passed the knife to Carr to cut the birthday cake, Richo had told the NSW Premier, 'One thing they tell you in the Labor Party is how to stab.' He had been playing to the Labor heartland that night, sitting on Table Nine with his wife Cheryl and old friends—people like Laurie Brereton and his wife Trish Cavanagh, Labor fundraiser Sam Fiszman and his wife Esther, former Labor NSW president Terry Sheahan, Labor identities Johnno and Pauline Johnson and John Gerathy, and his old mate Trevor Kennedy. Three and a half years after retiring from politics in March 1994 at the age of only forty-four, Richardson had cemented his position as a Labor legend.

Now, at the Regent Hotel, the scene was quite different. In the moment when Richardson stepped up to the microphone to begin a paean of praise for Rene Rivkin, the nagging incongruity of the night came into focus. Rivkin, standing there in the limelight, ready to talk about himself, was in his element. The punters were loving it already; they would talk about the evening for weeks. There was nothing out of the ordinary in that. But the real question on this October night in 1997 was this: What on earth was Graham Richardson doing standing here on the stage of the Regent ballroom?

In the backrooms and the front rooms of Labor politics in Australia there had been no more feared operator, ally or opponent. The man who had persuaded, threatened and negotiated his way to become one of the foremost politicians of his generation, who had reshaped the finances and the election tactics of the Australian Labor Party and who had been kingmaker for two prime ministers, was here reduced to acting as master of ceremonies at a tacky little get-rich seminar. How had it come to this? When exactly did the kingmaker decide to settle for life as Rene Rivkin's sidekick?

The really bizarre thing was that, as part of his introduction, Richardson was about to tell the audience how it had all happened.

If you want to understand Richardson in the 1980s and what he became, it is this moment in 1997 that is most telling.

'Nobody has benefited more from Rene's expertise than I,' Richardson assured the punters. 'I have never had a losing trade. Ever. I buy when I am told to buy. I sell when I am told to sell . . . I don't know anyone more honest and, given my background, that shouldn't come as much of a shock. No one has ever been robbed, conned or cheated by him. No investor big or small has ever been manipulated for his gain. Charities have benefited by untold millions, although no one will ever know by absolutely how much. He is a man of honour, intellect, generosity, humour and, above all that, knowledge . . . I'm proud to be his friend . . . it's Rene Rivkin I'm talking about.'

There Richardson was, celebrating the moment when he'd first decided to throw in his lot with his very good friend Rene in the joyous pursuit of mammon, when he had first realised there was a life beyond politics—a life even beyond the backrooms of the New South Wales branch of the Labor Party. It was the only time Richardson had ever been quite so forthcoming in public, and his comments were brimming with in-jokes and secret amusement. Indeed, the whole night was something of a private laugh. Yet if Richardson's praise for Rivkin that night was a little fulsome, there was good reason for it. He was at this time halfway through a tricky operation that would set him up with a new Swiss bank account that had a seven-figure cash balance. But these financial details would not emerge until years later.

Richardson is a man of private pleasures. In politics, though, he was known as the king of payback—he once remarked that the best kind of revenge was when you got someone back and they didn't even know it was you. At the Rivkin seminar, and at the Carr dinner two weeks earlier, Richo was sitting on his golden little secret—he was just a telegraphic transfer away from his million-dollar payout in Switzerland. And no one knew. The audiences at both functions did not have a clue. No one could ever call Richardson taciturn by nature, and that night at the Regent, as he introduced Rivkin, the conversational juices were in full flood.

There was a moment when his future became clear, he told the Regent audience. That moment was in 1988 at the Seoul Olympics, when he was staying in the hotel penthouse suite for a week as a guest of his very special friend Rene. The thoughts of the king-maker of Australian Labor politics may be many, deep and devious, but on this occasion he described them quite simply. As he settled himself onto the sofa in Seoul, he eased back with the thought, 'I could do with a little bit of this.'

Not that there is anything wrong with that. Richardson was very clear about this when journalist Ali Cromie suggested to him in 1998 that people said he only became friends with Rivkin because he wanted Rene to make him a lot of money. It was one of those rare occasions when Richardson was lost for words. The suggestion was simply outrageous. When he finally regained the power of speech he told her:

> As far as I'm concerned they can get knotted. And you can quote me . . . It's not what people say as a general rule. That's rubbish. Absolute rubbish. Some people say it because there are some jealous, greedy, grubby people in the world who will say anything. The idea that people say that as one walks down the street is rubbish. *Absolute rubbish*.

By the end of this outburst to the journalist, Richardson was actually shouting.

So what was the basis of his friendship with Rivkin?

It was the differences, Richardson told Cromie. 'We are very different and interested in the difference. He is interested in my sense of humour, and I am interested in his. We speak literally every day.'

There was a particular power dynamic to the mutual admiration of the humorists, this meeting of mirth. Once he left politics,

Richardson's relationship with Rivkin would never be an equal one. How could it be otherwise? Richardson could work the numbers in any faction room to the moon and back; he could project menace or marvellous bonhomie with the sort of laser-beam intensity that the Star Wars missile defence programmers dream about. But when it came to something simple like making money—serious money—Graham the kingmaker didn't know where to begin. After leaving politics he carved out a new career as a lobbyist and advisor but his principal relationship was with Rivkin. The price of becoming a partner of Rene Rivkin was that Richardson became, in effect, Rene's pet sea scout. In retirement he would work as a political fixer for Kerry Packer and others, he would be a player in media and political circles, but in the core relationship in his new life he would only ever be an acolyte. His role in life was now to be a faint reflection of Rene Rivkin.

Later they would do a radio show together. Everyone knew him as Richo, which meant that Rene had to be Richer. That became the title of their show on 2SM: 'Richo and Richa'. It was a little play on words. Rene's Swiss bank account at Bank Leumi was called Stilton, so Richardson's sub-account was a more lightweight Cheshire. When they set up two new sub-accounts in Zurich in December 2000, Rene's sub-account was called Senior, which meant Richo had to be Junior. But eventually, when Rivkin was being interviewed by the Zurich District Attorney in December 2002 about irregularities in his Swiss bank accounts, Rivkin would shop Richardson, casually exposing him as one of the Offset Alpine shareholders. Rivkin sold his old friend down the river for no apparent reason except that he felt like it. Why would Richardson settle for this?

In the 1990s, the two became great mates, sitting in adjoining offices. Though they had no formal links, they would meet and talk three times a day. But for someone who has been as powerful as Richardson, how much subordination is a few million dollars worth? The friendship went back to even before Richardson's

Eureka moment of realisation with Rene in the hotel suite at Seoul. Rivkin told the Zurich DA in 2001, 'He was the kingmaker of Australian politics and I was a very high-profile broker in Australia, well known in public life. He wanted to meet me. He invited me to an MP's birthday party and we were at the same table. So we met that way.' But it depends who is telling the story.

Rikvin had been attending Labor Party fundraisers organised by Richardson since 1982. Trevor Kennedy introduced Rivkin to Laurie Brereton, who introduced him to Richardson, who introduced him to Bob Hawke, the prime minister. 'I first met him in 1985 or '86,' Richardson told the Regent ballroom that night in 1997:

> The first time I got close to him was when I was in Seoul, in 1988, when I took him to Seoul as my wife. At the time I was Minister for Sport. I had to go to the Olympics and rather than take my wife, I took him. When I arrived there I had a very small hotel room. Twelve people had to have a meeting there, all of them Olympic officials, and they were all sitting on the bed. It was a disaster. So Rene went out and hired the presidential suite and I moved into it. He won me from that moment.

Richardson tells the story like the climax scene from *Jerry Maguire*, when Renee Zellwegger tells a suitably contrite Tom Cruise, 'You had me at "Hello".' It's a *romance*. Richo is the struggling young secretary swept off her feet by Rene, the glamorous older man. In reality Richardson had his own potent appeal for Rivkin, the old roué.

'Rene enjoyed the fact that he had a close friend who was a Minister and wanted to have him there,' Andrew Lakos concluded. 'Rene was the stockbroker for all these guys, helped raise money for them,' another old friend says. 'Rene loves the limelight, the political connections, the access, being able to pick up the phone and ring Laurie, or Graham or Bob or whoever.'

Richardson must have known this. But it made no difference:

> Another thing he did that won me—I was a boy from Kogarah,
> just getting accustomed to the ways of the rich and the famous—
> was when he said, 'Let's go shopping.' We went out to a duty-free
> store and Rivkin bought thirty-two ties. Thirty-two! I discovered
> he had some three hundred of them at home already. He bought
> thirty-two and gave me eight. If I can get a quarter of what he
> buys and sells for the rest of his life then I'll be a very happy man.

Rivkin's largesse did not end with changing hotel rooms and
tossing Richo a few neck warmers. Finding a taxi in Seoul was
difficult, so Rivkin bought a car and hired a driver. The previous
year, Richardson in his capacity as Minister for the Arts, Sport, the
Environment, Tourism and Territories had asked Rivkin to set up
a new fundraising foundation for the Australian National Gallery,
reportedly on the recommendation of Nick Whitlam, whose father
Gough was the gallery's chairman. So it was natural when the
foundation held a fundraising dinner in the capital that Rivkin
would fly Richardson, Gough Whitlam and Ita Buttrose to
Canberra in his new Falcon F20. And then there was the share
trading Rivkin did on his behalf—Richardson told his biographer,
Marian Wilkinson, that he earned $300 000 from share investments
in the 1980s.

Richardson was not the only politician Rivkin cultivated. In
October 1989, the new governor-general, Bill Hayden, put Rene
and his wife Gayle up overnight at Yarralumla. Around that time
a former Rivkin employee remembers seeing Paul Keating
coming out of Renee's stockbroking offices after a lunch. But none
of these relationships would develop the intimacy of the
Rivkin–Richardson liaison, which was fashioned in large part by
Richardson's past.

Of course, one needs to work out which version of Richo's past
you are hearing. It's all in the telling.

In some tales, he appears all coyness and reticence. In 1994, the man whom Senator John Button called the Minister for Kerry Packer published his autobiography, *Whatever It Takes*, without making a single reference to Packer in the index. Packer did appear in the text once, as an accompaniment to a paragraph about Rupert Murdoch. Rivkin rated just a couple of brief mentions in passing.

In other versions, Graham Richardson's most endearing attribute is his capacity to project candour. It is disarming. He says the unexpected while he admits freely to the most atrocious faults. He is frank, unrepentant, and often very amusing. He is eminently sensible, cynical and pragmatic. He says things that are true, and other things which clearly are not true, all in the most convincing manner. The effect can be mesmerising. One ends any conversation with him in apparent agreement and it is only later that the holes in the logic appear. And if charm does not work, there is always plenty of creative potential for threats. Bill Hayden did not dub him the Minister for Kneecaps for nothing.

That Richardson remains one of Australia's best political operatives, even today, is not simply because he is charming or persuasive, forceful or intelligent. He grew up in the heart of the Labor movement. He knows as well as anyone in Australia the concerns of working Australia, why the Labor movement matters. When he retired from politics in March 1994, he won a standing ovation after he concluded his farewell speech: 'When you boil it all down, if you battle in Australia, you've only got one hope. And when there are millions of people battling, all of us must understand that the dignity of those battlers isn't worth something. It's worth everything. When you walk away from it, you stop being human.'

Richardson draws that genuine concern from a childhood bound up in the union movement, in the bitter fights that his parents were involved in when his father was state secretary of the Postal Workers Union and his mother worked at her husband's side—both of them involved in fierce ideological warfare against the left faction. Richo grew up poor but desperately determined, familiar with the underhand tactics of union politics, where loyalty is everything, and betrayal can never be forgiven.

In 1988 in Seoul, Richardson had been at the height of his powers. As environment minister he conjured a magician's trick to win the next election for Labor, pulling Green preferences out of his hat to nudge the Hawke Government just over the line. Even today, conservationists speak with admiration of the forceful way he joined the environmental cause in Tasmania, in Queensland, and wherever else Green candidates could be persuaded to give their election preferences to Labor. He had grown up among slush funds that had been set up to house covert donations from businessmen who wanted to make sure the right side won union elections. Now in federal politics he adopted the same modus operandi, targeting senior business figures for donations to the Labor Party, public and otherwise. Finally, he turned his attention to Rene Rivkin.

The relationships that resulted from Richo's networking would be of critical importance to the events which unfolded three years later. That year, 1991, would be dominated by two epic battles. The first was Paul Keating's campaign to unseat Prime Minister Bob Hawke. The second was Kerry Packer's grab for the Fairfax newspaper group. Graham Richardson would be the key player in both sagas.

FIVE
Wrestling with emotion
1991

In March 1991, Trevor Kennedy dropped by the offices of the Australian Broadcasting Tribunal (ABT) for a 'friendly fireside chat', as he put it. It was time for some free speaking, frank exchanges of views, a few words of wisdom and counsel. It was the way the Sydney network liked to work problems out—no protocol or fuss, just a quiet little heart to heart. Trevor could always be depended upon to straighten out misunderstandings with a helpful, paternal word.

Kennedy had come to the ABT offices to talk about Sydney radio station 2UE. A little misunderstanding had arisen about who ran it. Kerry Packer had said previously that he had no control at all over the station—which was just as well because, under the cross-media laws, owning 2UE in addition to the Nine television network would have been illegal. It might be argued that, technically, Packer owned it. His Consolidated Press group would receive 99 per cent of any dividends paid. But Packer had sold 85 per cent of the voting shares to his accountant for $1, which meant Packer had no control. At least that is what his lawyers said. So it was a bit puzzling when former Test wicket-keeper Rod Marsh, who was one of 2UE's cricket commentators, made some unkind remarks on air about Channel Nine's coverage of the cricket and found himself out of a job shortly afterwards. As Kennedy was able to point out, this merely demonstrated a pleasing like-mindedness between 2UE management and the Packers. It certainly did not indicate that Packer was calling the shots at 2UE, which was the line of inquiry that the ABT had perversely decided to follow.

The House of Packer was no longer as close as it had once been to the ABT, in the days when Bruce Gyngell, the Tribunal's founding chairman, asked Kerry Packer to be godfather to his son David. The present chairman, Peter Westerway, was positively distant. As NSW general secretary of the Labor Party in the early 1970s, Westerway had tried unsuccessfully to block the appointment of Graham Richardson as a state organiser and his politics were more left than anything that Richo had time for. When the ABT persisted in wasting time on the 2UE inquiry, Cons Press sold its interest in the station on the day hearings were to begin.

Actually, the House of Packer by now wasn't as close to Kennedy as it had been either. Kennedy didn't seem too worried about that; his personal finances were going along quite smartly. At the end of 1990, new share disclosure laws had forced Kennedy to reveal that he owned 9.9 per cent of a Sam Gazal company called Sunshine Broadcasting. Kennedy also had some ambitious redevelopment plans for Horse Island, the property on the South Coast that he had received from Gazal for his help in the Bodalla Dairy takeover and asset strip. It's not clear whether Kerry Packer knew about the Horse Island deal but, if he did, it is unlikely he would have been overjoyed about it. While there was technically nothing wrong with Kennedy doing a deal with his mate Sam, Packer could hardly help focusing on the fact that he had already bought Trev a house—the harbourside pile at Elamang Avenue, Kirribilli. Kennedy had persuaded Packer to buy the house in 1984, several weeks after he discovered Packer had bought Rivkin's house as a favour when Rene went to London in 1983, before reselling it back to him. There was a world of significance in the Elamang Avenue purchase.

The North Shore, of course, is a marvellous place, full of wonderful boulevards and often quite nice people. The prime minister lives there; the governor-general has a house there as well. And Mosman is the heartland of the upper-middle class establishment that forged Sydney's cultural character. But, to be frank, it isn't the locale for serious money. At least it isn't any longer. For real wealth and power—an entry level of at least $50 million personal net worth—one buys in Bellevue Hill, Point Piper, Vaucluse or elsewhere in that sweep of harbour suburbs towards South Head. In Sydney, that is where the owners live.

The North Shore is populated by people who work for the owners. And a wonderful job they do of it too, as lawyers, accountants, merchant bankers and minor property developers—that class of superior employee who contributes so much to *res publica* and works so tirelessly in the interests of those who actually run society. Beyond them are the Upper North Shore suburbs, which are ground zero for Sydney's uppity middle class, solid burghers who are so not part of the network. South of the bridge, the power zone is quite contained. Bondi and Coogee are holiday homes for social climbers. Of the suburbs west of Paddington we shall not speak.

It's a simple rule: geography is destiny. The divine chain of being is codified by the street directory. According to one anecdote, perhaps apocryphal, Lachlan Murdoch wanted to buy Foxtel chief Mark Booth's house in Birchgrove after News Corp transferred Booth to Star TV in Hong Kong. Rupert Murdoch took his son aside and told him bluntly, 'People like us don't live in suburbs like that.'

When Packer bought Kennedy a house in Kirribilli in 1983, he was no doubt recognising him as a prince among men, a wonderful fellow and, really, an excellent employee. But what was Packer to make of an employee who owned his own island? In any case, why should Kennedy be getting another house, as reward for extramural work, when he was supposed to be working full time and being paid handsomely ($1.24 million in 1991) to spend twenty-four hours of each day looking after the interests of Consolidated Press?

The second coming of the institutions in the late 1990s blurred some of these social boundaries, creating a new wave of wealthy business figures who are employees and not players. One can only guess at Packer's feelings when he appointed Macquarie investment banker Peter Yates as head of Publishing and Broadcasting Limited (PBL) in March 2001, only to see him buy a house virtually next to the Packer compound in Bellevue Hill. It's said that when Al Dunlap, the abrasive American who succeeded Kennedy as head of Consolidated Press Holdings, expressed a desire to live in Bellevue Hill he was told in no uncertain terms where to go. Dunlap shuffled disconsolately off to the wilds of Woolwich. Sam Chisholm, that master of the small gesture, knew exactly what he was doing when he returned to Australia in the late 1990s after turning around Rupert Murdoch's BSkyB in Britain: he bought a place next door to the Packers at Palm Beach, and a country property near Canberra, not that far from Murdoch's Cavan property. The employee rule, incidentally, didn't work for everybody: Ita Buttrose had a company house near the Packers during her ACP heyday, and the current Cons Press chief, Ashok Jacob, lives just up the street—Jacob always had a deft touch with upward relations.

In 1991, Kennedy's difficulties at Cons Press went beyond housing. On the surface, everything Packer touched turned to gold. Packer's business acumen was legendary. But behind the scenes the picture wasn't as bright. For one thing, the business of being Kerry Packer had become incredibly expensive. There were the polo ponies, the Douglas DC8 to fly him around the world, the multiple residences, the casino jaunts, and Packer's readiness on any day to buy anything that caught his eye on any continent. In the mid-1990s, Sam Gazal was talking to Packer about the meaning of life and how little money either of them really needed. He confided, 'I could be happy earning just $300 000 a year.'

'Me too,' said Packer senior. 'I could be perfectly happy on that.'

At least, that's the way James Packer told the story. James couldn't believe it. '$300 000 a year?' he said. 'Try $100 million a year.' Or so the story goes.

In 1991, Packer's property developments were also looking rocky. In the middle of a recession Packer was stuck with problematic developments with the Grollos in Melbourne and Warren Anderson in Perth. He was not in financial difficulties, but it wouldn't take a lot of bad news on the property front to put him under pressure. And this was just the moment when an opportunity arose that Packer had been awaiting for decades.

On 10 December 1990, the banks appointed receivers to the Fairfax newspaper group. Investment banker Mark Burrows, who would supervise the sale of the business for the banks, laid out the ground rules for the great Fairfax auction. While publicly playing down his interest, Packer had already made his plans. On 28 November, just seven weeks after Packer's heart attack, Canadian newspaperman Conrad Black wrote to him about a joint bid for Fairfax: 'Could you bear in mind what I said at our meeting at Jimmy Goldsmith's house that I would be happy in principle if you were to participate in our deal?'

Packer faxed back the next day: 'I would be delighted to take an interest with you in Fairfaxes, but I do not believe the time has yet come to make our move. I will keep you fully informed and will consider you my partner in looking at Fairfaxes, so if at some stage you have a change of heart for some reason, kindly let me know.'

On 3 June 1991, Packer met with Black at the Savoy Hotel in London to finalise a joint bid for Fairfax through a consortium called Tourang. In the intervening six months, Malcolm Turnbull, who had been appointed representative of Fairfax's junk bond-holders, had put a deal together that virtually ensured Tourang would win. He had signed an agreement for the bondholders to deal exclusively with Tourang for a six-month period. Turnbull would sit on the Tourang board as the bondholders' representative. On paper the alliance looked unbeatable. However, Tourang faced two difficulties.

First, if its bid were successful, it would raise the foreign ownership of Fairfax to between 35 and 40 per cent. This was above the accepted government guidelines, and it would require careful lobbying in Canberra. The best chance lay with Packer's close links with the right wing of the Labor Party in NSW—which was to say, Tourang's hopes were founded on Graham Richardson. Unfortunately for Tourang, Richardson already had his hands full. On 3 June, while Packer was meeting with Black in London, Treasurer Paul Keating mounted his first leadership challenge to the prime minister, Bob Hawke. Keating lost and went to the backbench. As Keating's campaign manager, Richardson was now also on the outer.

The second problem was that the presence of Packer in the consortium would trigger widespread fears that he was secretly running the show. Packer could be a highly interventionist proprietor. There was still sensitivity over the David Dale affair the previous year. In March 1990, Dale as editor of the *Bulletin* had published an issue titled 'The Great Australian Balance Sheet'. The magazine listed forty-five Australian public figures who were assets to the culture, and another forty-five who were liabilities. A year before, Dale had produced a list of the country's 'Most Appalling People'. That issue had prompted an edict from Kerry Packer, whose friends had complained about making the cut, that there should be no more 'Appalling People' lists. 'The Great

Australian Balance Sheet' was a neat way around the ban. Alan Jones and John Laws were both prominent entries in the liabilities section, but they largely ignored it. John Singleton, on the other hand, had taken exception to the original list that rated his social appeal somewhere around that of the meningococcal disease. He made the traditional Sydney response to bad press, which was to call his very good friend, the publisher. Kerry Packer sacked Dale for breaking his ban on 'Appalling People' lists and ordered security guards to escort him from the building. Dale's timing could have been better.

Days earlier Packer had learned that American antitrust regulators were about to block Operation Happy, the $27 billion takeover bid he was making with Sir James Goldsmith and Rothschild for British American Tobacco. Packer could now say goodbye to the $1.5 billion profit that he had planned to make from Operation Happy. It was just the sort of disappointment to make Packer a little snippy, even before Singleton called to complain. The Dale sacking caused a flurry of publicity, which the Packers ignored ('Keep your nose out of other people's business,' Kennedy told the *Sydney Morning Herald*).

Despite the problems, in the winter of 1991, Turnbull had no doubts that Tourang could win approval from Canberra. On Monday 15 July, he took Steven Ezzes, the head of the Fairfax junk bondholders committee, to Canberra for lunch with Graham Richardson. Richo brought along the communications minister, Kim Beazley, so that Turnbull could put the case for Tourang directly. The next day, Tourang went public with its bid for Fairfax. The biggest news was that Trevor Kennedy was leaving Consolidated Press at the end of the month to head Tourang. 'I am personally very sad at this event but Trevor has chosen to pursue an opportunity as chief executive of a group which will try to acquire the Fairfax newspapers,' Packer announced to staff.

Conrad Black flew in on the Wednesday, ready to dispel any suggestion that Kerry Packer was calling the shots. 'Kerry will be very much a minority shareholder,' Black told the *Bulletin*. 'He will be a shareholder at the kind of level that normally gets you a free lunch and a tour of the plant. Kerry is not going to be controlling anything in that company . . .' Black then launched into the wildest account of how Kennedy happened to be working for him.

'Kerry's involvement arose out of me seeking to hire Trevor Kennedy as the prospective managing director of the Fairfax Group, were we to gain control of it.' It would have been a 'breach of protocol' if Black didn't first check this with Packer. 'When I did, he said he wouldn't stand in the way of any man's career, but if I did go ahead, he would like a piece of the deal.'

It was wonderful. In a town that values insincerity and narcissistic self-display, Black was a natural. How would he like to be seen? 'As the Samaritanly philanthropist that I am. I'm just here to help you, you know,' he admitted diffidently. The Samaritan would later tell US magazine *Vanity Fair* that journalists were 'swarming, grunting masses of jackals', 'a very degenerate group' with 'a terrible incidence of alcoholism and drug abuse' who were often 'ignorant, lazy, opinionated, intellectually dishonest and inadequately supervised'. As he told Quentin Dempster on the *7.30 Report*, he meant this in a nice way.

Two days later, Kennedy flew to Canberra with Black. He demonstrated his political connections by arranging for Black to meet with Prime Minister Bob Hawke and Treasurer John Kerin for an hour, and then to lunch with Beazley. There was a little hiccup when Beazley told Black the biggest obstacle to Tourang winning approval was 'the fellow sitting next to you'. Without a blink Black turned to Kennedy, 'Okay, Trevor, you're fired.' Everyone laughed. What a card that Conrad was. Despite these antics, unrest among the backbenchers forced the government to announce a senate inquiry into the print media.

With all the media attention focused on Tourang, no one noticed that Consolidated Press had quietly stopped furnishing financial information to Australian Ratings, which provides company debt ratings for creditors. Stopping the flow of financial information to your creditors is often a sign of trouble. Its 30 June accounts, when they later appeared, suggested that money was tight at this time. Packer's contribution to Tourang was to be only $75 million. Then within days of Kennedy leaving at the end of July, Cons Press was hit by bank demands for $650 million. The joint venture property deals set up on Kennedy's watch had hit the wall.

It was so avoidable. Warren Anderson had a joint venture development in Perth with Shimizu and C Itoh. It was in trouble, but everyone knew the Japanese did not let their partners fall over. Yet in October 1990, Anderson, who can be annoying at the best of times, managed to escalate into a major confrontation a minor difference over who was to pay land tax owing on the site. His partners appointed receivers to several Anderson companies on 9 August 1991. While this was bad enough for Anderson, it was pretty horrific for Kerry Packer.

Three years before, Packer and Anderson had ponied up $90 million as a down payment to buy the Westralia Square site in Perth. The rest of the sale price and the loan for construction didn't fall due until 1995. There was one proviso. If any of the Packer or Anderson companies in the deal went into administration, the bank debt fell due immediately. The moment the Japanese receivers walked into Anderson's companies chasing the money for land tax, the entire $360 million owing on Westralia Square became instantly due. And, because both Packer and Anderson were co-guarantors, the banks could now demand all of that money from Packer.

The bad news didn't stop. In Melbourne, the banks financing 120 Collins Street wanted their money back. Packer had sold down almost all his interest in the project to the Grollo brothers and now held only 1 per cent. But Cons Press was still liable for three quarters of the debt. That amounted to $288 million that Packer suddenly had to come up with.

Packer didn't go broke, of course. He had been playing with the idea of hiring Brian Powers, the American from US investment bank Hellman and Friedman who was working on the Tourang deal, as Kennedy's replacement at Cons Press (Stephen Mulholland, the South African later appointed to run Fairfax, described Powers in an Internet chat room in 2005 as a 'pushy, avaricious San Franciscan from whose scalp there grew mysterious and scrofulous tufts'). But instead of Powers, Kerry Packer called on Al Dunlap, the abrasive American cost-cutter known as Chainsaw (his reputation for turning around companies took a dive in 1998 when Sunbeam sacked him for fabricating profits—four years later Dunlap paid US$15 million to settle a class action by Sunbeam shareholders and US$500 000 to the US Securities & Exchange Commission to settle a civil fraud case without admitting liability). By late 1992, Dunlap would raise $2.8 billion in cash for Packer in a massive sell-off, but meanwhile in late 1991 Cons Press was stalling for time.

Anderson once described to journalist Mark Drummond a physical struggle he had with Kerry Packer over the Westralia Square debacle, actually wrestling with him on the floor of his Park Street office. It's a wonderful image, the two men thrashing about on the floor, arms and legs flailing. I think there must have been some grunting. At some point they knocked over a cast-iron stand holding a glass bowl of sweets, which exploded across the room. 'This bloody thing, I remember, it hit the deck and lollies went everywhere,' Anderson told Drummond. The episode was triggered when Packer first learnt in 1988 that he was tied to the Westralia Square debacle. That was when it merely looked as if Packer might be at risk in the project. One can only imagine Packer's feelings three years later when the banks actually came looking for their $360 million. This unhappy discovery marked the first of a series of magical moments that might be filed under the heading, 'Handling Adversity Badly'.

The next magical moment was at the Regent Hotel on 13 October, after the Tourang consortium members began a corporate game of Man Overboard. Conrad Black's lieutenant, Dan Colson, and Brian Powers had decided that Trevor Kennedy wasn't pulling his weight and he needed to be informed of their concerns. This would be no fireside chat. Their worry was that Kennedy could turn violent. 'Perhaps he will start throwing punches,' Colson quipped waggishly as they sat awaiting the arrival of their managing director in one of the hotel's rooms. Just to show how amusing this line was, Colson proceeded to hide various loose objects in a cupboard. There was a heavy ashtray, a letter opener, a pair of scissors—all much too dangerous to have around a snitty Trevor Kennedy. A less courageous man than Colson would have taken no chances with the television remote, the bar fridge, and some of the more lethal soft furnishings. Regrettably, the heated exchanges that followed were only verbal. Kennedy resigned from Tourang two days later.

The next moment was in the Botanic Gardens five weeks later, on Friday 23 November, where Colson had arranged a one-on-one session with an unhappy Malcolm Turnbull. Colson wanted Turnbull to resign from the Tourang board. Though neither of them had a letter opener or ashtray within reach, the prospect of Colson and Turnbull wrestling on the ground in $1000 suits amongst the bushes was jokingly entertained by the rest of the Tourang team as they waited at the Ritz-Carlton for Colson to return. However, while Turnbull had often described himself as a bomb thrower, he baulked at shrubbery. After a full and frank exchange of views, Turnbull told Colson he would resign. But by the next day, Saturday, he had changed his mind. Talks continued through the weekend.

Then came the most magical moment of all, on the Sunday night, when Peter Westerway found himself in a car in a darkened street in North Sydney, feeling so not like the head of the Australian Broadcasting Tribunal. He had been called late at night by someone he later described as 'a prominent public figure, who was also a principal in a major ownership and control case'. The caller wanted an urgent meeting because he had vital evidence that must be handed over in secret because he believed 'he, his wife and his family were all at risk'. So there was Westerway, feeling a little silly in the driver's seat, when the mystery figure climbed into the passenger seat beside him, 'where he passed across the material in a brown paper bag, like a character from a Len Deighton novel'. Westerway refused to identify the man in the car publicly, other than to say it wasn't Trevor Kennedy. And given the number of players in the Fairfax saga, it's impossible to say who the mystery man was. His claims about being afraid for his safety should probably be taken as a histrionic gesture, which ensured he had Westerway's complete attention.

Whatever the source, the papers inside the bag were dynamite. They were copies of diary notes that Trevor Kennedy had made around the time of his appointment in July to head Tourang, in which he gave his understanding of Packer's role in the consortium. Packer, Black and even Kennedy had, under oath at the print inquiry, been keen to stress that Packer would not control or influence the management of Tourang once it had secured the Fairfax newspaper group. Now it turned out that, privately, Kennedy had the exact opposite idea of Packer's plans. No doubt he had got hold of the wrong end of the stick, but dear old Trevor had written it all down in his diary. Now, by a stroke of luck, Westerway had a copy of these notes. This was not the same as getting hold of them officially, but it meant that the next morning he was able to draft a detailed order for Kennedy to produce the relevant diary notes. The Broadcasting Tribunal had the original diary notes in its possession by Monday afternoon. They were a showstopper. Westerway announced on Tuesday that he was opening an official inquiry into the Tourang bid—a lengthy process that would effectively put Tourang out of the hunt for Fairfax. Two days later, Packer announced he was withdrawing from Tourang. Packer, along with most of the Tourang camp, was convinced that Kennedy had leaked the documents to Westerway.

Kennedy was now persona non grata anywhere near the Consolidated Press circle.

Packer's departure left Conrad Black alone in the 'Big Brother' house. First Kennedy, then Turnbull, then Packer had been voted off the show. Then a week later, Conrad Black was told to pack his bags. On Thursday 5 December, the Federal Treasurer John Kerin, as head of the Foreign Investment Review Board (FIRB), decided to approve Tony O'Reilly's independent bid for Fairfax and reject Tourang's on the grounds that the level of foreign investment in Conrad Black's bid was too high. It was all over. Kerin's decision represented a complete defeat for Packer's and Black's plans, though the FIRB office would not inform Tourang of Kerin's decision until the following Sunday.

'It is sleazy, venal and despicable, I'm sure the Australian public are shocked and appalled by these tactics,' Conrad Black spluttered in London when he heard the news. Despite these brave words, Kerin's decision seemed to signal the end of the road for Tourang. But the battle wasn't quite over. One factor remained in play—that trusty friend of troubled media barons, Graham Richardson.

The major political events of that December—the battle for Fairfax and the climax of the Labor leadership challenge—could be written as two separate narratives, with only an incidental connection between the two. That connection would be Richo. Among his many other talents, Richardson would go down in history as a self-professed liar. He admitted as much in his 1994 autobiography, *Whatever It Takes*. It's part of the Richo legend. What is less well known is that when Richardson made this confession, he was talking about the events of late 1991.

In September, with Paul Keating on the backbench and his

failed challenge to Bob Hawke going nowhere, Richardson decided it was time to damp down leadership speculation. He saw himself as the key figure in the challenge, because of the votes he could deliver from the NSW right. He announced unilaterally that the challenge was over and went on radio with Hawke to talk about how matey they all were now. As he wrote later:

> This did not indicate treachery to Keating, but the difficulty I was having in helping him become Prime Minister without destroying the party. This sounds uncharacteristically noble, but having said that I have to add that to achieve that goal successfully I had to lie from time to time—which I did.

Getting back into the Hawke camp didn't just take attention away from the Keating campaign, which continued anyway, it also brought Richardson back into the counsels close to Hawke, who were debating what to do about Fairfax. But the whispering campaign against Hawke's leadership had quickened after Liberal leader John Hewson revealed his 'Fightback!' package for a goods and services tax on 22 November. Hawke's finance team of Treasurer Kerin and Finance Minister Ralph Willis were also not performing well.

The two dramas—Fairfax and the leadership challenge—both came to a head on 5 December. Kerin's historic, but as yet unannounced, decision to dump Tourang that day was entirely overshadowed by his disastrous performance at a press conference to release the September national accounts. The figures confirmed that Australia was in the middle of its worst slump in sixty years. In the course of his presentation, Kerin referred to the GOS figures:

> As you know, all of this is two to five months in the past. The Gross Operating, sorry the Gross, aah . . . [pause] share rose, Gross, aah . . . [pause] What's GOS?

At this stage in the self-disintegration of Kerin's career, a large sign up the back of the room that said 'Gross Operating Surplus, Stupid' could have changed history. Instead, Kerin's harmless but embarrassing gaffe became a sound bite that was played and replayed on television screens across the country. It was the final straw. Richardson advised Hawke, who still thought that Richo was on his side, to replace Kerin as Treasurer and to make a sweeping Cabinet reshuffle.

That private advice from Richardson, which was echoed by Victorian right-wing powerbroker Robert Ray, appeared on the front page of the *Sydney Morning Herald* the next day, Friday. By 11.30 that morning, Hawke had moved to appoint Ralph Willis to replace Kerin as treasurer as of the following Monday. (Kerin, his political career effectively over, resigned from parliament two years later, leaving his seat of Werriwa to the ambitious mayor of Liverpool, Mark Latham.) Richardson headed off for lunch in Rivkin's boardroom, where he was able to tell Laurie Brereton, Peter Barron and Rivkin that his advice to Hawke the previous day would destroy Hawke. Richardson had known, he later claimed, that even as he pressed Hawke for a full cabinet reshuffle the PM would jump the other way and only replace Kerin, an inadequate response that would not be sufficient to head off the Keating challenge. But Barron, who by now was Kerry Packer's chief lobbyist, and Rivkin, as Packer's sometime broker, would have seen much wider repercussions from Richardson's move.

It was quite the strategic masterstroke. Hawke's downfall would recharge Richardson's career and, whether or not Richo really was the deciding factor in Hawke's decision to sack Kerin, he would tell the story so many times that it became accepted history that he was. At the time he was advising Hawke, as a senior government minister Richardson would have known which way Kerin was leaning on the Fairfax decision. It seems inconceivable that he didn't know that Kerin had already formally rejected the Tourang bid. Of course, whether he actually knew or not doesn't make a lot of difference. In politics, it's how you tell the story.

The Fairfax auction had not yet closed when Kerin's decision was made public over the weekend. With Kerin now out of the picture, Tourang was free to submit a new, revised bid, and start the whole FIRB approval process all over again. By the following Wednesday, Tourang had restructured its bid for Fairfax to reduce foreign ownership to 25 per cent. The new Treasurer, Ralph Willis, only forty-eight hours into the job, had a month to make a response. He took just two days. On Friday 13 December, Willis approved the new bid without further inquiry. Three days later, the banks had sold Fairfax to Tourang, leaving the newspaper group at the mercy of Conrad Black's split infinitives and appalling syntax as the group's controlling shareholder for the next five years. Packer, meanwhile, was left to scheme endless ways, with all the relentless persistence of Wile E. Coyote, of getting Fairfax back.

Conrad Black had won Fairfax because Kerin was no longer treasurer. And the chief reason Kerin was no longer treasurer was that old wag, Graham Richardson. Even if Kerry Packer was no longer a shareholder in Tourang, as a payout for his departure he had negotiated a package of Tourang options, which he later cashed out for $60 million. Richardson had done many favours for Packer in his career. But this surely must have been one of the sweetest.

On 19 December, Keating defeated Hawke for the leadership. The next day he called around to Richardson's office to ask him what portfolio he wanted. And so Graham Richardson, the man who had already shown himself to be the Most Valuable Player for Team Packer, the politician to whom Kerry Packer owed the most, became the new communications minister.

PART TWO

Friends of James

GENERAL: But wait a bit. I object to pirates as sons-in-law.
KING: We object to major-generals as fathers-in-law.
          But we waive that point. We do not press it.
          We look over it.

Pirates of Penzance

SIX

Vapour trails

In Sydney, New South Head Road is the path that leads to money. You follow it out through the clutter of Rushcutters Bay and Edgecliff, past the discreet entrance to Darling Point, down the sweeping hill to Double Bay and then ascend beyond it to where a dizzying sweep of harbour beckons. And there you are: to your left the trees of Point Piper; rising up to your right is Bellevue Hill; Rose Bay lies before you. But right here, where you are, are the gates of Cranbrook School. The eastern suburbs . . . you're soaking in it.

Cranbrook's founders in 1918, besides having a great eye for property values, had a dry sense of humour when they plonked the school down beside the more austere Scots College. Scots is GPS; it is landed wealth; it is rugger. Cranbrook is the eastern suburbs' revenge. It is based upon, lives, breathes and propagates the network. In their choice of school motto the Cranbrook founders had also been pretty droll—*esse quam videri*: to 'be' rather than to seem to be—in other words, reality before appearance, substance rather than surface. It's a very Sydney exercise in self-deception. The real motto of course is more like *videri quam esse*.

In the Sydney network, appearance comes before everything. Bellevue Hill is a financial ecosystem, a food chain like no other, where the links between the very wealthy, their advisors, their lawyers, their accountants and, most of all, their friends create tides of investment that wash back and forth across Australian capital markets. In the desperately small world that is the eastern suburbs, the Packer compound on Victoria Road, Bellevue Hill, manages to be both the centre of gravity and the top of the food chain. Even a tiny piece of a Packer deal—or the appearance of a piece—can shower wealth indiscriminately on those close enough to catch it. The key is proximity.

How do you get close enough? Kerry Packer's uncertain health in the early 1990s meant that, at any moment, the young and inexperienced James Packer was a heartstop away from inheriting a multi-billion-dollar fortune. That made James potentially the single largest walking source of private capital in Australia. James Packer had become Sydney's ultimate honey pot, a lure that would draw spivs, fast money men, merchant bankers, earnest entrepreneurs and fundraisers from all over the country. The fights and intrigues to control James Packer would become a struggle between the Sydney and Melbourne networks, Australia's two centres of financial power. In the process, the Cranbrook alumni—ambitious networkers like Rodney Adler and Jodee Rich—would come into their own.

Kerry Packer's close friend Robert Whyte had a particular scorn for those he saw as arrivistes and would-be players. When the *Australian Financial Review* in 1996 was preparing a feature nominating a list of power figures from Australia's New Establishment (a concept borrowed from *Vanity Fair*), Whyte called the paper to, first, check discreetly that he was on the power list and then, once reassured, to share his views on some of the other names. Like

Frank Lowy. By 2000, with their shopping-centre interests here and in the United States, the Lowy family would rival the Packers as Australia's wealthiest family. As if mere money could atone in a town like Sydney. 'Very Second Eleven,' Whyte said dismissively of them, with a fine private-school disdain straight out of *Tom Brown's Schooldays*—or perhaps a Cranbrook School local equivalent, something like *Billy Bunter Does Double Bay*. No doubt Whyte would have picked up useful phrases like that when he was at The Kings School, or during the year he spent at Oxford in the mid-1990s, studying religion. It's a telling remark.

By 1991, the recession had wiped out almost all of the major and minor players of the 1980s. They were broke, or in jail, or in court. Besides Kerry Packer, only the technicians were left. They had spent the 1980s doing deals for other people. They had their little companies on the side, they knew the serpentine ways of fast money and modern commerce. They faced the same desperate struggle for survival that had decimated the real players of the boom, but they were sustained in their efforts by this one glimmer of hope: if they could wriggle past the grasping clutches of un-sympathetic bankers and ungrateful shareholders, predatory tax officers and over-zealous regulators for long enough; if they could keep the show going and away from the bankruptcy court for another couple of years, then the crisis would pass and they would be saved. Not just saved, they would be disgracefully rich. In the bright new decade of the 1990s, they would face no real opposition. This was to be a lacklustre era that would turn out to be tailormade for the B Team. Which would explain the advent of Rocket Rodney.

How to describe a character like Rodney Adler AM? In the hard times that have befallen him lately, it is hard to remember the air of success he cultivated so assiduously in the 1990s, when he was at full mega-wattage. Back then, everyone knew that everyone loved Rodney. He and his wife Lyndi appeared more than 400 times each year in the nation's press, where Rodney was described variously as a leading businessman, outstanding philanthropist, savvy investor, friend of the Packers, co-founder of One.Tel, society prince and national treasure. For journalists, Rodney's door was always open. He was that creature most cherished and loved by the media, a really great gossip. He understood the media contract: that in order to get a little, you have to give a little. The currency of exchange is information. In the 1990s whenever his name appeared in a social column, it was always fascinating to guess for which if any of the accompanying gossip items he was the source.

The practical consequence for journalists was that everything to do with Adler became personal. Everyone had a Rodney moment. The first time I called him, in June 1989, he could not have been kinder. His father Larry had died six months earlier, leaving Rodney at age twenty-nine in charge of a $3 billion insurance and investment operation teetering on the verge of insolvency. Up to that point, Rodney's life had been unremarkable and any business skills invisible. But he could certainly network. In addition to his father's links in the Sydney and Melbourne Jewish community, Rodney had attended Cranbrook, where his classmates included One.Tel's Jodee Rich, journalist Adam Shand, and Paul Brown, who became Richard Weisener's understudy as corporate fixer in Monaco. James Packer was several years behind Rodney, whose nickname was 'The Snake'.

Adler family life was shaped by Rodney's father, Larry, who founded Fire and All-risk Insurances after migrating to Australia from Hungary in 1949. 'We grew up with it,' Rodney's younger sister, Roxanne, said of the family business in 1994. 'We remember its whole life, and everything that went wrong . . . Dad wasn't a big chitchat man [but] in the last few years it was all we talked about.'

Larry didn't know too much about the niceties of insurance but he came into his own in the takeover frenzy of the 1980s. He was a bagman who did favours and held assets with no questions asked on deals arranged directly between principals with no messy paperwork. There was, after all, honour among financiers. The payoff would typically come in a large money transfer that didn't quite make commercial sense, but which could disguise the real exchange. In one instance, Christopher Skase's Qintex group paid $5 million to FAI for an insurance policy on Skase's life over a five-month period. To outsiders, the decision for the policy to run just for that period was hard to understand. It appeared as if the effect of the deal was to transfer money from Qintex to FAI.

Deals that weren't really deals were the trademark sign of the network. They signalled the real business had been done behind closed doors. The 'honest brokers' who organised the deals, warehoused the shares and held or loaned the money were called 'bishops', and Larry Adler was one of them. Larry was respected, but he wasn't loved. The 1987 Crash—which interrupted Rodney's honeymoon with Lyndi—wiped out two thirds of FAI's value. Larry Adler's empire, like its founder, was living on borrowed time. When he died in December 1988, *Australian Financial Review* journalist Ian Thomas spent an entire afternoon trying to find someone to say something nice about him for his obituary, but failed.

After the shock of Larry's death, Ray Williams at HIH Insurance quietly suggested a takeover that would have left the Adler family with about $240 million. A year before, the Adlers' shares had been worth $1 billion. The family wasn't ready to sell.

Rodney was soon faced with the uncomfortable discovery that his legacy was threadbare. Larry held markers from all over town in messy deals that Rodney had to untangle. Rodney himself had little experience and few prospects. It was fortunate then that Rodney could turn to his father's investment banker, Bruce Corlett, who quietly became deputy chairman of FAI in December 1988. 'Bruce is extraordinarily good at sorting out difficult situations,' an associate of both men said. It was Corlett who worked out the strategy and negotiated most of the trickier deals. FAI would never see the $562 million it had loaned to Alan Bond. Corlett grabbed what he could instead—a Queensland coal mine and the St Moritz Hotel in New York—while Rodney talked the talk.

With the media, Rodney was affability itself. When I telephoned him in mid-1989 about a recent share deal in which Skase's Qintex group seemed to have given FAI a $15 million straight-out gift, Rodney was only too pleased to talk. It was a very interesting matter and well worth querying, he said. Unfortunately he had only a perfunctory memory of the affair. After a few general remarks he said he really thought he ought to look at the file before saying anything else. Could he call me back? No one could be more helpful. Rodney was a giant among men . . . though he did seem to be taking a while to get back to me. After several days of silence I called his secretary, who broke the bad news. She told me quite kindly that Mr Adler had indeed looked at the file but he didn't think there was anything he could add. That was when I realised I was dealing with a pro.

Blatant insincerity of this order is a rare gift. It's why I've always admired Rodney, though his own feelings for me have been more ambivalent. In 1998, he wrote to say he was cutting all links—he would not answer my calls or speak to me, and any letter from me would be dumped unopened in the waste bin. A year later he did reply to a letter, out of 'corporate politeness', to tell me:

> In essence, every time you write a story that refers to me or is about me, you cause significant damage either between my family, with the companies I am associated with, or with the Tax Department . . . Your figures are totally inaccurate—this is why I say you are a dangerous journalist. Neil, the principle of public accountability and freedom of the press is important but you take that to such an extreme that you actually take away the joy of being an executive or non-executive director. You actually stifle entrepreneurship.

That was pretty gentle for a Rodney letter. Back in January 1991, he was detonating tactical nuclear devices in his correspondence with Coles Myer chairman Solomon Lew, who, besides being 'impertinent and dishonourable', owed FAI $50 million. 'Don't write to me in sarcastic tones about our daily cashflow,' he wrote. And again, 'What in God's name are you people playing at? Does honour and one's word mean nothing in your state? Whatever happened to morals and ethics in business?'

In February 1990, FAI had been stuck with a load of overpriced shares it didn't want in Lew's company, Premier Investments, from a share underwriting deal that went wrong. Lew had been stalling on his promise to take $60 million of the shortfall, basically because he didn't have the money. FAI was struggling as well and the mood between Adler and Lew wasn't pretty. Happily the stand-off was resolved on 21 January 1991, when FAI announced that it had received $39.4 million from Lew's private company to settle the matter. What the announcement didn't say was that most of the money came from a deal that Lew's people had arranged the previous year for FAI to sell the shares to a $2 company called Yannon. The money to cover Yannon's losses in the trade came from the Coles Myer super fund, and ultimately from Coles Myer itself.

This miraculous resolution of their dispute should have been great news for Solly Lew, if only he had known about it. The Yannon deal would be highly controversial when it came to light four years later, but Lew was able to assure the Australian Securities Commission that the executives who arranged the deal never told him any of the details. I suppose the clue for Lew should have been that Rodney was no longer threatening to amputate his arms and legs, or words to that effect.

But that wasn't the only significant consequence of the Yannon deal. Its successful completion meant that, on Tuesday 1 February, Rodney Adler and FAI had a little spare money when an old friend dropped by.

It's difficult, even for those who lived through it, to remember how harrowing those days in the early 1990s were. Corporate Australia seemed to be falling apart. For every major corporate crash like Bond Corporation or Adelaide Steamship, dozens of minor ventures were foundering. Public companies, large and small, would see their share price slip a little, dip further, and then plummet, down and down, until their bankers lost their nerve, froze their funding and finally called in their loans. Most entrepreneurs' wealth was tied up in their companies. They faced personal as well as corporate shipwreck. This was not a matter of facing a little bad news. The prospect here was financial annihilation. In order to survive, they had to find a way to maintain public confidence, to keep that share price up. The question was, what were they prepared to do to achieve this?

Rene Rivkin had never really recovered from the 1987 Crash. He had survived since then with the odd trading coup while otherwise maintaining a precarious balancing act between his many creditors. Year by year it became harder. His broking business, Rivkin & Co, depended upon support from his public company, Oilmet, to keep its doors open. But Oilmet was struggling. It had 115 million shares on issue, and the only people who seemed remotely interested in owning them were friends of Rivkin. Larry Adler bought some shares in 1988, then sold out again. Robert Whyte believed Oilmet was a good investment and his public company Audant Investments bought ten million Oilmet shares in 1989. Rivkin had a similarly high view of both of Whyte's public companies, Audant and Trafalgar Properties. Rivkin bought their stock via Oilmet, then bought even more shares through his Swiss accounts. Whyte said he knew nothing of this.

For the most part though, Rivkin resorted to buying his own

stock. Rivkin bought huge lines of Oilmet shares, then parked them in nominee accounts managed by Rivkin & Co. He secretly owned or controlled nearly half of the company's shares. This kept the Oilmet share price from collapsing completely, but it was a blatant breach of the Takeovers Code, which required Rivkin to make a full takeover bid when he kept buying over the 20 per cent limit. Rivkin's approach to the Takeovers Code was to ignore it. He simply claimed the shares were being held for clients. And no one asked any questions. Yet behind the bravado, maintaining the charade was a delicate business. It began to unravel in early 1990 when Rivkin made his unhappy bet on the future of the Japanese market and ended up losing $10 million. As his credit lines dried up, Rivkin started selling assets. In March 1990, he pocketed $1.4 million when Oilmet bought Rivkin & Co. Later in the year there were cars and shares and apartments for sale.

In April 1990, the Australian Stock Exchange (ASX) noticed that something funny was happening with shares in Rene Rivkin's company. Share trading in Australia is monitored by a tiny division of the stock exchange called ASX Surveillance. Jim Berry, who set up Surveillance and ran it from 1987 to February 2005, is a large square man with a lively sense of humour and a tendency to come at any subject from an angle. While Surveillance rarely rates a mention in the media, by dint of sheer determination, shrewdness and a little guile, Berry built the division into the sharp end of corporate law enforcement in Australia. In general, ASIC only investigates share trading after ASX Surveillance has done its own investigation and referred the matter on. Berry operated in a shadow world based partly on technology and the computer programs that monitored share trading, and partly on his private intelligence network of contacts.

While senior ASIC officers would spend much of the 1990s scoffing at the idea that insider traders or market riggers regularly operated in the Australian share market, Berry knew the truth was very different, because he saw it every day.

In March 1990, Berry began looking at a trail of suspicious trades in Oilmet stock. His inquiries showed that Bank Leumi le-Israel had recently bought 4.7 million shares. The way the sales went through made him suspect that Rivkin was behind the trading, using it to prop up his share price. While Berry referred the matter to the ASX listing committee, no direct action was taken. In the United States the Securities and Exchange Commission regularly prosecuted investors for market manipulation, but for Australian regulators in the early 1990s it was all new territory. It was easy to dismiss Berry as a conspiracy theorist.

Berry had caught a glimpse of a far wider operation. Rivkin had been selling Oilmet shares he held in nominee companies in Australia to Stilton, his Zurich account with Bank Leumi. Actually, Rivkin had been doing this for years. It was a way of bringing money into the country from Switzerland, in this case to cover the losses from his bet on the Japanese market. It also pushed up Oilmet's share price. Unhappily, Rivkin appears to have also been using Stilton to buy Japanese futures, notching up $US3.3 million in losses. By mid-year, Rivkin was in trouble in Zurich as well. Stilton's only assets were twenty-two million Oilmet shares. Against that, Rivkin owed Bank Leumi close to $6 million. Leumi's new private client manager, Ernst Imfeld, wanted some fast money.

Rivkin never talked about the events that followed. When he was asked about it twelve years later by Zurich District Attorney Dr Nathan Landshut, Rivkin flatly denied any knowledge of what Landshut called the 'Stilton disaster'. Landshut dragged it out of him line by line. Back in September 1990, when Rivkin was facing financial ruin both in Australia and Switzerland, he went back to the one place he had always got money—his father. 'It never entered my head, I know nothing about it,' Rivkin insisted when Landshut suggested that Walter had bailed him out. Walter didn't have a name for his account, just a number, 8405. Rene went behind his father's back and signed a guarantee agreement that froze $3.5 million of 8405's funds to secure the money Rene had lost in Stilton. In his 2002 exchange with Landshut, Rene denied this up to the moment when Landshut produced the guarantee agreement Rivkin had signed in Zurich on 5 September 1990.

The stilted transcript of the 2002 interview, which has been translated from English to German and back to English, still rings with Landshut's flat incredulity at what Rivkin had done:

> So you were using the account of your father, with whom you hadn't spoken for years, and who was desperate to hang on to his assets, as security for your speculative account. Is that right and did your father know that? Did he know that rather than having about A$4 million in his account, he really actually had only A$500 000?

Walter Rivkin didn't know. Rene told Landshut that, as he was his father's only living child, the money would come to him anyway: 'I now remember that I did have the right to sign on behalf of my father's account and Mr Imfeld had made it clear to me that he would exchange security between those two accounts—Stilton and 8405.' Clearly it was Imfeld's fault.

Rene wasn't looking back. The day after Rivkin signed the guarantee document in Zurich, Oilmet announced a new start under a new name. It would henceforth call itself Stroika Limited. Rivkin would spend the rest of his life telling the world at large how awful his father was, but Zurich would not feature in this account. The sad thing was, even ripping Walter off for $3.5 million wasn't enough to save Rene. Five months later Rivkin was forced to go to the lender of last resort.

On 1 February 1991, a peculiar meeting unfolded in Rodney Adler's office in the FAI building in Macquarie Street—a meeting shrouded in so much mystery that even years later no one was prepared to talk about it. In the desperate days of the 1990–91 recession, the deal consummated that day seemed trivial. Yet it would be a milestone for the Sydney network. This was the survival moment that turned it all around. It was the occasion when two casualties of the recession, battered and bruised and still taking damage from those penurious times, stood up and said they weren't going to take it anymore. In short, it was the day when Rene Rivkin, that moral pillar of the broking community, appealed to the noble character of his very good friend Rodney Adler and hit him for another little loan. Today, the only evidence of what followed is a fading paper trail and a strange whiff of aviation fuel.

It looks quite simple in the public filings. On that date, FAI Leasing Finance made a loan to several Rivkin companies, including Simdock Pty Ltd, a $2 company that owned a $3.5 million corporate jet. FAI took a mortgage on the jet as part of the security for the larger group loan. The mortgage document describes this as 'the Falcon F20 Jet Aircraft (Registration No. VH-RRC) together with fixtures and appurtenances and equipment connected there together with all engines, spare engines, appliances, parts, instruments, replacements or other equipment . . . and all income arising from the aircraft . . .' You can see the document today because it still sits on the public record. The mortgage was never discharged and in theory is still in force.

That's where it gets a little unusual. If you look up aircraft records, there is indeed an aircraft currently registered as VH-RRC. There is one problem. It's not a $3.5 million Falcon jet. VH-RRC is a kit aircraft, called an RV-6A. It comes in a couple of biggish boxes with an instruction manual that shows you how to build it yourself, if you are nifty with a few spanners and a machine lathe. The RV-6A is a nice little plane, worth perhaps $75 000, but it's a little on the small side—it's doubtful if Rivkin could even have fitted inside one without the use of surgical lubricant. The RV-6A currently registered as VH-RRC is privately owned and has nothing to do with Simdock, or Rene, or FAI. So what happened to the Falcon jet?

Corporate jets are large objects, and generally they are quite difficult to misplace. The obvious explanation for the disappearing F20 is that someone slipped up with the paperwork. When the debt was paid out and Rivkin sold the Falcon, someone forgot to file the release form on the mortgage. So it just sat there. Yet that doesn't explain the real puzzle, which is the way the paperwork was drawn up in the first place.

When you borrow $20 000 to buy a car, the finance company makes careful note of the make, the registration, the vehicle identification number, chassis number, modifications—anything that can identify the car—in the contract, along with the various nasty little clauses finance companies like to slip in, like selling your children into slavery if you miss the first payment. Aircraft financiers are no different. All aircraft have an identification plate with numbers that identify the frame and the engines. Spare parts and engines are valuable too so, in addition to quoting the identification plate data, standard loan documents for aircraft include an exhaustive list of parts. None of that happened with the Simdock loan. It looked an impressive document but, in reality, the moment the Falcon F20 flew out of Australia and was re-registered overseas, it had no connection with FAI or any missing money. It was a bit like borrowing money secured against something documented as 'the red Mazda in my driveway'. The moment you drive down the road, it's no longer the car in your driveway, so the security you've provided is worthless. Except in this case it's as though your collateral switches over to the red bicycle you left behind. Whichever way you read it, this was not a conventional loan document. It had the hallmarks of one of those special deals where the real transaction takes place elsewhere. What was going on?

The air of mystery extended to the rest of the loan agreement. Rodney had agreed to replace Tricontinental Corporation as Rene's personal banker. The Simdock mortgage was merely collateral to the main event, which was the loan FAI was making to Rivkin's main private company, Timsa 69, which operated a family trust. In addition to the disappearing jet, the FAI loan was secured against Rivkin's main asset—shares in his public company, Stroika. But they slipped up on the paperwork here as well. A decade later, long after FAI had been taken over by HIH Insurance, those Stroika shares were still on the public record as being under mortgage to FAI although, like the jet, they had long since been sold off. When questioned in 1995 about FAI's loans to Rivkin, Rodney Adler said he was unable to comment other than to say that 'any relationship we have with Mr Rivkin has always been at arm's length, commercial and successful.'

One of the consequences of this new banking arrangement was that, in early 1991, Adler and Rivkin began buying shares in each other's company. A year before, Jim Berry at ASX Surveillance had suspected Adler of artificially pumping up the FAI share price, at the same time that Rivkin was doing the same thing for Oilmet/Stroika. Berry now reported to ASX's broking committee that Adler and Rivkin were manipulating each other's share price. Between April and July 1991, Rivkin repeatedly bought tiny parcels of FAI stock in his own name just before the end of trading, which gave FAI a higher closing price. FAI operated similarly, buying Stroika shares.

The FAI funding that Rivkin had secured in February gave him breathing space and he was spending freely. He bought another eight million Stroika shares offshore for his EBC Zurich accounts, then bought 7.2 million more shares for EBC from Hobkin Nominees, a nominee company owned by horse breeder John Messara. Rivkin now secretly owned 60 per cent of Stroika.

It was such an expensive business being Rene Rivkin. Over time his debt to FAI would rise to close to $20 million, while Rodney Adler made personal loans to Rene on top of that. But what the documents Rivkin signed on 1 February showed was that if the Stroika share price ever turned around, the major beneficiary would not be Rivkin, it would be FAI. Rivkin would make a huge windfall on these shares, but much of the payout would go to paying off his debt to FAI. In the drama that followed, Rodney Adler would be the big winner.

SEVEN

Solid work among the shrubbery

1992

In the slow days that marked the 1991–92 summer, a steamy calm enveloped the entire eastern seaboard. The nation headed for the beach to frolic in waves so irregular and half-hearted that they could only have been scheduled by Sydney's State Transit Authority. Bereft of any real news, the fourth estate fell back on that old summer perennial: the latest news from the front on Operation Yabby Pump, the Australian government's noble campaign to extract Christopher Skase from his hidey-hole in Majorca. There was the inevitable footage of what Australia's favourite holidaymaker would look like strolling along the beach, if anyone was actually on the beach in Majorca in early January without NASA survival gear.

There is a rough, homespun appeal about someone who misplaces a billion dollars. We want to take him home, tickle him under the chin and ask him where he put it. When Skase decamped from Australia after the Qintex crash in 1990, like Hansel and Gretel he left a trail behind him as he travelled—shipping containers filled with antique furniture, Rolls Royce Corniches and BMWs, and some $50 million in bank transfers from Sydney to London, to a Landesbank branch in Vienna, back to Ireland, then on to the Carribbean and the Cayman Islands.

Despite the headlines, nothing was really happening. Indeed, life would have been entirely mundane and unremarkable that summer if it had not been for one of Australia's more endearing exercises in corporate ineptitude, when Coles Myer's private security force quietly wandered off the reservation.

It began five days before Christmas 1991 with a bunch of private detectives outside the Terrey Hills home of John Forsyth, the chief executive of the Dymocks book chain, deep in Sydney's leaf belt. Not that anyone would have seen anything out of the ordinary. These people were professionals. The detailed reports they submitted did not actually state where they were hiding— behind the azaleas perhaps, loitering inconspicuously among the lesser shrubbery, or blending in between the No Parking signs. As Joyce Kilmer would have put it:

I think that I shall never see
A poem lovely as a private detective pretending to be a tree.

Or maybe they just sat in the car.

'We're very cunning about where we sit,' a helpful private detective once told me. 'For instance, we don't sit in the front seat, we sit in the back seat. No one notices you there, particularly under a blanket.' You know the sort of inconspicuous blanket he means. The sort that operates a video camera.

There wasn't a whole lot going on at Mona Vale Road that day. Or on any day during the two weeks they camped outside. But when something did happen the gumshoes were all over it. Like the suspicious types they saw coming out of the house on Sunday morning, 22 December: 'At 9.35am . . . we saw and filmed three (3) people exiting the property on foot. We followed . . .' No doubt using natural cover, the chaps in trenchcoats followed the three (3) suspects all the way to the house next door. 'They entered, closing the double gate car access behind them. No further movement observed.'

That was the neighbours sorted out. There was an even more suspicious fellow ('male, 20–24 years old, slim build, wearing a white shirt VIDEO FOOTAGE OBTAINED') who emerged from the property each morning. He drove off in a yellow VW kombi van, registration number PQI 191. Or was it the green kombi campervan registration number RQI 191 they reported the next day? Or maybe it was the bright lime-green van that the sleuths tried to follow, only to lose it in peak hour on Eastern Valley Way, one of the main back roads to the city from these salubrious parts. You can almost hear head office explaining the problem to the client: 'Hey, our boys are good at this, but it was a lime-green kombi in slow-moving traffic—*a lime-green kombi*, for pity's sake. Our boys never had a chance in hell.'

That was pretty much the way it went. Day after day, the surveillance team wrote down conflicting details as Forsyth's son James drove to work, and only once caught sight of Forsyth senior, who was the reason they were there.

Meanwhile, another firm of private investigators had contacted estate agents Laing & Simmons on 20 January about renting a room at 424 George Street. It was the Dymocks building, and the detectives took quite a fancy to Room 10 on the second floor. Room 10 was directly above the Dymocks boardroom. A week later they were ready to sign the lease, in the name of a fictitious opal mining company called Black Thunder Lightning Ridge. On 28 January the detectives reported: '03.35pm—Attend Dymocks, sign lease, phone "NICK", wait for "BERNIE", hand over key.' 'Nick' and 'Bernie' were Coles Myer security officers, so deep under cover that even the private detectives put inverted commas around their names. Someone in the Corporate Security and Loss Prevention Department of the Myer–Grace Bros department store division in Melbourne had obviously been reading way too many airport paperbacks.

It had started harmlessly enough with a few secret identities. Everyone needs a 'John' and a 'Robert', a 'Brendan', 'Nick', Bernie' and 'Ken' in their life. They needed American Express cards to go with the fake names. And taking planes and hiring cars meant some fake ID to go with it. Maybe a driver's licence. A smarter management would have been thinking cross-promotional opportunities here, with 'Nick' and 'Bernie' action figures. And there you had the Coles Myer A Team, dodgy credit cards at the ready, set to save the world with its first big assignment. Which turned out to be surveilling a Sydney book retailer.

It was called Operation Dragonsong and it cost at least $81 000. Coles Myer wanted to expand its Grace Bros store in George Street by redeveloping the Dymocks site next door. Coles Myer was offering $40 million but Forsyth refused to sell the Dymocks property for less than $70 million. The security team had a broad brief, to find out something useful about Dymocks and its staff. In fact, the Coles Myer operatives found out quite a lot about what was happening at Dymocks, which may or may not have been related to the fact that they had rented the room above the Dymocks boardroom, bought a closed-circuit television system and paid $25 000 to an electronics specialist for 'confidential services'.

It was all useless, of course. Dymocks never sold, and Coles Myer's expansion plans for the George Street store had to be shelved. Details of the affair were leaked to Bill Pheasant at the *Financial Review* in 1995. With allegations of telephone tapping, Federal Police investigated but no charges were laid. Coles Myer's own internal investigations concluded that none of its senior executives knew anything about the affair, which just goes to show how successful the group that controls 40 per cent of Australia's retailing is at encouraging initiative in its junior staff.

Little more was heard of the Coles Myer security wing, despite unfounded claims later in 1992 by barrister Laurie Gruzman QC that someone was following him, tapping his phones and had searched his office, after he headed a shareholder campaign asking Coles Myer to be a little less secretive about its business arrangements. Gruzman's comments were outrageous, according to Coles

Myer's deputy chairman, Baillieu Myer. He told Gruzman sternly: 'Frankly, I wonder that a man in your position should assume that any possible surveillance of his activities is necessarily unlawful, or that it is in some way authorised by this company.' What could Gruzman have been thinking?

Coles Myer's major shareholder, Solomon Lew, later declared publicly that he had no knowledge that Coles Myer was involved in the Yannon affair in 1990, which had got Lew out of a sticky jam with Rodney Adler. Given that state of ignorance, there was little prospect that Lew—or indeed any of Coles Myer management— had any inkling of the entirely unrelated events that unfolded in Operation Dragonsong, one month after Lew became sole chairman of Australia's largest retailer.

Dragonsong had underscored the way that the line between Sydney's private worlds and its public world was blurring. NSW Premier Nick Greiner would get quite a different take on this in the unhappy repercussions that flowed from a private meeting he held on 27 February 1990, around the time the Dragonsong team were packing up their handyman tools. Greiner's secret meeting would later become all too public. It was his biggest political blunder and it began when he agreed to have a drink with his former education minister, Terry Metherell.

Reconciliation is an overrated virtue in politics. Graham Richardson never believed in it. He saw it as a matter of principle. 'If they've ratted on you once, they'll rat on you again,' he wrote in his autobiography, *Whatever It Takes*. Greiner had scraped back into power in the May 1991 election with what was in effect a one-seat majority, with the support of a conservative Independent. Five months later, he lost that majority when Metherell resigned from the party in a shower of sparks and angry recriminations. Metherell announced his move without warning, during a live interview with journalist Quentin Dempster on the ABC's *7.30 Report*. He told Dempster he had decided to abandon the Liberal Party because he was 'disgusted' with the recent state Budget and the way the government had failed to help 'battlers'. Metherell had resigned from the education ministry the previous year while he sorted out a minor embarrassment with the Tax Office over unpaid back taxes. He said his hissy fit had nothing to do with the fact that Greiner had reneged on a promise to return him to Cabinet after the election.

A very angry Greiner was now left with a minority government, dependent on the vote of Metherell or one of the three other unaligned Independents—John Hatton, Clover Moore and Ian McDonald—to get any legislation through. The smoke had barely cleared in February 1992 when newly elected backbencher Brad Hazzard, who was a friend of Metherell, set up a meeting between Greiner and Liberalism's wayward child at 10 p.m. on a Sunday night. Despite initial nerves, it all ended well and Metherell and Greiner went back to being the best of buddies. 'Anyway, from the first mineral water we were back on old terms,' Metherell wrote in his diary that night.

You might think that anyone who could actually write a line like that is sure to come to a ghastly end. 'Old terms' meant they talked about Metherell retiring from politics to take up a $110 000-a-year job with the Environmental Protection Agency. The government would get back its majority after the ensuing by-election, and Metherell would have an honourable and profitable retirement. When this appointment was announced on 10 April, however, a political firestorm broke out and the Independents teamed with Labor to vote to refer the matter to the Independent Commission Against Corruption for investigation. In June, ICAC Commissioner Ian Temby, after a week of hearings, handed down a finding that Greiner had acted corruptly in offering Metherell a job in return for him leaving parliament. Nick Greiner was political roadkill. The Supreme Court would later conclude that Temby got it wrong, that he had misinterpreted the ICAC Act. Greiner was vindicated for doing the sort of deal that politicians have been doing forever. But the vindication came too late. Under fierce media pressure, Greiner had already been forced out of politics.

Corruption scandals have been a staple of Australian politics since the Rum Rebellion. But the Metherell affair illuminated the way the rules for media coverage and public accountability were changing. It set up a model for the powerful role that the electronic media would play whenever corruption allegations were bandied about. The media hydra would re-emerge from time to time when certain stories had achieved critical mass. A similar process occurred after Greiner lost his job in 1992 and left his successor, John Fahey, to feud endlessly with Clover Moore and the other Independents. The media mechanics that had driven the Greiner–Metherell scandal were not lost on the opposition leader, former *Bulletin* journalist Bob Carr, who was now just one no-confidence vote away from winning power. All he needed was to find a way to wedge the three swinging Independents away from Fahey. That opportunity came two years later when Labor supported a motion by John Hatton to set up the Wood Royal Commission to investigate corruption. This would prove the most explosive outcome from the Greiner–Metherell affair, and the change in power it precipitated. Two years of sensational hearings would reinforce the role of media and public watchdogs, as Wood uncovered vast levels of corruption in the NSW police force, captured on colourful videotape footage.

At a more pragmatic level, when Carr came to power in 1995 he understood better than anyone the threat posed in the modern news cycle by the attack dogs in the press and talkback radio. Overnight coverage could become an out-of-control monster that could break any politician who misread the way the media cycle works. Carr's solution would be to grow closer and closer to the shock jocks, embracing them as part of his personal network. Alan Jones, John Laws and Col Allan, the editor of the *Daily Telegraph*, had the power to change government policy overnight—particularly on police and education. This accounted for Carr's dismay, in 2003, when Sam Chisholm played kingmaker for Alan Jones, conjuring up a deal that lured Jones away from 2UE and made him a multimillion-dollar shareholder in John Singleton's 2GB. This removed Jones from the cosy State Labor circle that Carr had so laboriously built up and positioned him strategically closer to Prime Minister Howard. Carr was left bemoaning, 'Hey dude, where's my network?'

But back in 1992, while Carr was waiting and hoping for the wheels to fall off the Liberal Government after Greiner's departure, the Carr household also had aspirations in the private sphere. Carr's Malaysian-born wife, Helena, a senior executive in the printing industry, was trying to buy a business from her husband's old employer, a little concern called Offset Alpine Printing. However, deals in the Packer circle are never quite that simple.

For almost a year, the links in the network had been fraying. Kerry Packer had been deeply angered by Trevor Kennedy, whom he blamed for his humiliating exit from the Tourang bid for Fairfax in November 1991. The man who had been Packer's chief lieutenant for years was now blacklisted. Across Sydney, Kennedy was discovering the difference between those friends who stuck by him, and those who didn't. One of those who stuck was Rene Rivkin, who offered Kennedy office space. But Rene had his own problems.

Everything was falling apart. The old Australian Establishment, after two decades of turmoil, was making its last stand. The Establishment had once defined itself by its inherited wealth, its clubs and its directorships. It was a closely ordered hierarchy. At the top were the board positions of the great Establishment companies—the four major banks together with blue-chip giants like BHP, CSR and Elders. At the other end of the spectrum there was a lot of kudos for sitting on the boards of the minor banks, state banks and finance companies. They offered an entry level for aspiring networkers, a springboard for higher positions. But these positions had been among the first casualties when finance companies foundered in the property busts of the 1970s. The fallout of the 1980s claimed most of the state banks. Now in the early 1990s, the major banks faced the blowtorch. Inherited wealth had been decimated by two decades of inflation. By the mid-1990s, clubs would be irrelevant in Sydney.

Finally, the key networks that defined the traditional Establishment were coming apart, as company boards full of men born in the 1920s struggled against the avalanche of economic disaster. In Melbourne, the ANZ Bank faced a torrid ordeal that would claim executive chairman Will Bailey. In Sydney, Westpac wrote off $1 billion in bad and doubtful debts in November 1990, but was predicting an economic recovery in 1991. Two months later, chairman Sir Eric Neal warned that the bank had another $2.5 billion in problem loans, just as the Westpac Letters fiasco revealed what a mess the bank had made of foreign currency loans. Its finance company subsidiary, AGC, needed an emergency bailout in mid-1991. By November 1991, Westpac's problem loans were up to $5.2 billion. That was just before Sir Eric announced that the worst was over, in January 1992. And then things really got ugly.

Poor old AMP. In a bid to show how modern it was, in 1992, for the first time in its history, it held its annual meeting outside Sydney. NSW policyholders could probably have lived with that—if it had been anywhere except Melbourne. 'Why on earth would an annual general meeting be moved to a provincial capital?' an elderly policyholder quizzed AMP chairman Sir James Balderstone in 1993, when the AMP meeting returned to its rightful place. Sir James explained delicately that he and several other AMP directors actually lived in Melbourne, which didn't help matters at all; the aforesaid policyholder was then incredulous to learn that AMP policyholders who lived outside New South Wales actually had voting rights. There were, he warned, 'some *very cunning* people [in other states] who had some *very cunning* habits.'

Unhappily, none of these cunning types worked for AMP, which in June 1991 had forged a strategic alliance with Westpac, ostensibly to build a financial powerhouse. In reality it became a way of propping Westpac up. AMP pumped $423 million into buying Westpac shares and promptly lost more than $100 million as the bank's share price spiralled down. By May 1992, Westpac was writing down another $2.6 billion in bad debts. With its equity base now under serious threat, the bank had no option other than to announce a $1.2 billion share issue. With its position worsening almost daily, it took months to finalise a prospectus that directors and underwriters would sign off on. The share price went into free fall below the $3 issue price and the bank's underwriters were left holding an $883 million shortfall.

Sir Eric and four other directors resigned. Westpac was in play; nobody loved it. Bad news kept on coming—the stock exchange called Westpac's 1991 results misleading, then its US arm reported a previously undisclosed US tax liability and the share price went to $2.58. And then, when things surely couldn't get any worse, Kerry Packer pounced. He picked up a 9.8 per cent stake in Westpac and demanded to be made a director, along with his aggressive chief executive, Al Dunlap. The new chairman, John Uhrig, duly invited Packer and Dunlap on to the Westpac board with the sort of warm hospitality the Romans would have shown when offering holiday accommodation packages to Attila the Hun and his horde.

The turmoil at Westpac was a mere ripple compared to the waves that were engulfing smaller companies. Now even the life-line that Rene Rivkin had extracted from Rodney Adler seemed to be running up short. The clearest sign came when FAI executive director Bruce Corlett joined Rivkin on the Stroika board on 9 September 1991. Rodney Adler later denied he had sent Corlett in because he was concerned about Rivkin's financial problems. Adler had merely given the nod for Corlett to take a little time out from FAI to help out an old friend. 'It was just a favour to Rene,' Adler wrote in a letter in June 1995. On another occasion, Adler was less sanguine: 'Rene likes to buy a lot of things . . . [but] he is not a good seller.' Adler's view was that Corlett was Rene's confidant, while he himself had a more commercial relationship.

Despite what Adler says, it looks like Corlett was sent in to sell up Rivkin as well as his public company, Stroika. This must have been awkward because, as another old friend put it in the mid-1990s, 'Rene doesn't regard Bruce as an equal. He regards Bruce as working for him. He's a very close friend, very trusted, very loyal, but not exactly an equal for Rene.' Within a month Stroika had sold its large shareholding in Dart Corporation (which was secured by an FAI loan); the Falcon F20 had been sold offshore; another Stroika investment, the Takeover Trust of Australia, had been wound up; and FAI had taken a mortgage on more of Rivkin's Stroika shares. By mid-1992, after Stroika's last major asset, a large block of land on the Gold Coast, had been contracted for sale, the company announced it would pay out $20 million in capital repayments and that was pretty much the end of the ball game. Rivkin controlled 62 per cent of Stroika at this point so most of the money went to him. For his Australian shares he received $4 million, which helped him a little with his FAI debt, but not enough. His Swiss bankers picked up

$8 million, which still left him in default there as well. Stroika was dead in the water and he had run out of options.

Rivkin had always closely linked money to happiness. 'Money gives him a great deal of enjoyment on the basis that he is right in what he is doing and that his judgement is correct,' Andrew Lakos once said of Rivkin. 'If I lost my wealth tomorrow I would feel suicidal,' Rivkin mused in 1997. 'There is no question of that. Because I would lose most of what is me.'

He couldn't work as a broker—Rivkin & Co had been closed down earlier that year, and the group of young brokers who had worked for him were dispersing. Rivkin had stepped up his use of Prozac. From his own account, by the mid-1990s he wasn't seeing a psychiatrist and was virtually self-medicating. He even stopped giving media interviews.

In 1992, he appeared in the press a paltry sixty-three times, an all-time low. He might as well have been invisible. He was the cleverest person he knew. He had been breaking rules all his life. He secretly controlled two thirds of his company's stock, for pity's sake, and he still couldn't stop the share price imitating the *Titanic*. All this subterfuge, and still he had ended up hard on the ocean floor. How fair was that? In this atmosphere of deep professional and personal failure, the jaded old broker cast his eyes around and decided to settle for a little rougher trading.

EIGHT

Packer's trifecta

1992

Sydney has always had a soft spot for the ambitious, diligent and physically active type; for the go-getter, can-do people who won't take no for an answer; for natural leaders, whose personal style is brash, forceful, sometimes even a trifle brutal. These worthy sons and daughters of the city do well wherever they find themselves, and they do particularly well in Kings Cross. The Cross, that dirty half mile of streetfront, halfway between the city and the mansions of Edgecliff and Darling Point, is a hotbed of capitalism, market forces and free enterprise. The keen business minds there, ever aware of market opportunities, are always trying to extend into Double Bay or Oxford Street, following the economic faultlines.

The start of the 1990s saw these captains of industry temporarily in retreat. Even the Double Bay Bridge Club—a time-honoured institution which, in its heyday as one of the better illegal casinos in the 1970s and '80s, once had the police commissioner on the payroll—had been forced to close, a victim of police crackdowns and tougher economic times. Ironically, in the 1990s, Gayle Rivkin would be one of the pillars of an unrelated association also called the Double Bay Bridge Club, where people actually played bridge—some people have no sense of history.

The Cross was doing it tough as well, though on the surface little seemed to have changed. As the Wood Royal Commission would reveal, the area was dominated by four major heroin and cocaine distributors, eight major drug outlets, seven strip clubs running prostitution and a solid phalanx of standover men. Victims disappeared; killers beat murder charges; police officers stole drugs and money from dealers, ran protection rackets, made up evidence and threatened witnesses. Business as usual, it seemed. Detective Sergeant Trevor Haken had just been appointed head of the drugs squad. Haken's old buddy Inspector Graham 'Chook' Fowler was head of detectives at Kings Cross and Darlinghurst. 'I love the NSW service; I served it; I hate to see what's happening to it,' Fowler told the Wood Royal Commission in 1995.

The city's media also had a soft spot for the Cross—by which we mean the strip—everywhere except Darlinghurst Road tries to salvage some self-respect by calling itself Potts Point or Darling-hurst. At one point in the early 1990s, an axe murderer was thinning out the tourist population in the Cross on a random basis but it rated barely more than a brief mention in the press. But behind the happy façade, even the Cross was feeling the recession.

Bill Bayeh, the brother of that better-known Friend of the City, Louie Bayeh, who would feature prominently in the Wood Commission, was said to be so down on his luck in 1991 that his one-time protégé, Danny Karam, lent him $50. The money drought hurt everyone, even the sensitive souls who ran the protec-tion rackets. Standover man Anton Skoro would later testify that the drug dealer who paid him $2500 a week to operate in the Cosmopolitan Cafe regularly resorted to paying him in caps of heroin rather than the folding stuff. 'They were always running out of money,' he complained. 'They were the poorest drug dealers that I've ever known.'

Impoverished drug dealers. Don't you hate that? Yet the tide was turning. By 1993, Bill Bayeh was back in the pink, running four heroin and cocaine outlets in Kings Cross—the Laser fun parlour, which reportedly turned over $20 000 a night, the Penthouse billiard room, the Downunder hostel and the Cosmo Cafe.

It wasn't all crime and laughs. A resurgent Cross economy saw opportunities on the right side of the law as well. On 15 November 1991, as the last scenes of the Fairfax sale to Tourang were being played out, an ambitious thirty-year-old Lebanese businessman called Joe Elcham signed a lease on a restaurant property in Victoria Street, Kings Cross, which he opened as Joe's Cafe. Elcham had the skills to turn a grubby establishment into one of the Cross's fashionable meeting places. Its exotic clientele gave the cafe an appealing, racy edge among the Cross's modish daytime population. In 1996, when the *Daily Telegraph* wrote a profile of John Ibrahim, the young Lebanese nightclub operator said to be a former Bill Bayeh protégé and described in the Wood Royal Commission as 'the new lifeblood' of the drugs trade in Kings Cross, Ibrahim did the interview sitting at ease at Joe's Cafe. He described life in the Cross, his pastimes, and the way he worked out at the City Gym on Victoria Street. He denied the 'lifeblood' claim and said he never touched drugs.

While such connections have given Elcham a colourful reputation—in 1997 the Casino Control Authority found he was not a fit person to work at Star City Casino—his reputation is otherwise unblemished. But he knew a business opportunity when he saw one. Which is why, within days of opening the cafe in 1991, Elcham cold-called Rene Rivkin as the former broker drove past in his green Bentley.

'I tapped on the glass,' Elcham told journalist Ali Cromie in 1998. 'He looked. I'm sorta a little terrifying looking 'cause I've got a growth and I'm quite dark. If you didn't know me I look quite mean. I'm not. I'm a real softie and he wound down the window half an inch.' Rivkin appeared unfazed by the growth. Elcham told him he had been a big fan of his for years. 'I've got this little cafe across the road and I'd love you to come in one day and have a coffee,' Elcham said. 'The next day, he was there, saying, "Okay, show me this great coffee".'

For the next four years Rivkin would be a habitue of Joe's Cafe, cultivating a set of athletic young men who hung out there when they weren't exercising at the City Gym. 'Rene is an animal who thrives on conversation,' was Andrew Lakos's verdict. 'He hates to be alone.' He hired one of the young men, a former bouncer and would-be tattooist called George Freris, as his chauffeur. For the rest of the 1990s he would take groups of his cafe pals on holidays with him, and they would duly lounge about in the sun and vie for his attention. With the rest of his life falling apart, Rivkin still had the trappings of wealth.

The great appeal of the Bright Young Things to Rivkin was that they would do what he told them. The appeal was the power imbalance. 'I have good older friends, but I like my young friends more,' Rivkin said later. 'Old friends are my equal. If I was out with my old friend Trevor Kennedy, and I said I wanted a nap, he'd say, "No, you can't have one." My young friends will do what I want to do and my older friends will not do what I want.' That meant that when Freris wore an earring that Rivkin didn't like, he paid him $200 and Freris took it off. 'At the time, $200 was a lot to me,' Freris told the *City Weekly* in October 1996. Rivkin would play mind games with his group of yes men. He would say to one of them at random, 'George Freris thinks you're an idiot. What do you have to say about that?'

'I like controlling people,' Rivkin told *Australian Lifestyle* in 1998. 'I don't know why, but I do it for their benefit.' Like medicine, it was no good if it didn't hurt a little. That's the pleasure of power. Rivkin put it bluntly to Freris: 'I don't want to pay people to do things they want to do. I pay people to do things they don't want to do.'

All of this didn't help the Rivkin bank balance, so it was wonderful timing in late 1992 when Rivkin got a call from his very good friend Graham Richardson. It had been a disastrous year for

Richo. He had begun with high hopes as the new communications minister. He had been able to head off a few threats posed to the Packer television interests by pay-television proposals, largely by postponing any consideration of the issue. Then he had gone off on a world tour to inspect pay-television operations around the world. He said later the highlight was a round of golf at the famous Augusta course in Atlanta, Georgia, that Kerry Packer and Greg Norman had arranged for him. He stayed in Rivkin's flat in London and used his Rolls Royce. In return, Richardson's office was helping the immigration application for a young Scandinavian barman whom Rivkin had taken it into his head to employ. It was a whim of Rivkin's, and how pleasant it was that a senior government minister would feel compelled to act.

In May 1992, though, after less than five months in office, Richardson was forced to resign from Cabinet over revelations about assistance he had given to Greg Symons, an old friend and the husband of his cousin, who had been charged with a passport scam in the Marshall Islands. It was the biggest professional setback Richardson had had. Yet it wasn't all loss. He said later that it was only after his demotion from Cabinet that he began to make some modest share investments. And in the winter of 1992, Richardson became involved in meetings of a new faction of the Labor right in state politics called the Terrigal group. It met in the Terrigal beach house of Eddie Obeid, the Labor power-broker for the Lebanese community. It was here that Richardson helped persuade left-winger Michael Knight to defect and join the right. Much later, when Knight became Olympics minister, he appointed Richardson mayor of the Olympic Village.

By late September 1992, Obeid had told Richardson about his interest in acquiring a little printing business owned by Kerry Packer, which did a little printing work for trade unions. The business had been run for half a century by three generations of the Hackett family, starting out in 1938 with Ronald Hackett senior as the Offset Printing Company. By the time Kerry Packer took it over in the 1980s, the operation had become Offset Alpine and it was run by Ron Hackett junior and his son Garth. Trevor Kennedy sat on the board. By 1990, it was turning over a tidy little profit each year of $4.5 million to $5.5 million before tax. But its presses were ageing and the company needed some serious investment to keep it competitive.

Packer loathed printers and the printing business—he had convinced his father to sell the *Telegraph* to Murdoch just before Sir Frank died. But he had kept Offset Alpine because he wanted an alternative printer for the ACP magazines as a negotiating point when printing contracts were being worked out. That pressure had lessened now that it was possible to outsource the work to high-quality printing outfits in Singapore. Bob Carr's wife, Helena, and her business partner, Max Turner, had been negotiating for months to buy Offset Alpine from Consolidated Press. Previously Carr and Turner had run Leigh Mardon, the communications and packaging arm of Amatil, until they lost out in a management buyout deal in 1990. They had experience in specialist printing, but not enough money.

Just how Eddie Obeid got involved has never been clear. He had run the Arabic newspaper, *El Telegraph*, for years, but his property investments were struggling in the recession. He subsequently said that he heard Offset Alpine was on the market and raised the matter with his good friend Graham Richardson. All Richo could do was to flick the deal to Rene Rivkin. By October 1992, the Offset sale had quietly switched from a deal with Carr and Turner to a sale to Rivkin's public company Stroika. The terms of the sale had become a bit sweeter as well.

On 16 October, Stroika announced it was buying Offset Alpine for $15 million, with the seller, Packer's newly listed magazine arm, Australian Consolidated Press, lending $5 million of the purchase price to Stroika. Rivkin later described it as the best deal of his life. It seemed ridiculously cheap. In the previous three years Offset Alpine had earned that much in pre-tax profits. And it was going to get better. In the past Offset Alpine had got less than 10 per cent of its business from ACP: now Stroika announced that the deal included increased printing work for ACP.

The value of Stroika's shares jumped by $10 million after news of the deal. Rivkin controlled 63 per cent of the shares by now, most of it through Swiss accounts, so a majority of the benefit from this deal went to him. But it turned out the Swiss shares weren't all his. Ultimately more than $35 million would flow out of Rivkin's Swiss accounts in the wake of the Offset deal. But to whom did it go?

In December 2002, Rivkin testified to Zurich District Attorney Dr Nathan Landshut that when the shares in Stroika (by then renamed Offset Alpine) were sold in December 1995, 7 per cent of the proceeds went to Graham Richardson, Trevor Kennedy received 12 per cent, and the rest was Rivkin's. Kennedy's interest was via Brampton, an investment vehicle he had set up in the 1980s in the Bahamas. He says he did not control Brampton or even know what it was investing in. ASIC officers who searched Rivkin's office in November 2003 found correspondence between Rivkin and Alex Fundulus, the private client manager at EBC Zurich, which referred to Brampton buying Stroika shares in 1992 and 1993. Kennedy says he knew nothing about this and the documents show the deals were organised by Rivkin. Richardson had been using one of Rivkin's EBC accounts to disguise his interest, Rivkin told Landshut. Rivkin's Stilton account at Bank Leumi shows several large cash transfers to unknown parties from 1992 to 1995, so there may have been other shareholders who cashed out of Rivkin's Swiss investing fund early.

Quite apart from the Swiss holdings, Richardson told his biographer, Marian Wilkinson, that he held a small parcel of Offset shares in Australia. Sam Chisholm, the former head of Channel Nine, had bought some Stroika shares in his wife's name. Governor-General Bill Hayden owned Stroika shares as well, and there was talk of a number of other political figures making a timely investment. There is nothing wrong in buying stock like this, so long as the investor does not have confidential, market-sensitive information.

Eddie Obeid said he did not own Stroika shares but Kate McClymont later reported in the *Sydney Morning Herald* that Obeid claimed that he held an option to buy 20 per cent of the printing business. This seems a strange bit of accounting—when could Obeid have exercised such an option after the deal was done? It is hard see to how the option would have worked out in practice, since Stroika shareholders had not been told about it and any attempt to exercise such an option would presumably have required Stroika shareholder approval and independent advice. In any event, if there was such a contract, Obeid said he did not have the funds to exercise it. The day before the deal was finalised, Obeid's son Paul joined Rivkin and Corlett on the three-member Stroika board, adding his experience, which was in 'property investment, property construction and international trading'.

The Offset Alpine sale made a lot of money for a lot of people who had shares in Stroika. Did Kerry Packer intend to be this generous? It seems unlikely. In 1992, Packer wasn't about to do any favours for anyone or anything linked to Trevor Kennedy. This looked like an Al Dunlap deal. He was still running the show at Consolidated Press Holdings, selling off any part of Packer's empire that wasn't welded on. It was hardly the first time Chainsaw sold assets for less than they were worth. However, while Packer had not intended it this way, a number of politicians were better off as a result of the Offset Alpine sale. There is nothing like the bonding that comes from a successful financial transaction. Packer must have built up a bank of political goodwill from the windfall he had inadvertently delivered. This was a new role—Kerry, the patron saint of the political battlers. What a solid fellow he was, a benevolent Santa Claus, quite unlike the ravenous figure he was usually painted as. It proved rather fortunate timing because Packer was about to bounce back into the headlines and he needed Canberra to cut him a little slack.

The Offset Alpine deal was settled on 19 November 19 1992. Seven days later, Consolidated Press announced that it had bought 8.3 per cent of Westpac. Within days the stake was nudging 10 per cent and Packer and Dunlap were talking about what needed to be done to turn the troubled bank around. In contrast to Westpac, Packer's empire was back in robust financial health. Al Dunlap, that shrinking violet of the management classes, had hacked and hewed at everything he saw at Cons Press, raising more than $3 billion in cash for Packer from floating both the magazine division as Australian Consolidated Press and the US inserts business as Valassis Communications. Unlike almost everybody else, Packer believed Westpac would recover, that its franchise was too strong not to bounce back. 'Kerry basically thought that Westpac was unfuckable,' a former Westpac executive said later.

Part of Westpac's appeal for Packer was the huge property port-folio the bank now controlled after foreclosing on problem loans. In addition, Westpac and its receivers controlled both the Ten and Seven television networks, the rivals to Packer's Nine. Seven would later be sold in a public float, with News Ltd and Telstra taking the largest stakes. Packer had very strong views about how Ten and Seven should be run and what sort of rivals he would end up with. Packer wanted Ten to be a no-frills operation that would not challenge Nine's dominance or bid up the price of US programming or sports rights. In the best of all possible worlds, it would broadcast the test pattern all day, perhaps with a little background music. How Westpac sold the two networks and who ended up owning them would be critical for the future of Nine and for Packer himself. This is where Packer's Westpac move became controversial—because of the restrictions of the cross-media laws.

Mid-year, Westpac had actually taken ownership of Ten to help the resale process. Packer and Dunlap could not join the board until the network had been sold. The bank had been in negotiations with Canadian Izzy Asper's CanWest group, but finding an acceptable way to keep voting control of Ten in Australian hands, as was required, had been difficult. Westpac CEO Frank Conroy was under pressure to finalise the sale of Ten so an impatient Packer could come on board. As a temporary measure, Packer and Dunlap were invited to a Westpac board meeting on Thursday 17 December as observers. Conroy finalised the Ten sale at 3 a.m. on the day before for $242 million, but it didn't save his job. After discussion with Packer and Dunlap, the board gave Conroy his marching orders on the Thursday, leaving Packer in the box seat to determine who Conroy's successor would be. Meanwhile, Ten had been sold to a consortium in which two close friends of Packer's, Robert Whyte and John Singleton, played leading roles.

Most of the Ten sale price was debt. The cash part of the deal was only $90 million. To get around the foreign investment restrictions, Izzy Asper, a one-time Canadian tax lawyer, set up the deal so that while CanWest came up with more than half the cash it held only 15 per cent of the voting stock. The rest of the voting shares were parcelled out between Laurence Freedman and Brian Sherman (who invested via Telecasters North Queensland), investor Jack Cowin, Melbourne tax lawyer Izzy Leibler, Singleton and Whyte. It made for a delicate balancing act. On one side the Canadians had put in the bulk of the money. On the other Telecasters North Queensland held the biggest voting block with 40 per cent. And perched there on the catbird seat between them with the balance of power were Kerry Packer's good friends Whyte, with 15 per cent, and Singleton, with 10 per cent.

Whyte became acting chairman, and he and Singo were both on the four-member executive committee that ran Ten in the early months. Their combined investment had cost a mere $11.4 million, yet this modest amount gave them enormous power as they held a quarter of the voting capital of one of the three major networks. It turned out that the views of the new Ten board coincided with some of Kerry Packer's. The directors under Whyte (who later became deputy chairman) were very much in favour of Ten running no-frills programming that would not challenge Nine's supremacy. When CanWest put forward a budget in 1993, the board sent it back to them insisting on more cuts.

There was some surprise that Whyte and Singo managed to raise the $11.4 million to pay for their stakes. Singo was reputed to be broke and Whyte had privatised most of his public company, Audant Investments, in a share buyback scheme in October. Whyte was always a smooth operator but for once he was having to scrimp and scrape. The independent expert's report described the share buyout that Whyte organised for Audant as 'not fair but reasonable'. In the language of such reports that means the deal isn't fair but shareholders don't have much option but to accept. Whyte was operating on the 'pay later' principle as he scrambled through a series of deals to pay for the buyback. On 23 December, as Whyte raised money from Rodney Adler to complete the Audant buyout, Whyte's other public company, Trafalgar Properties, reported that Audant 'will have no cash resources after meeting the payment'. A week later Whyte borrowed even more as Audant paid $6.8 million for its Ten shares.

Things looked tight for Whyte but now he played his trump card. Three years before, Audant had done a great deal to buy a 9.9 per cent stake in Advance Bank for $25.3 million. Remarkably, at a time when commercial interest rates were up to 25 per cent, Audant's financier, State Bank, charged no interest on the loan other than the Advance dividends paid on the shares. In return, State Bank was entitled to half of any capital gain, an arrangement that suited Whyte very well. If Advance Bank's restrictions on its shareholdings were ever to ease, State Bank probably hoped or expected to buy these shares from Whyte. By early 1993, bank stocks had started to rise, and Whyte eased his financial pressure by selling the Advance shares for $38.4 million. It was a nice return, even after the profit share arrangement with State Bank. Only it turned out that the Advance shares he sold hadn't gone very far. They popped up in nominee accounts held by Challenger Capguard Securities and Macquarie Bank. It was never identified who was behind these accounts but they offered Whyte an even better deal than State Bank. The mystery investor agreed to give Audant the right to buy the shares back several years later for $37 million—that is to say, for $1 million less than the mystery person had paid for them.

The return for the unknown investor in the deal would come in the form of the franked dividends it earned from the Advance shares. This seems an advantageous deal for Whyte. However, a party involved in the 1993 deals described them as 'commercial transactions negotiated at arm's length', and said that 'any view which regarded the transactions as unusual or unique demonstrated commercial naivety and lack of knowledge of available structures to finance complex commercial transactions'.

The only party ever linked to the share deals was a Packer company called Consolidated Press Finance, which loaned money to Audant in May 1993. In return for the one-month loan, Packer's company took a mortgage over some of Audant's Advance Bank shares. When asked about this in 1998, a spokesman for Whyte would only say that Consolidated Press provided bridging finance on an arm's length basis, and on commercial terms. Cons Press did not comment.

What made the loan from Packer's company different from most commercial loans was the list of conditions that put the loan into default. One of these conditions read: 'Investigation: any person is appointed under any legislation in respect of companies to investigate the affairs of any transaction party.' That is, any official inquiry into any of Whyte's companies triggered the default, and the whole funding structure collapsed.

Back at the end of 1992, however, Kerry Packer had every reason to feel pleased. It had been a lucky few months. He had taken a commanding position in Westpac and was now poised to make a financial killing. The bank had sold the Ten Network to a consortium that featured some of Packer's closest friends, one of whom he later helped with some bridging finance. The no-frills business plan adopted by Ten was the best possible outcome for Packer. And there was not a peep from Canberra, where a lot of politicians had done very well out of a share investment that Kerry Packer had turned into a windfall.

Packer wasn't the only one feeling comfortable at the end of 1992. Across town on Christmas Eve, Rodney Adler was helping another up-and-coming businessman in Cabramatta. Phuong Ngo was a thirty-four-year-old Vietnamese entrepreneur with an eye for the main chance. In 1992, Ngo had talked Adler into backing his new venture, a registered club called the Mekong. When it came to lending money, Adler kept a broad church at FAI.

Several blocks away in the CBD, a young blonde model called Caroline Byrne was introducing her new boyfriend to her family on Christmas Day. Gordon Wood was a fitness instructor at Club World of Fitness on Castlereagh Street in the city. He hadn't quite swept her off her feet—she insisted that he take an AIDS test before the relationship went far. Caroline moved in with Wood over the Christmas break. The two were still celebrating on New Year's Eve when Wood introduced Byrne to her first ecstasy tablet.

NINE

The Phantom

1993

Some mornings it is a wonderful thing to be an attorney at law. The fraternity of the Bar, the simple courtesies that characterise relations between learned counsel and the Bench, the lighthearted banter between opposing barristers, all reflect that simple and dignified camaraderie which distinguishes those who serve in the courts of justice. At such times one knows the law is a noble profession, its practitioners right up there with merchant bankers as tireless workers for the public good. Thursday 22 April 2004 was not one of those mornings. On the sixth floor of St James Hall, next to the Supreme Court on Phillip Street, the fraternity of the law was taking a bit of a battering.

The essence of the complaint Charles Augustine Sweeney and his family company, Sweeney and Vandeleur Pty Ltd, later laid against his colleagues and the management of the barristers' chambers on the sixth floor was that they were interfering with the quiet enjoyment any occupant is entitled to have when they rent property. Sweeney, being of Senior Counsel, actually said quite a bit more than this, Justice Haylen noted in his subsequent judgment in the NSW Industrial Relations Commission. The cause of the hubbub was a visit that officers of the management company, which is to say his fellow barristers on the sixth floor, made to Sweeney's office. They got in by 'falsely informing the Clerk to the floor that the respondents had made an arrangement with Mr Sweeney QC to enter his chambers and by obtaining keys and access for that false pretence,' Haylen quoted from the statement of claim that Sweeney had filed. The entry was, as Sweeney put it, 'unlawful, high handed, outrageous, abusive, oppressive, dismissive, contemptuous and an invasion of privacy', it was 'calculated to humiliate' and amounted to unlawful breaking and entering. Onlookers regarded it as a miracle of self-control that Sweeney had not found a way to include the adjective 'contumelious'.

The appalling indignities did not end there. Sweeney's statement of claim alleged: 'Prior to their entry, the respondents [that is, the management of the floor] had clandestinely engaged a private inquiry agent or investigator to conduct an investigation of the applicants and to examine the telecommunications facilities connected for the benefit of the applicants' chambers to the telecommunications board in the premises.' Not just that, the management of the chambers was threatening to change the locks and not to let him in.

The issue that had ignited the staid chambers was a dispute about fees. Haylen found that Sweeney, who had been in the rooms since 1990, apparently wanted to offer some suggestions about how the operation of the floor might be changed, which the management had declined to discuss. It was 'a perhaps rash response' by Sweeney and his family company to refuse to pay floor fees until he was listened to, and 'the unwarranted response' by the management company had been to try to kick him out. And then naturally they called in the private inquiry agent. The significance of the telecommunications gear Justice Haylen didn't try to fathom. As Haylen noted, the relationship between the two sides was 'so poisonous and so lacking in mutual trust' that it wasn't clear how the situation could be resolved, though Sweeney's statement of claim went on to suggest that payment of $780 000 in damages might help to rebuild some bridges. Unfortunately the Appeals Court didn't see it that way and ruled against Sweeney's case.

Sweeney's fellow barristers hadn't seen much of him during the fourteen years he had been in these chambers. He maintained rooms in Melbourne, was reported in 1999 by a New Zealand paper to be based in Auckland, and also practised in the Pacific Islands. In July 1999, the Australian Securities and Investments Commission (ASIC) had tried to catch up with him when they launched a civil case against him, accusing him of $3.25 million of insider trading and share manipulation; but Justice Austin in the NSW Supreme Court at that time found that Sweeney no longer lived in Australia. He had in fact flown out on 26 July 1999, the day before ASIC lodged its case, and had not been back since.

The office in St James Hall sat Sweeney-less during those two and a half years, still with the shingle up and instructions arriving regularly from Sweeney to his lawyers from an unknown address. ASIC had made extensive efforts to track Sweeney, tracing him once to Colorado and even writing to him care of a post office box in Vanuatu. At one point ASIC lawyer Peter Riordan managed to speak to Sweeney on his mobile phone, Riordan later told the court, only for Sweeney to tell him it was three o'clock in the morning in Copenhagen. While this was no doubt true, telephone records showed that Sweeney was in New Zealand at the time, Riordan testified. (Sweeney later produced airline tickets to show he was in Denmark, and his New Zealand mobile phone was on global roaming.) When ASIC sought court approval for substituted service by serving the court documents on Sweeney's lawyers, the lawyers said they could not accept ASIC's writ because they didn't know where their client was either.

The ASIC case was full of interesting philosophical questions: where exactly does a Senior Counsel live? Are chambers without a barrister half empty or half full? The *Sydney Morning Herald* reported that Sweeney's lawyers had taken to referring to their client as 'The Phantom'. It's surely a compliment. Not every man can look elusive in a pair of striped underpants, a mask and a special ring. In this scenario, the later unauthorised entry into his room at St James Hall by the management company would be akin to breaking into the office of the 'Commander of the Jungle Patrol', and riffling through the safe to work out how the 'Ghost Who Talks' left his orders. You can see why he would be upset.

In January 2002, ASIC threw in the towel and reached a settlement with Sweeney. They dropped their case in return for Sweeney agreeing not to manage a company for the foreseeable future. 'ASIC was well aware that since I had not managed a corporation for many years and had no intention of doing so now, their offer was one which I could not refuse,' Sweeney said in a statement. 'The substance of the settlement is that ASIC's case has been abandoned with no order for the costs of the action or of the investigation . . . The settlement reflects the fact that there was no evidence to support any of ASIC's allegations. They should not have been made.'

Having emerged from the affair with his reputation unsullied and above reproach, Sweeney was free to write a new *Commerce Act* for the Cook Islands, where he also practises. The *Cook Island News* described the fruits of his labour as 'the saviour of the Cook Islands economy . . . based on theories of fair trading and perfect competition, theories many believe to be found wanting in the capital, Rarotonga.'

Sweeney's adventures with ASIC were a legacy of the network wars of the early 1990s, when Sydney and Melbourne networks were jostling over who would win the honorary title of 'James Packer's Best Mate'. The unhappy lesson of 1993 was to be that being a mate of the Packers' was a risky business. As with any network, there would be winners and losers. When deals go wrong at the big end of town, the show still goes on. But someone is left behind in the water.

House Packer had begun 1993 badly. Unfortunately, even in a crisis, you can only push the Establishment so far. One false step and it will turn on you. On 14 January 1993, with Westpac apparently at his mercy, Kerry Packer made that misstep. In December, Packer and Al Dunlap, having forced the resignation of Westpac's chief executive Frank Conroy, bagged the bank's management all across town. At the January board meeting, even before they had been officially appointed as directors, Packer and Dunlap had been pushing their own suggestion for an American as Conroy's replacement but, when he proved unavailable, they pressed for an immediate sweeping overhaul of the bank. The embattled Westpac board, under new chairman John Uhrig, was being pushed into a corner but, instead of capitulating, the directors voted to elect their own American candidate, Bob Joss, and opted for slower change. Packer stormed out of the meeting in a rage, which turned into a spirited exchange in the lift with Dunlap, who had no doubt whose fault it was. 'I couldn't believe the excessive display of stupidity,' exclaimed Dunlap, who had any trace of tact surgically removed from his personality at birth. Their row escalated and a month later Dunlap was no longer on the Packer payroll.

After walking out in such dramatic fashion, it would have been difficult for Packer to return to the Westpac board—and in any case Packer didn't believe the current board could turn the bank around. In May, Packer sold his Westpac stake to Lend Lease for $600 million. His six-month foray into banking had yielded a $100 million profit, but to sell at this time proved a dreadful decision—he had bought in for less than $3 a share and a decade later Westpac stock was selling at $19.75. While it wasn't apparent at the time, Packer had walked away from a $2.5 billion profit. The huge returns and influence that would flow from this block of Westpac shares would go instead to the suits at Lend Lease. The institutions were edging back into the driver's seat.

Elsewhere, Packer was focused on the looming threat from pay-television. His friends in Canberra had already blocked Steve Cosser's maverick plans to build a pay-television operation. Cosser had been buying up licences for a local broadcast system called MDS to pre-empt government plans for a satellite pay-television service. Startled out of their complacency by Cosser's move, Packer and Rupert Murdoch and Telstra announced they had joined forces as the Dream Team for pay-television. The soap opera this became would prove every bit as entertaining as it promised. The PMT combo would be unbeatable—except the service took so long to materialise that Packer lost interest and hooked up with Optus, which had its own plans for a cable pay-television service. The government's auction of satellite licences became a farce, with the bidding dominated by $2 companies. At the end of the day the satellite licences ended up with . . . Steve Cosser in Monaco, in what became Australis Media. Telstra and News Limited looked positively lead-footed as they pressed on with plans for a cable service called Foxtel.

In Canberra, Keating had beaten John Hewson against the odds in the March 1993 federal election. Keating offered the post of US ambassador to Trevor Kennedy but he turned it down. Keating then offered the post to Graham Richardson but, instead, Richo opted to return quietly to Cabinet as health minister.

Meanwhile, James Packer had a new pair of best mates. The first was Theo Onisforou, a barrister turned property consultant who had rooms in St James Hall across the hall from Sweeney. Onisforou had been on the Consolidated Press payroll as an investment strategist until Dunlap torched him in 1992. By this time Onisforou was so tight with James, who was eleven years his junior, that the two went into business together in a company called Dorigad to do some modest property developments the following year, with Rodney Adler never far from the deals. Theo wasn't a favourite with Kerry—one story, perhaps apocryphal, has James once smuggling Onisforou into the Packer compound in Bellevue Hill in a car boot. Eventually, Onisforou muscled his way back into the Cons Press circle, only in early 1998 to fall out badly with Packer senior, who flung him back into uttermost darkness. Or at least out of the Packer companies.

James Packer was determined to prove himself by making money on his own account; the endearing thing about his new friends was that they were equally determined to help him. When Packer and Onisforou began marketing their property developments, the Friends of James formed an instant queue. They loved Packer's Medina executive apartments near Randwick Town Hall, which went on sale in November 1994. Rodney Adler was naturally there with his cheque book, buying twelve apartments for $2.8 million for a family company. Packer advisor David Gonski and his friend and fellow lawyer Jillian Segal outlaid $4.7 million on apartments. Kim Oxenham, County NatWest's operative in Monaco, shelled out $1.84 million, as did Melbourne entrepreneur Andrew Kroger, working through his lawyer, Guy Jalland. James's childhood friend (and Kerry Packer's godson) David Gyngell paid $868 000. A rising Consolidated Press executive with his eye on the main chance, Michael Karagiannis, also plonked down $860 000 for four apartments.

Karagiannis was playing out of his division. He was on the fast track at Consolidated Press, where he handled accounting and administration for 'various houses, a couple of aeroplanes, some helicopters, various farming interests and things of that order', but his pay packet was only $130 000. To buy the apartments he had mortgaged his house and 'my entire life', he told the Administrative Appeals Tribunal (AAT) in 1998. That was the cost of upward mobility.

James Packer's other best new buddy was Andrew Kroger, the 1980s whiz-kid of stockbroker Macintosh Hamson Hoare Govett who was living in semi-retirement in a spacious country mansion on the Mornington Peninsula near Melbourne. Andrew Kroger is a personable man, as amusing and engaging as his younger brother Michael, the Liberal Party bovver boy, is not. Like all the 1980s entrepreneurs, Andrew Kroger had ended the decade deep in debt but he had stayed out of the newspapers—at least he had until the New Zealand Opposition Leader, Winston Peters, tabled in the

Kiwi parliament a vast jumble of documents that had been discovered in a winebox. The papers were internal memos from Euro
Pacific Banking Group, an investment bank set up in the Cook
Islands, apparently with the noble intention of ensuring nobody
ever paid any tax ever again. Not that there was anything wrong
with that. Euro Pacific were a particularly shy lot. Their standard
borrowing contract contained a clause that the client would be
charged a $150 000 fee by Euro Pacific if either the media or tax
authorities ever heard about the loan and investigated. Andrew
Kroger was one of the few Australians who appeared in the
winebox documents.

In July 1988, Kroger had taken control of an investment
company called Strand Holdings, with the help of Larry Adler at
FAI. Within two weeks Strand was working with Euro Pacific in
a deal to take over a New Zealand farming company called Agland
Holdings. Strand needed the New Zealand government's Overseas
Investments Commission approval for the deal but the Euro
Pacific documents showed that the bank had not waited on the
formalities. On 16 August, a bank memo stated: 'EP has warehoused Agland shares; between EP and [Strand] we already have
control [51 per cent] of Agland. EP . . . will put the parcel to a
Strand nominee when OIC consent is obtained.'

Despite the references to warehousing, New Zealand author-
ities never suggested there was anything improper with the deal.
Kroger was involved in another exchange of communications eight
months later, when Guy Jalland, a former lawyer who worked for
Rene Rivkin before joining Euro Pacific, wrote to his brother-in-
law, James MacKenzie, who ran Euro Pacific's trustee business in
Hong Kong. Today, Jalland is a senior executive at Consolidated
Press while MacKenzie, who was a Strand director, went on to run
Victoria's Transport Accident Commission and later Norwich
Life. On Monday 17 April 1989, Jalland wrote to his superiors that
Kroger had approached him the previous Friday with an urgent
need for a $3 million loan by Monday. 'Documentation is being

signed today, with money running overnight in Singapore,'
Jalland reported. 'Publicity risk while present is acceptable.' The
deal was a $3 million back-to-back loan from a Singapore
company controlled by MacKenzie to Euro Pacific, which then on-
loaned the money to Kroger. There seemed little commercial logic
in the deal. MacKenzie's company was making an unsecured loan
at less than market rates of interest, with no hope of seeing its
money back if Kroger's finances dipped. Kroger owed substantial
debt on his Strand shares and Rodney Adler, who was running
FAI after his father's death, was charging him 29 per cent interest.

In 1995, I spent more than nine hours talking to MacKenzie,
Jalland and Kroger, trying to convince them to explain the two
Euro Pacific deals on the record. I told them they needed to be
more proactive in handling publicity—like Rodney Adler, for
example. They never did go on the record; the explanations they
offered off-the-record seemed to me to be wholly unconvincing
(though the fact they didn't give me a credible explanation doesn't
mean there wasn't one). But they did introduce me to the way the
network handles its little problems.

It was my last attempt to get a comment from Kroger. He was
in Sydney for the day and arranged to meet me in the FAI offices,
where he said he would borrow a room. Instead I was shown into
Rodney Adler's office, where I discussed for hours with Kroger,
Jalland and Adler how we could clarify this situation. Rodney's
role as mediator was to say at regular intervals in his inimitable
manner, 'I hear what you are saying, my very good friend Neil.
But I think what my very good friend Andrew is trying to say is
that . . .' No one wanted to know about Euro Pacific. 'That's old
news, Neil, old news. No one wants to hear about stuff in the past,'
Rodney would say, searching for some neutral ground. 'But let me
interest you in this other story. Now this is a current story.'

It was hard to keep a straight face. Simply to make small talk,
as I left I mentioned to Rodney that ASIC had forwarded a brief to
the Director of Public Prosecutions that alleged FAI Life had

manipulated the share price of more than fifty public companies on the last day of one financial year in the mid-1990s. But he wasn't to worry, because I didn't think there was anything to the story (and no charges were ever laid over this investigation). It didn't seem to lift the gloom that had descended upon the meeting. After another three-hour session we gave it away.

Meanwhile, the networks' obsession with the Packers continued. Sticking Close to James was now recognised as a pursuit sport. Going into 1993 Onisforou held the yellow jersey through his property deals with James. But Andrew Kroger now emerged as a challenger, introducing James to what proved a mining play in the purest Australian sense, which is to say that at no point in the proceedings did it involve any actual mining.

In 1993, Bendigo Mining was a company that had the nice idea of reopening the old goldfield underneath the modern town of Bendigo. Kroger's run began on 19 February when he paid $200 000 to take a placement of four million Bendigo shares. Almost immediately, Bendigo Mining's share price began to rise. It had reached 15 cents by 7 April, when Kroger took a further twenty million shares at 5 cents, while James Packer's company Dorigad took another fourteen million shares. The Bendigo share price kept moving up as other investors piled in. James Packer began selling immediately. By 30 June, he had sold out completely for a $4 million profit. Kerry Packer was impressed, and that's where things came unstuck. Packer senior wanted a piece of Bendigo Mining too. He was so keen that he invited his friend Sir James Goldsmith along as well. At three minutes past noon on 1 October, Bendigo announced that Goldsmith and Packer were investing $7.5 million together in a placement of fifteen million shares at 50 cents. All the ingredients were there for a market killing. Several institutions were also taking shares, pushing the total placement to twenty million.

The news was leaked with the usual nods and winks to the financial press: here was another Packer masterstroke—just watch the price soar as everyone gets on board. Unfortunately that didn't happen. What no one had foreseen was that the placement coincided with the Australian share market taking off on its biggest rise since the 1987 Crash. Stocks were moving up sharply everywhere and fund managers, who normally would have followed the Packer lead and bought into Bendigo Mining, were faced with a feast of other investment opportunities, including several mining companies that actually had mining operations. While other stocks roared up, Bendigo went sideways, slipped a little and eventually dived. Andrew Kroger quietly sold down. He walked away with an $8 million profit on a net outlay of $580 000. The Packers were not so fortunate. Even allowing for James's earlier profit, the net position for House Packer was $600 000 down. Goldsmith lost nearly $4 million—but Packer senior lost face. And a far greater problem was emerging.

Kerry Packer is one of the world's great gamblers. On one occasion he won twenty blackjack games in a row in a Las Vegas casino at $300 000 a game. He has regularly chalked up wins and losses of more than $20 million in a session. When bored and far from the great casinos of the world, he had taken to dropping into the Consolidated Press foreign exchange desk at Park Street. At times he treated the foreign exchange markets as his personal casino, good for a few hours of play. A decade before, Packer had said, 'Betting is like a disease which is not understood by those who do not have it.' Early in 1993, he made a big gamble. He and another billionaire friend both made bets of some $1 billion on a basket of currencies against the US dollar. Instead of rising, though, the greenback dropped. Kerry Packer held his nerve for months, but, according to one account, by October James Packer was growing concerned that his father was betting the family fortune and spoke to him directly about it. In the days after the Bendigo Mining failure, Kerry Packer blinked. On 15 October, Packer closed out his currency position, closed down his foreign exchange dealing room, and wrote off $450 million. Packer's only comment when a journalist asked him about the loss months later was, 'Fuck off!'

It had been a disastrous year. First Westpac, then Bendigo Mining, and now this. It didn't help that the US dollar subsequently turned around and started firming. Packer's friend, who made a similar-sized punt though with a slightly different mix of currencies, reportedly emerged close to even in the end. These were waves big enough to bother even a major-league tycoon; for the smaller players in the networks that revolved around House Packer, the effect was catastrophic.

In mid-September 1993, a fateful little meeting unfolded in the Woollahra Hotel on Queen Street, a leafy avenue in the heart of the eastern suburbs awash with money. Michael Karagiannis was there with his close friend, solicitor John Barbouttis. They were having a quiet drink with Gerard Farley, their stockbroker. Farley, who started out in real estate, had been running State Bank's broking operation, First State Securities, since April 1992. It's said that when Farley joined State Bank in 1992, his first move was to get a bank loan for $10 000, which he used to buy for himself BHP options at one cent each. BHP shares rose strongly and Farley made a lot of money. There was nothing suspicious about the trade. 'There was no way he could have known the whole market was going to rise,' a senior market observer commented.

Farley was just a lucky punter. He was also the son-in-law of former NSW Chief Justice Sir Laurence Street—whose father and grandfather had been Chief Justice before him. Farley lived in Wolseley Road, Point Piper; he played polo, was a convivial regular in the Packer crowd and got a lot of business from the network. He would later testify that James Packer and Onisforou were two of his biggest clients (a Consolidated Press spokesman denied this), and press reports linked him to Gretel Packer's then husband, Nick Barham. Farley had also got to know Karagiannis, who was a co-director with Onisforou of Dorigad. Karagiannis was also Dorigad's company secretary and he handled the paperwork on its share transactions.

By August 1993, Farley was buying Dominion Mining and American Boulder stock for Karagiannis. There was a good relationship between the two men, albeit with a little niggle. 'He knew my financial predicament, he used to joke about my living in Blakehurst, in the southern suburbs,' Karagiannis later said of Farley. 'You might see me trade a fair bit, but that was because I was trying to emulate others that were making money.' The two men referred to their favourite stock, Bendigo Mining, as the Bendy Dogs, or just 'the Doggies'.

Farley's saga with the Bendy Dogs unfolded five years later in a hearing before the Administrative Appeals Tribunal. Farley had appealed to the AAT after ASIC imposed a four-year order banning him from working as a stockbroker. The deputy president of the AAT, Bruce McMahon, subsequently confirmed the banning order. The details of the story which follows are drawn from McMahon's judgment.

Farley claimed that at the Woollahra Hotel meeting in mid-September, he was introduced to a new client, Theo Onisforou's friend Charles Sweeney QC. Sweeney was a commercial barrister whose clients included the Trade Practices Commission, the Australian Broadcasting Authority and Westpac. In 1990, he had been lead counsel in a private fraud prosecution that Westpac brought against two of its former currency traders, the Halabi brothers.

The Halabis had obtained copies of some damning legal advice a law firm had sent to Westpac in the mid-1980s, which suggested the bank had ripped off clients with foreign currency loans. The Halabis tried to use the documents, which became known as the Westpac Letters, as a lever to force the bank to drop the fraud case against them. When that failed, the letters were released to the press. Westpac's lawyers obtained court orders banning publication of the documents by a string of media. But the documents got out anyway. Sweeney's legal advice had been sound, but the affair was a public relations disaster. He had been a little luckier on the homefront. His wife had bought a house in Wentworth Avenue, Point Piper, in April 1986 for $1.55 million. Less than three years later, Monaco resident Richard Weisener bought the house for $6.075 million and knocked it down for a tennis court.

Farley would later testify to the Administrative Appeals Tribunal that, when he was introduced to Sweeney, he understood that here was a person of wealth, influence and repute. Indeed, he believed he was 'dealing with some of the most creditworthy people in Sydney'. They needed to be, because Farley's employment contract at State Bank stated that if his clients didn't pay, his own company had to make up the shortfall. 'It's an honour business and you have to believe people will behave honourably,' he told the Tribunal. A casual conversation in the pub with the right people was all it took to secure someone's bona fides. Karagiannis said he had no recollection of the Woollahra Hotel meeting.

On Thursday 30 September, Farley received instructions from Sweeney to buy Bendigo Mining. By midday Friday, when Bendigo announced it was issuing twenty million shares to Packer, Goldsmith and some institutions, Farley had bought more than one million Bendy Dogs for a Sweeney company. Sweeney was also using a second broker, Hambros Equities, to buy another four million Bendigo shares in the last days of September. Farley testified that he didn't know Sweeney was using two brokers, 'which is quite bizarre . . . which means you are competing against yourself . . . It's clear to me that he's gone out and bought some five million shares . . . on the day before a major announcement.'

When Farley made these comments at the Administrative Appeals Tribunal hearing in 1998, his evidence about Sweeney could not be tested because Sweeney was overseas (his barrister applied unsuccessfully for a court order banning any press mention of his name). ASIC questioned Sweeney about these trades in five separate Section 19 hearings (compulsory interrogations under oath, under Section 19 of the *ASIC Act*), asking if he had inside information about the Packer placement. He denied knowing anything about it.

In October 1993, however, Farley faced a far more pressing concern. According to McMahon's judgment Sweeney hadn't paid for his shares. Sweeney owed First State and Hambros $3.25 million and he was still buying. By 13 October, he had bought more than one million more Bendigo shares, taking the bill near $4 million. Sweeney paid $300 000 as a part payment to First State on 8 October, but that was all, McMahon found in his judgment.

Farley had already received a stern talking to from his boss the month before about the number of his unpaid accounts. Farley was a great believer in 'quick turns', buying shares and reselling them before settlement day five days later, when the client had to come up with the money (today the settlement period is three days). That was fine if the share price went up—very dangerous if it fell. Farley might be mixing with the top end of town, but State Bank had wanted the unpaid accounts fixed by 30 September. Instead, the Sweeney trading had blown out even further. How does one get members of the network—important and influential friends of friends—to pay up?

Helped by the strong buying by Sweeney and by others, the Bendigo share price had jumped 22 cents in the week before the announcement on 1 October. On that Friday it climbed another 11 cents to 76 cents, before dropping to 70 cents. In the following days it stalled, then fell back. There would be no quick turns on the Bendy Dogs. Farley's clients, meanwhile, were saying they had not ordered the shares Farley had booked to them. But then they would say that, Farley's lawyers later argued. 'Parking [an American term for warehousing or holding shares in someone else's name] was the only excuse they could come up with' which would save them from having to pay for trading losses, Farley's counsel, Paul Roberts, told the AAT hearing in 1998. Farley did admit to some unauthorised trading—for example, with the account of writer and former rugby inter-national Peter FitzSimons—but otherwise he insisted the trading was authorised, and that clients were aware of the trades almost immediately because contract notes were issued automatically. Farley had also booked Bendigo shares for his sister, his bankrupt brother, and a one-time roommate in Melbourne who was also bankrupt, as well as various entities around the world.

The circle was closing. Farley's protest to his boss, First State managing director Graham Hand, that most of the unpaid shares belonged to an unidentified 'senior person' failed to sway him. Hand ordered Farley to cease acting for certain clients. Hand testified at the AAT that much of First State's business came from clients close to Consolidated Press, and Farley feared that tough action to extract debt from one client might alienate others close to him. Farley told Hand he was 'unable to push the client or sell the shares given the status of the client in the business community'. But the debt situation was getting out of hand.

Sweeney went to see Hand in mid-November. He promised early repayment, then took a month to confirm that he would pay the debt in January. 'It was clear from the terms of this letter that Mr Sweeney had no intention of paying until such time as it suited him,' AAT Deputy President Bruce McMahon found in his judgment. Sweeney had, as McMahon put it, 'an unorthodox attitude to credit' and had spoken frankly to investigators about his manoeuvres to extend unauthorised credit, taking care not to buy assets in his own name. 'It was clear from his evidence [to ASIC] that he was not particularly concerned as to the ostensible owner of shares, so long as Mr Sweeney was not to be responsible,' McMahon said in his judgment.

Farley was stuck in the middle, his vulnerability exposed. He was a creature of the network. He later testified that his livelihood depended upon retaining access to the circles around the Packers. A knock-down brawl with Sweeney could threaten this. Instead of following Hand's direction, Farley continued to trade for Sweeney, buying even more shares and flicking share parcels back and forth between a series of companies that McMahon found were controlled indirectly by Sweeney, though Sweeney denies this. In return, Sweeney did favours for Farley—he loaned Farley $40 000 for two days, and later $50 000. Perhaps Farley believed in late 1993 that his situation was now so dire it could not grow any worse. Which just goes to show how even the cleverest of market operators can get it wrong.

PART THREE

Hot news

SERGEANT: Such expressions don't appear,
POLICE: Tarantara! tarantara!
SERGEANT: Calculated men to cheer
POLICE: Tarantara! tarantara!
SERGEANT: Who are going to meet their fate
            In a highly nervous state.

Pirates of Penzance

TEN

A very good fire

1993

A little money has a wonderfully restorative effect on a culture. While the Bendigo Mining plotters were coming unstuck, happiness was breaking out all over a rising share market. For six years, market players had sat stranded as the stock market went sideways. The All Ordinaries Index had ended each financial year since the 1987 Crash back at 1500. But now the old crocodiles in the trading rooms felt the wash of a rising tide. By December, the All Ords had topped 2000 for the first time since Black Tuesday in 1987. Brent Potts's Swiss bank account, that bellwether of economic change, reflected the giddy new era. Rivkin's old partner had been reduced to investing his offshore cash on the money market, with an occasional trade through Remgus, his Bank Leumi account with a Liechtenstein address. All that changed as the market turned. By July, Potts was using Remgus almost daily to dip into mining stocks like Zapopan, Coplex Resources and Dominion Mining, aided by the amiable Ernst Imfeld, the client manager at Bank Leumi.

It was a time for new beginnings. In April, Michael Kroger put his political ambitions on hold and opened a boutique merchant bank, J. T. Campbell. Rodney Adler was his first client. Life was also looking up for another of Adler's partners, Phuong Ngo, who prevailed upon Governor-General Bill Hayden to open the Mekong Club in Cabramatta on 6 August. Adler was encouraged enough to go into a Vietnamese newspaper start-up with Ngo.

Market booms—and the traders who make them—follow a set pattern. As former ASX Surveillance Director Jim Berry would put it: 'The guys are back. They're like fish who sit in the mud while it all dries out but then it rains again and they're swimming around. And they're shoaling.'

There is an old British investors' joke that goes: What do you call an Australian mining operation? Answer: A hole in the ground owned by a liar. That's the British for you—they have no imagination. Two centuries have established the surest way to success on the Australian share market is to build a better gold mine. In early 1993, Australia's favourite ultra-Orthodox mining entrepreneur went one better than this. Rabbi Joe Gutnick produced, with a little flourish . . . a diamond mine. Actually it was pretty tight timing because, after losing his shirt in the 1987 Crash, Gutnick had remade his fortune supported by a prophecy from Lubavitcher Rebbe Menachem Schneerson in New York that Gutnick would find huge gold and diamond deposits by 1 October 1993. And who would want to mess with the Rebbe?

Gutnick had wangled the first leg of the prophecy when he snared one of the country's biggest gold prospects, Bronzewing, near Mount Keith in Western Australia. His Great Central Mines company then announced it had found a handful of tiny diamonds at its Nabberu joint venture in Western Australia. The stock soared to $18 and Great Central's market value went to more than $1 billion. Regrettably, it turned out that the micro-diamonds he discovered were so small and sparse that laboratory staff were still using optical equipment to try to find them again after one of them sneezed. But Gutnick's supporters decided that it was close enough to fulfil the prophecy.

By now gold mines were so last week. Even before the market had thrown itself into micro-diamond madness, there had been a new tack . . . *Diamonds at Sea*! In December 1993, the share price of a tiny company called Cambridge Gulf Exploration took off amid wild rumours that it had found diamonds the size of golfballs in the Joseph Bonaparte Gulf off Australia's northern coast. After the stock exchange suspended the shares, Cambridge reported some very promising results from its dredge, the *Lady S*—so promising that the company might be able to earn up to US$1.3 billion profit a year from diamonds, plus another US$135 million from mining gold, platinum and palladium. Cambridge shares surged when they came out of suspension on 23 December. By the following day, the company's shares were worth $417 million, before they began a slow descent.

Unhappily, the diamonds the *Lady S* had found were worth only $815 and it turned out later the crew had made a mistake and had been dredging on someone else's lease. As Christmas Eve 1993 rolled around, the record for spec stocks was looking a little tatty. Reopening old gold workings, Lubavitch prophecies for micro-minerals and swimming for diamonds were all investment concepts whose time had not yet come. Who would believe then that on this very night it would turn out that the best little spec stock of the year belonged to Rene Rivkin, who had managed to turn his printing business into a veritable El Dorado.

On Monday 4 October—as Charles Sweeney began worrying about his quick turn in Bendigo Mining; as Kerry Packer was deciding he had really gone off foreign currency trading; as Joe Gutnick was sweating on the Rebbe's prophecies; and as the crew of the *Lady S* on Bonaparte Gulf were getting mixed up about where to take gravel samples—no one noticed a new addition to the workforce. Gordon Wood, indolent gym instructor turned man about town, put on his best togs and set off to report to his new boss, Rene Rivkin.

Caroline Byrne had left Wood a month before. She told her father Tony Byrne, who was a property manager, that Wood spent his time doing nothing and going nowhere. 'There's no future with Gordon,' she told him. 'He lies in bed until lunchtime [and] apart from a few gym classes he doesn't work.' Wood was distraught over the breakup and even approached Tony Byrne for a job as a concierge. At thirty, Wood was older than most of the crowd he hung out with at City Gym and Joe's Cafe. He was born in Bath in 1962. His family had emigrated to South Africa, then moved to Queensland in 1978. His friends would find the stories he told about his past colourful, but hard to believe. 'He said he lived in Cape Town—he said he went to the Bishops School there—you know, the elite school,' an English friend said later. 'Yet he also went to a grammar school here. A lot of the things didn't make sense. I could never distinguish what was true . . . He's obviously incredibly intelligent.'

In the seven years since he had graduated from the University of Sydney with a Bachelor of Economics in 1986, Wood had acted in small bit parts in television, worked as a ticket seller at the Sydney Opera House and later an aerobics instructor at Club World of Fitness, and been a personal trainer for patrons of City Gym. While popular with women, they sometimes had an ambivalent response to his tall, blond physique. 'He's obviously incredibly good looking,' said a workmate who knew him in Britain in the late 1990s. 'My wife said he was probably gay. He was so fastidious. The way he would shine his shoes and wear clothes that were fitted. His tie he would tie and retie until it was absolutely right. He was always coming up and adjusting the knot on my tie. He was always commenting on what men were wearing. The males, not the women.'

Almost immediately after breaking up with Wood, Caroline Byrne began a new relationship with a Polish baker and part-time model called Adam Baczynski. Meanwhile, Wood had heard that Rivkin needed a replacement for George Freris, his twenty-five-year-old driver/gofer. Big George Freris, who would remain a Rivkin favourite for the next decade, was the smartest of the young men hanging out at Joe's Cafe and City Gym. He was a former nightclub bouncer with a slow John Travolta smile and a knock-about past. His curriculum vitae included experience in building work. His sometime business partner, John Compagnon, ran a string of companies with names like 'Compagnon's Commandos Plant and Equipment Hire', 'Blasting Dynamics' and 'Demolition Engineering'. Freris was a man of many talents and, in September 1993, Rivkin offered to set him up as a tattooist. In November, Freris received planning authority to open his tattoo shop, Skins and Needles, which he ran with a New Zealand friend, Gary Redding. Meanwhile, auditions were on for Big George's replacement as Rivkin's gofer. So Gordon Wood put on his briefest gym outfit and headed off to Joe's Cafe. Rivkin already knew Wood—that spring he had taken half a dozen of the Joe's Cafe crowd on a holiday with him to North Queensland, including Wood. Gordon caught Rivkin's fancy, and life suddenly changed.

It had been a quiet year for Rivkin, with nothing much to do besides overseeing a rather mundane printing operation. Stroika had renamed itself Offset Alpine Printing Group. Offset Alpine/Stroika had made two capital repayments to shareholders in 1992. This had channelled $8 million into Rivkin's Swiss accounts and $4 million to his Australian company, Timsa 69. But Rivkin was still deep in debt to FAI and to Rodney Adler, although he would never admit it to anyone. He still had his boat, the *Troika* (the precursor to *Dajoshadita*), and his London apartment at St James, and could always be counted on for a story about his latest extravagance, but his Swiss bank accounts told a different story. Underneath all the appearances Rivkin was basically broke, at least by his standards. He had no serious money and for the next two years he would fund his lifestyle by selling Offset Alpine shares.

Timsa 69 would sell about $500 000 in Offset Alpine shares every six months. According to Timsa's corporate filings the shares were supposed to be still under mortgage to FAI. That must have been an oversight. Rivkin seems to have forgotten the paperwork again.

In fact, Rivkin was selling these shares to himself. On 21 September 1993, Timsa 69 sold 200 000 Offset Alpine shares for $176 000. The buyer was Rivkin's Stilton account at Bank Leumi, which shows an entry of $179 202.41 for Offset Alpine shares. So the share sales went on, month by month, sometimes selling to Bank Leumi, sometimes to his accounts at EBC Zurich as Ernst Imfeld and Axel Fundulus, his accommodating Swiss bankers, advanced him the money to buy the shares. Really what Rivkin was doing was borrowing money in Switzerland and transferring it to Australia to finance his lifestyle, a transfer he disguised as share sales. This wasn't just self-indulgence. Rivkin needed the money to keep up the appearance of wealth and success until better times came. Rivkin's life was about playing for time.

In mid-1993, Rivkin had smelt the change in the market. He did a few quick trades in his Bank Leumi account in stocks like Independent Holdings, Valiant Consolidated and Hydromet. Then he made a shrewd options play on Advance Bank, where his friend Robert Whyte had made a lot of money, and cleared $102 000 five months later. It was hardly Master of the Universe stuff. But Rivkin didn't have much money to trade with. In fact, he had little to keep him occupied besides his new friends at Joe's Cafe, who still treated him like royalty when he threw a little pocket money their way. They were the very best of friends. They were so easy to please.

Offset Alpine had ordered $11 million of new presses to replace its ageing equipment to be able to meet the new printing contract with Australian Consolidated Press. The new presses were due to arrive in early 1994. When the company's insurance policy fell due for renewal on 31 October, it made sense that the new policy would cover the replacement value of Offset's old presses—$6 million for the building and \$33 million for plant and equipment—rather than their actual value. The presses were in the books at just \$3 million. The policy also covered the cost of any lost business while a claim was processed. Offset's insurance broker, Sedgwick James, placed the policy with Commercial Union Assurance Co. of Australia (which would later become CGU, and later again be part of IAG, the former NRMA Insurance), which took 33 per cent of the cover. FAI took 7 per cent of the slip.

There was nothing unusual in this. Offset Alpine's deputy chairman, Bruce Corlett, had resisted the temptation to steer a little insurance business towards his company, FAI. Corlett said later that he did not even know that Offset Alpine had taken out new insurance: 'I had no involvement at any stage in FAI's general insurance underwriting activities.'

There had been some unhappiness reported at FAI over the policy. An FAI manager who inspected the plant complained that the equipment was old, the presses badly laid out and the operation antiquated. 'As soon as we got there we knew the place was a very ordinary insurance proposition,' the manager told Jennifer Sexton of the *Weekend Australian*. In a statutory declaration quoted by Sexton, the unnamed manager said, 'In my report to my superiors I advised that Offset Alpine represented the highest possible insurance risk and I therefore recommended against writing the business.' Perhaps for this reason FAI reinsured most of its cover, cutting its own share of any payout to less than 1 per cent.

The last member of the family that founded the Offset business, thirty-six-year-old Garth Hackett, left the company on 30 November. His father Ron had left on 30 June. With challenging times ahead, it was not unusual for the Offset board to issue share options on 1 December to two directors. Kerry Packer's cousin Rob Henty, who had joined the Offset board in June, received 50 000 options exercisable at 77 cents. Bruce Corlett picked up 200 000 options. Similarly there was nothing unusual in issuing 500 000 options to Offset employees on 23 December. It was a little unconventional that no options went to the other two board members—Paul Obeid and the chairman, Rene Rivkin—but then again Rivkin probably didn't need any incentivising because by this time he secretly controlled 66 per cent of the company. He had sold shares in Australia, but his Swiss holdings now accounted for 48 per cent of the share register. Obeid, however, must have later regretted that he did not insist on being part of the options pool.

The annual meeting had approved a share issue to help pay for the cost of the new presses. On 23 December, Offset announced it had placed 4 095 000 shares at 69 cents. The biggest parcel would go to FAI, which was putting up $1 million for 1.45 million new shares. Bankers Trust put its hand up for 800 000 shares.

Friday 24 December was a scorching summer day as last-minute Christmas shoppers formed queues in stores across the city. Trying to get service on Christmas Eve is a long row to ho, ho, ho. The buying was no less frantic on the stock market, where Cambridge Gulf was defying gravity to reach its all-time high. The Adler family had their own concerns. Lyndi Adler was busy signing a cheque for $150 000 to the Mekong Club. Nine months later, when it came to light during a Liquor Administration Board investigation, the cheque would raise eyebrows. The cheque, which helped the club pay licensing fees, was banked as petty cash and noted as a director's loan in the club accounts, which it clearly wasn't. In any case, loaning money to Phuong Ngo at the Mekong Club was a risky business.

Nine weeks later, on 3 March 1994, Vinh Loc Nguyen, a Vietnamese businessman who was pressing Ngo to repay a $300 000 loan, was forced at knifepoint in Ngo's office to forgive the debt and sign over another $300 000. Then he had his right hand staked to a telephone book with a hunting knife. Ngo gave his victim a towel and a band-aid, Malcolm Brown reported in the *Sydney Morning Herald*. Ngo also had some innovative ideas about how to use the petty cash drawer. Apart from extracting cash advances of $68 000 from the club, in April 1994 Ngo used Mekong Club funds to buy a .22 Ruger, a .22 rifle, a .32 calibre pistol and, later, a .45 Magnum. He spent that month organising his first three failed attempts to shoot the State Member for Cabramatta, John Newman, whom Ngo didn't really like. Clearly Lyndi Adler had no idea of any of this when she signed her cheque. Neither did her husband Rodney. Somewhere along the line, his Rolodex of business partners had lost the quality control button.

None of these matters troubled the Offset Alpine staff as they closed up the plant at Silverwater for the Christmas break after a barbeque for the 150 staff in the loading dock. The company ran twenty-two hours a day year round, apart from this two-day break. There was a big order to fulfil on the day after Boxing Day; in preparation, double quantities of printers' ink, rags and the forty-litre cans of solvent used in the offset process had been grouped around each of the eight presses ready for use. Staff had gone home by 4.30 p.m. The head cleaner, Tae Hun Yung, was the last out; he turned off the lights and locked up at 6.30 p.m.

The fire alarm inside the Offset Alpine building went off at 11.04 p.m. A fire had broken out in a drum that contained rubbish collected from the barbeque, plus some old rags and solvent. While parents across the city were wrapping up presents and practising Santa impressions, firemen on seventeen appliances from fourteen stations battled a fierce blaze at the plant for more than two hours. 'The fire quickly increased in magnitude up to the second floor and through the roof,' Silverwater fire station officer Dennis Hinchey said in a report for police. 'The building was eventually totally destroyed.'

By the time the fire was finally extinguished at 1.20 a.m., the intense heat had melted the high-quality steel of each of the presses. While the new pre-press equipment that had just been installed was untouched, the old presses were a write-off. The police report described the cause of the fire as unknown. 'Due to the intensity of the fire, causing major structural collapse of the roof over the greater portion of the building, examination of the fire scene was hampered,' district fire officer William Powell said in his initial report. A week later he concluded: 'Because of a lack of direct evidence, no determination could be made on a source of ignition for this fire.' Police found there was no evidence of accelerant, nor any sign that the fire had been deliberately lit. A re-investigation of the fire in 2005 by police found no sign of arson. It was suggested that smouldering material from the barbeque probably had ignited the flammable printing chemicals in the drum. Privately, sources close to the new investigation said that, while it was possible someone had planned the fire, they could find nothing to suggest this.

Rene Rivkin was in Singapore when news of the fire reached him the following morning. He called Gordon Wood to tell him he was coming home immediately and to pick him up at the airport. Wood was spending Christmas with the Byrne family after winning Caroline back. Rivkin later claimed to have advised Wood how to woo her—though again, Caroline insisted both she and Wood be tested for HIV. Tony Byrne had walked into his apartment one lunch time and found Wood sitting with his daughter on the couch. 'Daddy, Gordon got a job,' Caroline had said. 'He's going to work for Rene Rivkin.' She then moved back into Wood's flat.

The young couple spent New Year's Eve house-sitting the Rivkin mansion, Carrara, at Rose Bay Avenue in Bellevue Hill, while Rene and Gayle Rivkin were out celebrating. Not without cause. On 28 December, Offset Alpine had told the stock exchange that it had extensive insurance: 'The company has been advised that the fire was accidental but at this stage no cause has been determined. Contrary to one newspaper report the cause of the fire will not affect the insurance.' That is, even if someone started the fire, the company would still get the money.

The news saw Offset Alpine's share price jump from 70 cents to $1.85. Around this time someone with smelling salts must have been telling the chief executive of Commercial Union, Philip

Clairs, that the insurer was about to be hit with its biggest individual insurance claim in thirty years. The total payout would be $53.2 million, though after reinsurance Commercial Union's share of the cheque was a fraction of this. In 1995, Rodney Adler told me that after its reinsurance cover FAI's net payout came to $450 000. On the other side of the ledger, FAI was well ahead from the rise in the share price. FAI made a $4.2 million profit on the Offset shares that it had just acquired together with a parcel of old Stroika shares that it had bought from Robert Whyte in 2002 (FAI had bought more shares by the time it sold out in 1995 for a $5.9 million profit). The other plus was that Rene Rivkin was now in a position to pay off his debt to FAI. It would take time, but Rivkin would eventually raise $10.2 million from his Australian shareholding, and another $28 million from the Offset shares held in his Swiss accounts. Bruce Corlett's options were worth $396 000, and Rob Henty's smaller parcel would make $99 000. The employee options issued the day before the fire would provide a cool $1 million profit.

All in all it was 'a very good fire', Kerry Packer commented later, with no sign that he was amused. What was there to laugh about? He had lost a fortune on foreign currency, he had lost face on Bendigo Mining, and now Rene Rivkin had scored big on a lucky fire. In a crying injustice, Kerry Packer, the previous owner of Offset Alpine and its kindly benefactor, wouldn't get any of it. Sometimes life is hard to bear.

ELEVEN
Under The Toaster
1994

Deep under Circular Quay, in one of the secret places of the city, a man stands rigid with outrage, racked with that species of intense pain that only Sydneysiders can truly know. He is only metres from the Opera House, deep below the water level of Sydney Harbour. The silent chamber around him pulses with intrigue, passion, ambition and aggression. Water is dripping. And there's a whiff of engine oil. After an extraordinary journey the man has made it here into the first circle, to take his place in the new hub of social and business power in Sydney. He has made it into this car park. But now someone has pinched his car space.

It's not just any car park. This is the parking palace for 1 Macquarie Street, the apartment complex whose striking lines—hailed as an architectural tribute to kitchenware of the world—earned its nickname as 'The Toaster'. The site is less than a stone's throw from the spot where Governor Phillip came ashore that day in January 1788 with the First Fleet. I like to think that Phillip had a vision of the fair metropolis that would grow on the spot where he was trying not to get his feet wet. I can imagine him laying it all out: 'Over *here* will be a cultural pavilion for the people, set with odd white sails, an international landmark that will house something useful. Perhaps opera and aid relief concerts.

Or professional wrestling. Over *there* we need a bridge, a mighty structure, the largest span of its kind within—oh, say, three or four miles. An overpass would be useful to blot out the view of the north shore. And *here* we will have a large apartment building in the shape of a modern kitchen appliance.'

The AMP Society must have known it was playing with fire when it built The Toaster. The building is aimed at people whose natural habitat is Sydney's eastern suburbs, that subdivision of Utopia that stretches from Vaucluse to Double Bay, known for its spacious homes, gracious living and ferocious fights over building applications for pergolas and garages. It is a Sydneysider's inalienable right to quarrel with the neighbours, particularly about anything that affects the view, and there is no feud like an eastern suburbs feud. To take these people out of their natural breeding ground and leave them living cheek by jowl with no yards, no fences, and no potential for relieving tension by arguments about the view—frankly, it's hellishly dangerous. To move into the anonymity of The Toaster is to leave much of the old life behind, beginning with your wardrobe. ('They are tiny apartments, you can't own too many clothes,' observed one resident.) It's a change-of-life move that is all about control. The territorial imperative of the eastern suburbs is confined here to the only place residents are likely to meet, after passing through two smartcard-access doors, a security guard station and being tracked by a remote television camera. In the car park.

There is one inviolate rule in this hidden community: don't touch my car. But car parks are a world of mystery, where rules are sometimes broken.

Paul Makucha, a reborn billboard millionaire, had been living in The Toaster for a year when he drove his black Mercedes into the car park on the afternoon of 9 January 2003 to find a green Verada parked in his space. The temerity of driving a Verada into this car park, to nestle among the crowd of Ferraris, Aston Martins and assorted upmarket motors, is the most remarkable aspect of this saga. Makucha harrumphed and complained to the front desk at The Toaster, which was run by a company called My Sydney Concierge. They didn't know whose car it was, so Makucha left his Mercedes in the Opera House car park. As the hours passed, Makucha's mind turned to what the foreign car could be doing there. He told the concierge staff that the Verada had a funny burning smell. Was it about to burst into flames? Taking no chances he sprayed it with a fire extinguisher, leaving a residue of fine dust on the car.

This was in the days after 11 September and before the Iraq war, when the government's fridge magnets were telling people to look out for attacks on spots like the Opera House—to 'Be Alert, But Not Alarmed'; to 'Be Worried, But Not Anxious'. Of course, what they should have advised for situations like Makucha's was, 'Be Annoyed, But Don't Go On About It'. Makucha decided the Verada might be a car bomb and that he should discourage any potential act of terrorism by partly deflating its tyres. There was some logic in Makucha's thinking inasmuch as, for anyone wanting to blow up the Opera House, hitting the car park next door would be the easiest way to do it.

Makucha was to testify subsequently that it was only several hours later, after he had asked My Sydney Concierge staff to report the car to the terrorism hotline, that one of them said they remembered whose car it might be. The staff denied this and said they called the police about Makucha, who then received an irate call from property developer John Boyd, whose secretary had parked in the critical car spot. Boyd, who counts Kerry Packer as a close friend, asked Makucha, 'Do you know who I am?' As it happened, Paul Makucha did know who John Boyd was. It went downhill from there—police were called, and went away again; there was a scuffle between Makucha and a security guard—it was always going to end in court.

In February, after he said his smartcard key to The Toaster suddenly stopped working, Makucha took out Apprehended

Violence Orders against Boyd, the security company, the security guards and others. Several days after the AVOs were issued, Makucha went to his car to find someone had splattered eggs over it. They did it again the next night, with such force that it cracked the duco, causing $3500 damage. The culprit was never discovered. Makucha had also taken out AVOs against the directors of My Sydney Concierge, one of whom is Australia's public relations doyen Ian Kortlang, who thus found himself in the back of the court at the AVO hearing on 28 May 2003, surrounded by a crowd of rather tough-looking employees whose dress code seemed to borrow heavily from *The Sopranos*. Boyd was busy elsewhere as a character reference for Rene Rivkin, who by then was up for insider trading.

One of the appeals of The Toaster is its complete privacy. It is perfect for a secret meeting or rendezvous, or an illicit affair. Cars drive into the Opera House car park, then immediately turn right into The Toaster car park. Residents go directly from the car park to their apartment. It isn't clear how the residents of The Toaster felt about the revelation that My Sydney Concierge, the company which manages the electronic security system that records every time they arrive and leave, and automatically films them and whoever is accompanying them, is controlled by Kortlang, a former intelligence operative and political operator. Not that anyone was suggesting Kortlang would ever have access to such information. In any case, as one of the guards testified, in recent years the cameras had become more blurry. They certainly caught none of the action around the Makucha parking space. In fact, that footage had been lost.

The AVO hearing unfolded as a comedy of manners. Four barristers were there to represent their clients, while Makucha represented himself. Makucha in court was painfully slow, and often quite funny, with the air of a man who feels he has been kicked around by the big end of town. In personality he resembles a tabloid newspaper: aggressive, dogged, often crude, hugely cunning, but with a certain rough charm. His business style is something like Ted Turner, the founder of CNN, who is generally perceived as brilliant but mad.

'I've lost interest in the case,' Kortlang said. 'Mr Makucha clearly has an opinion; I think the rest of the people represented in court have another opinion.'

The most wonderful moment was when a process server stepped up during an intermission to serve Kortlang with a bankruptcy notice. It was actually addressed to Makucha, and nothing could have been more civil and a testimony to the fading art of social discourse than the way in which Kortlang deftly explained to the server he had the wrong man, but if he stepped *this way* and peered through the window he would see there at the front of the courtroom the very chap he was looking for. The case was adjourned in May and when it resumed seven months later Makucha ambushed his opponents by hiring a QC. The magistrate urged all parties to settle, which they did, each side paying their own costs. Kortlang and the My Sydney Concierge staff signed declarations denying they had acted in the manner alleged by Makucha, but undertaking they would not deliberately engage in conduct that intimidated Makucha, or assault, molest, harass, threaten or otherwise interfere with him.

Makucha derived great amusement when Kortlang's lawyers mistakenly sent him a copy of their bill, which showed that Kortlang spent $8415 on this little episode. But Makucha had made a strategic error—he had made himself a person of interest to the media. He now found himself typecast in the role of comic relief and the newspapers had a fine old time with him. Makucha was now characterised as an obnoxious troublemaker who deserved everything that came to him, as a person who had no friends and no social graces. He was his own worst enemy; his failures and setbacks seen as humorous, something to be richly enjoyed. That was the media line, at least. It was a manifest injustice. Even in a town that judges people as shallowly as Sydney, Makucha had the credentials to be taken seriously. He had put together building projects worth more than half a billion dollars. In little more than a decade he had left his mark indelibly across the city. Visually he would be one of a handful of people whose work dominates Sydney, from the Airport Sheraton site to the huge billboards on Qantas Drive, from the signs of numerous pedestrian overpasses to the Balmain wheat silos. His personal and his professional life fell apart and he put it all back together again and made another fortune. He could turn his hand to so many things; yet he could not network to save his life.

There was a terrible inevitability about his downfall. What other outcome should there be than that he be stripped of his wealth, that receivers be appointed to his companies, that debtors dun him to the point of bankruptcy and hound him out of his home, that his intellectual property be appropriated, that he be mocked in the gossip pages and, finally, that he should be arrested, stripped of his $1000 suit and searched for concealed weapons in the holding cells of the Magistrates Court on Elizabeth Street. Which is where he ended up after Magistrate Pat O'Shane charged him with contempt of court. He had been representing himself in a civil case in a fight over fees with a surveyor. Makucha was desperate to introduce as evidence an expert opinion that the surveyor had made a critical error. He was arguing that the case should not proceed until he had obtained a transcript of a previous day's hearing when O'Shane took objection to his behaviour in the court and called the bailiffs. Minutes later Makucha was behind bars and facing a strip search. 'They told me, "Lift your scrotum, Makucha, lift your balls",' he told me later that day. He was released on bail and a year later he was still waiting for a trial date on the contempt of court charge.

Of course the dispute in the car park was not really about car spaces. Like all Sydney feuds this one had a history. The world, it turns out, is a small place. And The Toaster car park is not much bigger. On the afternoon in January 2004 when he saw the Verada, Makucha had just begun the paperwork needed to lodge a private fraud prosecution of Westpac. In the car park he was confronted by one of the figures from a traumatic past; a shadow from the heady days of 1994.

Paul Makucha's parents were Ukrainians, conscripted into slave labour by the Nazis. Some twelve million Ukrainians died during World War II, amid appalling suffering. The Makuchas survived through two years of what they called 'a walking tour of Europe'. The rigours of this forced march killed their two children. At the end of the war they were in Kiev, confined to a displaced persons camp there for four years before they were approved for migration to Australia. A third child, Paul, born in 1946, came with them. They settled in Brisbane, living in a hut made from kerosene tins hammered flat and lined with hessian. A fourth child died of encephalitis because the parents did not have sufficient English to explain to the doctors the ominous symptoms they had observed.

In 1961, Paul's mother walked out, taking the family savings with her. His father had a breakdown, locking himself in a cupboard with an axe. It was his fifteen-year-old son, Paul, who had to disarm him and take him to hospital. He would see his mother sometimes, crossing a nearby busy intersection, but she would ignore him. Paul Makucha had just enrolled himself at Brisbane Church of England Grammar School and now, besides having no parents, he had no money. But he was big and strong and had the ferocious survival instinct bred in the DP camps of Europe. He sat down with the school bursar and worked out an arrangement where he would pay his fees week by week, by working as a builder's labourer on the weekend. 'If I didn't have that background, I wouldn't have the personal strength to stand up to three or four lawyers at a time in court,' Makucha explained later. He also became the school bookie.

One of his school friends was David Jull, who would later be the Liberal member for the Queensland seat of Fadden and chair of the parliamentary committee that oversees Australia's spy agencies. Ian Kortlang was another contemporary growing up in Brisbane, though their paths never crossed then. After finishing school Makucha went broke running a fish-and-chip shop, around the time Kortlang was dropping out of his law degree and going to Vietnam. Makucha drifted first into electronic repairs, then trading in electronic parts, and finally into aviation. By the 1980s, he had a worldwide business trading in aircraft parts and integrated circuits. In 1984, aged thirty-eight, he tired of travelling and settled at Sydney Airport. He bought up narrow strips of land around the airport and leased others, with the idea that he would build a monorail. With part of his land he secured government approval for a $250 million Sheraton Hotel development. He sold the site and plans for $13 million, though not, he says, before a fight with Kortlang, who was by then director-general of the Office of State Development. This fight ended with Makucha having to pay the NSW government $1.5 million to reduce the width of the footpath. Kortlang told me in 2004 that he thought State Rail handled the matter, with some 'tangential' role by OSD, but that he did not recall the incident.

Makucha had dropped the monorail idea but he realised the long strips of land were ideal for billboards and car parks. Ever the lateral thinker, Makucha also approached state transport minister Bruce Baird in 1989 with an offer to build pedestrian overpasses over busy streets for the government, on which he would attach advertising signs. The government adopted the idea but barred Makucha from the tender, which was won by John Boyd. In Makucha's mind, this was another strike against Kortlang. Makucha also developed plans for a billboard on top of the wheat silos on Glebe Island, but he later lost his intellectual property ownership of this idea. In the end it was Boyd who built billboards on the site.

Makucha now concentrated on his airport sites. He had a four-kilometre strip of land, most of which was between two and five metres wide, sandwiched between the railway and Federal Airport Corporation land along Mascot Drive. 'It was the most unlikely piece of land, and he'd got hold of it and managed to turn it into something that was going to make a lot of money,' a businessman who knew him said. But as the economy turned down, Makucha's relations with his financier, AGC, came under strain. Makucha's development plans had been delayed by lengthy court battles with councils and the FAC over planning approvals. Westpac, meanwhile, had taken over the AGC loans and was itself struggling for survival. Makucha had designed some of the biggest billboard structures in the world but by mid-1993 the Westpac executive assigned to handle Makucha's loan was complaining that 'revenues are down, expenses are up, bank interest is unpaid and outstanding creditors have grown to an inordinate level'. The bank questioned whether Makucha had the execution skills to complete his billboard projects. Part of it was a personality thing.

'Mr Makucha may be a difficult man to deal with,' Justice Davies noted in the Federal Court in July 1993. 'Mr Makucha finds it difficult to accept the answer "no" to any action which he considers should be undertaken . . . Mr Makucha is a man of action.' Which was quite a mild way of describing an elemental force. When the federal government sold 40 per cent of Qantas to British Airways, Makucha splashed 'No British Airways Owner-ship of Our Qantas: Piss off Poms' across one of his billboards. 'It's a figure of speech,' he said when the Equal Opportunities Board complained. When Paul Keating offended Malaysian Prime Minister Mahathir Mohammed, Makucha wrote a giant 'Sorry'. Part of this reflected Makucha as a walking tabloid news-paper. Part of it was a marketing ploy to draw attention to his billboards.

Makucha now found himself at an impasse with Westpac. The bank had given him a deadline of 31 December to reduce his loan by $15 million. In July, Makucha arranged to sell a car park on Baxter Road for $14 million. It was well over the valuation price on the land, but Westpac blocked the sale. The Westpac account executive who refused permission said the car park was a major cash-producing asset and without it the Makucha group would be making a net operating loss.

Relations with the bank were breaking down. Makucha wrote back to ask what an acceptable payout figure would be for the car park, or for any other property in the group: 'If I do not have [a] payout figure for an individual property then I cannot repay the bank the $15 million because in order to repay the bank I will sell a piece of property or a business unit or units.' Makucha never received these payout figures from Westpac, despite repeated requests as the 31 December repayment deadline loomed. On 4 January 1994, with the debt standing at $40 million, Westpac hired insolvency expert Richard Grellman to prepare a report on what to do with the Makucha group. Makucha now played his last card. He called in The Phantom.

Makucha understood how important connections can be in a town like Sydney. Since 1986, he had used Theo Onisforou as a barrister and property advisor. But the two men had fallen out in August 1993 after Makucha learned that Onisforou was a partner in property ventures with James Packer's company Dorigad. Makucha now turned to Onisforou's friend, Charles Sweeney QC, for legal advice about whether he could force Westpac to allow him to sell part of his property. Thus, in late 1993, while Sweeney's share problems worsened with Gerard Farley and the Bendy Dogs, he was developing a closer business relationship with Paul Makucha. What followed is detailed in a series of documents that David Jull tabled in federal parliament in August 2001.

The bulk of the two large folders that Jull submitted consisted of letters which Makucha had written to Westpac executives, directors and a wide range of government officials complaining about his treatment by the bank, with accompanying records and related documents. Jull told parliament he was submitting the material as an example of what he called a moral injustice. Makucha's legal efforts are self-taught and his letters range over a very wide field, coloured by the intensity of his beliefs and his unhappiness that the bank had not agreed to the asset sales he had set up in 1993 which might have saved him. Makucha's letters and other documents show that, in the first weeks of 1994, he decided upon a change of strategy.

Makucha had been impressed with the high standing Sweeney enjoyed among senior Westpac executives after his work in the Westpac Letters affair and believed Sweeney could help sort out his loan problems. On 25 January, Makucha appointed Sweeney as chief executive of his companies. Sweeney now began writing to Westpac about his plans for the group. Talks were in hand to raise more than $25 million from asset sales. Sweeney also wrote about his own pay arrangements. He was already charging the Makucha companies $10 000 a day. In addition, he now proposed a pay package totalling $8 million that would fall due by July the following year. He would also get to keep the two company cars, a Mercedes and a BMW.

As talks proceeded through February and March, relations between Makucha and Sweeney soured. Makucha believed Sweeney should be paid his bonus only if the asset sales eventuated. Sweeney insisted he should be entitled to the $8 million for eighteen months work, irrespective of what happened. The two men had a fiery argument about it on 28 March. Sweeney no longer insisted on keeping the cars, but now wanted his money by December that year.

It was an extraordinary series of demands but Makucha was desperate. Sweeney strenuously denies there was anything inappropriate in what was a commercial relationship. Westpac was anxious for Sweeney's position to be clarified and had been kept informed of the details of the remuneration agreement. The bank now took a decisive role. Westpac wrote to Sweeney on 12 April that there was 'cause for concern' about dissension in the Makucha group regarding Sweeney's continuing role:

> We would therefore like to receive from you by 14 April 1994 your written assurance that there is now no dispute, particularly on behalf of Mr Makucha ... concerning the terms of your ongoing involvement with the companies ... We need this confirmation in order to decide whether further negotiations [about the loan] are justified.

Makucha was over a barrel. Westpac had told him if he wanted to extend his $40 million loan, he had to resolve the dispute with Sweeney. He had forty-eight hours.

Unbeknown to Makucha, another drama had been playing out behind the scenes. Gerard Farley's case in the Administrative Appeals Tribunal in 1998 provides a different picture of Sweeney's activities in early 1994. AAT deputy president Bruce McMahon in his judgment spelt out the financial predicament that faced Sweeney. On 1 February, the week after Sweeney took the helm at the Makucha group, both First State and Hambros Equities decided to sell the Bendigo Mining shares he had bought four months before. On top of the $4 million Sweeney owed to First State and Bendigo, ASIC records show that his company filings listed a further $13 million of liabilities in his family trust and related companies, against assets of $8 million. Sweeney was also involved in a legal case between his family's trustee company and the Bank of New York.

McMahon's judgment gives a detailed account of a series of share trades executed by Farley in companies that had no apparent link to Sweeney, but which, McMahon said, were 'accustomed to act in accordance with Mr Sweeney's directions'. The trades had the effect of moving the liability for Sweeney's debt further and further away, though Sweeney denied any knowledge of the trades.

'These transactions were structured to give the very false impression that there was real trading going on, where shares were merely being moved from place to place, where each place was his [Sweeney's] place,' John Agius QC, counsel for the Australian Securities and Investments Commission, told the AAT hearing. Sweeney was not present to contest this.

McMahon found the deals 'give a false impression of commercial reality. In fact, if one regards [the companies] as the alter egos of Mr Sweeney, there was no change in beneficial ownership'. Sweeney denied any attempt to mislead the market and has pointed out that ASIC dropped a civil case against him which alleged this.

The Bendigo Mining shares ended up in an obscure American company and a Cook Islands shelf company with a post office box number in Western Samoa. Both companies later proved impossible to trace, according to evidence presented to the AAT. McMahon found in his judgment that 'entities associated with Mr Sweeney were indebted to the extent of almost $3 million', but First State now had no record that Sweeney was linked to any of its unpaid shares—and indeed, Sweeney himself denied any involvement in the companies or in the share trading.

Farley, meanwhile, had lost his job. He was due to leave First State on 31 March and was faced with a bill for $5.5 million in unpaid client accounts. According to McMahon, Farley believed Sweeney was negotiating to buy out the First State broking operation, which would wipe the slate clean. The tapes of Farley's telephone calls in those last days, played five years later in court, showed a mixture of panic, forced jollity and downright desperation as he called Sweeney, Consolidated Press executive Michael Karagiannis and others—people he thought of as his friends and comrades, his lifeline to the network—to ask for help.

'I am hurting badly . . . but you know, what can I do?' Farley told Karagiannis on Wednesday 30 March, the morning before he left. Karagiannis asked Farley: 'Do you want to see if I can do a rescue package for you?'

'Tell me what you mean . . . I basically need about five million bucks,' Farley said, before asking if Karagiannis would approach Onisforou to buy some shares. But the assistance never came.

Farley called Sweeney. 'We should meet tonight. I mean, it's suicide if we don't. Complete and utter suicide,' Farley told him. Sweeney cut the call short.

Then it was back to Karagiannis again, as the realisation sank in for Farley that the rescue would not take place: 'Uncle, Uncle, Uncle Michael . . . you know all good uncles do a favour now and then.' This was a preamble to hitting Karagiannis for a $40 000 loan.

Nothing had been resolved by Thursday afternoon when Farley packed up his desk. In the days that followed, Farley and Sweeney held talks about buying out First State but nothing eventuated. In 1999, ASIC accused Sweeney of creating the appearance of a false market with the Bendigo Mining trades, a civil charge that Sweeney vigorously denied. The charge was dropped when ASIC made a settlement with Sweeney in 2002.

While Sweeney may have played his cards ruthlessly with First State, he emerged with no adverse findings against him and his reputation clear. However his actions raise serious questions about Westpac's treatment of Makucha. By 12 April, Westpac was applying huge commercial pressure to force Paul Makucha to agree to pay $8 million to a man who had just extricated himself from his $3 million debt to First State. There's no indication Westpac knew anything about Sweeney's share trading but the question remains: exactly what did Westpac know about this man who it had now decided was the key to a $40 million loan?

Makucha had had enough and on Sunday 17 April he sacked Sweeney. Four days later Wesptac appointed Richard Grellman as a receiver to Makucha's companies. The debt stood at $40 million on properties earning $6.8 million a year. One of Makucha's last acts had been to commission a valuation by Heron Todd White, which concluded his properties were worth $75 million.

Makucha's little drama went entirely unnoticed as other news filled the headlines. Everyone seemed to be having their troubles, even Kerry Packer, who had just lost the tender for the Sydney Casino licence. On 6 May the Casino Control Authority awarded the licence to construction group Leightons, in partnership with the Showboat casino group in the US. Three days later, Packer's friend John Boyd telephoned Leightons chief executive Wal King and asked for a meeting. He told King that Packer didn't want to have a war over the casino thing. He suggested that Leighton sell Packer a shareholding in the casino. King declined. King would release details of the meeting days later when the Packer camp launched a media assault on the bona fides of Leighton and Showboat.

In early 1995, Grellman sold the Makucha properties and business to Manboom, an investment trust owned by Kerry Packer, Robert Whyte and John Singleton, for $15 million. Makucha had development approvals in place for additional billboards that would cost $3.3 million to build. Within short order Manboom was earning more than $9 million a year. As part of the deal, Makucha had to sign over his rights to all intellectual property for the sites for $10. In his correspondence tabled in parliament, Makucha claims that his former advisor, Theo Onisforou, negotiated with the receiver on behalf of Manboom. Makucha claims to have seen correspondence with the receiver on Consolidated Press letterhead signed by Onisforou. In contrast, press reports have Robert Whyte as the one who made contact with Grellman.

It was a vivid demonstration of the differences between Sydney's winners and Sydney's losers. Within five years Manboom's investment was worth $200 million. It made Rene Rivkin's Offset Alpine deal look ordinary. In 2001, Manboom sold a little over half the

Makucha properties to the Ten Network for $125 million. The remaining land was reported to be valued at a further $75 million.

John Boyd was another winner. In 1999, he was reported to have received $30 million for the sale of 75 per cent of his advertising business, Boyd Outdoor, 'which is famous for its huge billboards on the wheat silos at Glebe Island and on six pedestrian bridges around Sydney', the *Sydney Morning Herald* reported.

It wasn't all happy endings. First State reported Farley to the Australian Securities Commission (ASC) and pursued the unpaid accounts. Michael Karagiannis was shocked in March 1995 when State Bank's lawyers hit him with a demand to pay $279 000 for his Bendigo Mining shares. Karagiannis exploded and demanded that Farley sign a letter stating Farley alone was responsible for the debt.

'You threatened Mr Farley with physical violence if he didn't provide you with what you wanted?' Farley's counsel asked Karagiannis at the AAT hearing.

'I had a number of conversations . . . I did have one conversation when I was very emotional with Gerard,' Karagiannis replied.

When he was interviewed under oath by the ASC, Karagiannis ditched his old friend. He gave an elaborate story about how Farley had booked the shares to Cazworth, Karagiannis's family company, without telling him anything about it. ASC investigator Peter Riordan heard him out and then played the tape of his phone calls with Farley on Farley's last day at First State. Karagiannis's story collapsed.

'I'm not proud of what I've done. It was the wrong thing to do,' Karagiannis said of his lies at the AAT hearing in 1998. 'Gerard Farley had a responsibility for that account as much as I did. I was in a position where my family would have been out of a home . . . It was the welfare of my family.'

In November 1994, secure in the belief that he would not have to pay the debt to First State, Karagiannis had spent up big, using

Cazworth to buy apartments in James Packer's Medina development. He had mortgaged his family home in Blakehurst as well. If Cazworth went, everything went.

Karagiannis turned his courtroom confession into a Greek tragedy. 'I've confronted everybody about my situation. I've confronted my family, my friends, my employer, my religion. This story had to be told,' he said. It didn't seem to hurt his career. A year later he had a promotion at Consolidated Press, and the year after that he and his wife moved out of Blakehurst into a $1.46 million waterfront home at Kyle Bay.

Makucha had disappeared seemingly without a trace. His penthouse in Darling Point, his $400 000 Bentley, his twelve-metre yacht (*Lady Fun*), all had to go. He moved into a renovated shipping container on a site he still leased near the airport between O'Riordan and High streets, Alexandria. For the next five years he would sleep there, above a sewerage pipe next to a rat-trap factory, with an outdoor shower he built himself. 'I call it the Shithouse Hotel,' he said. His marriage had broken down and he was drinking heavily. Yet miraculously he pulled himself together and began rebuilding another billboard venture based around a site on O'Riordan Street.

Westpac, for its part, strenuously denied any suggestion that it had acted with impropriety towards Makucha and his companies. In correspondence with their former client which was also tabled in parliament by Jull, the bank firmly rejected his allegations of misconduct. 'Westpac again rejects the allegations of impropriety you make against it and its officers,' one executive wrote in 2001. 'Otherwise I do not believe that [your letter] merits a response.' The letter reminded Makucha that under the deed of release for his debt which he had signed in September 1998, he had agreed not to communicate in any way with Westpac employees or directors; the bank was also closing his accounts.

By 2002, he had moved out of the shipping container and leased an apartment at The Toaster. In January 2003, he quietly launched the legal campaign he had been planning for nine years: he began the process for launching a private prosecution of Westpac. He would claim the bank had placed 'unreasonable demands on the said Paul Makucha which [Westpac] knew he could not comply with, with the intent to cheat/defraud the said Paul Makucha and the Makucha group of companies'. He was at a delicate stage in these proceedings when he arrived home one day to find someone had taken his car space. After all these years, John Boyd had ended up in the next-door parking space and, when Boyd's secretary went to see him, she got his car space number mixed up. How else would you expect such a Sydney story to end?

Makucha served his summons on Westpac in June 2003 but the case went nowhere. The Director of Public Prosecutions quietly took over the prosecution of Makucha's case. He looked at Makucha's brief of evidence, but in the end judged it inadequate and no-billed it. 'He didn't tell me it was a trivial prosecution,' Makucha consoled himself, but this was meagre comfort. His financial affairs were plunging once more into crisis. And the newspapers were loving it. That Makucha. What a card.

PART FOUR

Strange days, Mama

RUTH: But all in vain the quips we heard,
　　　 We lay and sobbed upon the rocks,
　　　 Until to somebody occurred
　　　 A startling paradox.

Pirates of Penzance

TWELVE

Rivkin's party

1994

Gordon Wood had taken to writing notes to Caroline Byrne to assure her how much he loved her. Love letters are tricky things. Not everyone can hit the right note. In 1994, Gordon Wood had the happy thought that he could endear himself to Caroline by posing as an erotic biscuit. Rene Rivkin's driver and personal assistant chose Australia's favourite chocolate treat, the Tim Tam. 'You've heard of the packet of Tim Tams that never runs out, well, I am giving you the dessert that never runs out—and it is sweet and pure and full of goodness,' Wood wrote to his beloved. 'That dessert is my passionate, undying and deepest love for you. You can tuck into this dessert whenever you want, as often as you like, and what is more, eat as much as you can and never fear—it is endless, limitless . . . and will be there as long as we both shall live.'

There was much, much more: 'You are my purpose in life . . . I am on this planet to love you . . . this is the meaning of love . . . I now believe it is a crime to use the word LOVE in any way that doesn't relate to you . . . Not only are you my princess and my goddess, but in my eyes you are Miss World, Miss Universe, Miss All-Time Greatest and Most Beautiful Woman.'

Excerpts from the letters appeared in *Woman's Day* shortly after Wood left Australia in 1998. *Woman's Day* ran even more earnest outpourings by Wood, but the Tim Tam line was the high point. Personally I would have seen Wood more as an Iced Vo Vo, and there's not a lot of people I would say that about. It's hard to project just the right quality of coconut flakiness. In 1998, Rene Rivkin, that old Arnotts All Sorts, put it more prosaically and with fewer biscuits: 'I knew how much he [Wood] loved her. He called her "Chicky babes" and she called him "Gordy".' Actually that pretty much summed up a common reaction people had to Wood's romantic sallies: 'Oh Gord!'

Gordon and Caroline had eased effortlessly into the latte society of eastern Sydney. There had been no more talk about drugs. Caroline's friend Natalie McCamley said in a statement tendered at her inquest in 1998: 'I'm not sure if Caroline used the drug [ecstasy] any other time but Gordon one other time said that he knew a guy that could get it for me. He said to me, "It's safer to get it off somebody that knows what they're doing, rather than buying it off some stranger."'

Wood later told police he and Caroline had had 'a couple of puffs' of marijuana. Another friend, Narelle Cook, said, 'I remember Caroline talking to me one time in her flat in Elizabeth Bay that she and Gordon had used the drug ecstasy. I think she also said that they used speed. She said it was just to see what it was like. This was very unlike Caroline because she was always so conscious of her body. I remember at school there would be some of us smoking cigarettes but Caroline wouldn't even have one puff.' It's not thought that Caroline ever went beyond these experiments with drugs.

Rene Rivkin had his hands full with Offset Alpine. From 14 December 1993, Rivkin had become an avid trader of Offset Alpine stock, along with a former Rivkin operative, Nigel Little-wood. One or other of them—often both—bought Offset shares on eleven of the last twelve trading days in December. Rivkin was back in the market on 4 January, and traded throughout January. The shares surged after Christmas with news of the fire but, even with Rivkin's continued buying, the price did not lift above $1 in the first week of the new year. Then, from 10 January, Rivkin began buying bigger licks of shares through his Stilton account at Bank Leumi. Stilton outlaid $446 000 to buy Offset shares from Rivkin's Australian holdings, and the share price rocketed to $1.70. There's no indication Littlewood was involved, but Rivkin's Swiss trading looked like a classic move to ramp the share price up—selling it from one bank account to another. But why bother? Here was a man who had just had (or back in mid-December was about to have) the luckiest break of his life. The insurers would have to cough up $53 million in cash. Why did Rivkin need a high share price?

It's critical to remember that behind the impressive façade and the million-dollar lifestyle, Rivkin still didn't have a lot of money. He had FAI financing him in Australia, and Leumi and EBC Zurich funding him in Switzerland. In each case, he had been loaned money against the value of his shares (sometimes it looks like FAI and Bank Leumi, unbeknown to each other, had mortgages over the same shares). The higher his share price went, the more Rivkin's bankers would lend him. The money from Offset's fire insurance would not begin to flow for another six months. And when it did, the money would go to Offset Alpine for replacement presses. If it didn't, even if the insurers would wear that, the money would immediately become taxable. So while the fire payout was a windfall for the Offset Alpine business it would not benefit Rivkin directly until someone either bought his shares or bought the business. This was the cruel paradox that would drive the human drama that unfolded over the next two years. Rivkin had money, money everywhere, but not enough to spend.

Rivkin had a bundle of friends and supporters holding Offset Alpine stock. Chief among these was Trevor Kennedy. Offset Alpine's Top Twenty shareholders list in September 1993 showed he had bought another 225 000 shares in the previous year, either before Stroika bought Offset, or in the months since. By September

1994, Kennedy had bought another 300 000 shares and now held 3.5 per cent of the company. In 1995, this would be worth $2.7 million. That was on top of his share of Rivkin's EBC Zurich shareholding. Kennedy's total return from Offset Alpine would come to $5.8 million.

Between them, Rivkin, Kennedy, Graham Richardson and FAI owned 70 per cent of Offset Alpine but there was still sufficient Christmas cheer to spread around the diaspora. Kennedy's former Consolidated Press colleague, Sean Howard, would clear half a million dollars on his Offset investment—in October 1994, Kennedy and Howard came together again when they joined with Malcolm Turnbull to back an Internet service provider company called Ozemail, which Howard had bought from Consolidated Press Holdings. Turnbull and Kennedy each shelled out $450 000 for a quarter share. Other lucky Offset Alpine investors included real estate agents and old China hands Bart and Ronald Doff, Nora Goodridge and Rivkin's former butler, Thomas Mann. But the most persistent Rivkin supporters were Ray and Dianne Martin. Rivkin had been doing finance spots with Martin on the *Midday Show* since 1990. By May 1995, the Martin household had bought no less than four parcels of Offset Alpine shares. The Top Twenty shareholder lists would show Dianne Martin held 100 000 shares while Ray held 83 310. There was also a joint holding of Ray and Dianne with another 52 800. Then there was another 25 000 for Ray, this time with an address care of Channel Nine rather than the family home. In all, the Martins held 261 110 shares, which eventually cashed out for $710 219 in 1995. Sam Chisholm, the former head of Nine, had bought shares in the name of his then wife, Rhonda, back in the Stroika days before the Offset deal. The shares eventually would be worth $85 000. 'That was all Sam,' Rhonda Chisholm said. 'I didn't see any of it.'

It made for a powerful lot of good feeling directed towards Rene by his many friends and supporters. This was no minor thing as Rivkin approached his fiftieth birthday. But first there were the technicalities of obtaining the payout from the fire. The police report on 9 January concluded that the cause of the fire was 'undetermined'. On 18 January, Offset Alpine announced that the underwriters had accepted liability for the fire: 'On the basis of claims to be submitted by the company, the underwriters will be making progress claims as and when required.'

The nature of the negotiations now changed. The primary insurers were now concerned with verifying the replacement value of the old presses, which had been worth only $2.8 million in the books, and with getting the new facilities up and running. The longer it took to restore operations the more they would have to pay out to cover Offset Alpine's losses from disrupted business. The burden of investigating the fire now passed to Australia's two biggest reinsurers, Munich Re and Swiss Re. They would provide the largest share of the payout, reportedly $10 million apiece. It is exactly at this delicate point in the payout process that friction can often arise between the various parties involved because there is the danger, when an insurer pays out on a claim, that the reinsurer may later deny it, leaving the insurer with the total bill. In 2004, Jennifer Sexton of the *Weekend Australian* reported that investigators for the reinsurers had made contact with the FAI assessor who had originally recommended against them accepting the Offset policy. He now complained that his file on Offset had disappeared.

There is nothing very unusual about any of this. In an article he wrote for the *Australian Institute of Insurance Journal* in 1995, loss adjuster Tony Morgan described the fire as a textbook example of an insurance payout: 'Despite rumour, anonymous phone calls and uninformed speculation, exhaustive inquiries by forensic experts, investigators and the police failed to establish any evidence which implicated any interests associated with Offset Alpine.' It's a careful choice of words. It would be simpler to say there was no evidence of arson; but even if there had been evidence, it would not have been sufficient to thwart an insurance claim. Insurers would have needed not just to show arson, but to link it with parties linked to Offset Alpine. In the meantime, all Rivkin could do was wait.

Elsewhere the year had begun with mixed fortunes. On 23 January, Mark Latham was elected the new Labor member for Werriwa; he replaced John Kerin, who had retired two days before Christmas. He had never really recovered from his demotion and humiliation in 1992, engineered in part by Graham Richardson. Only days remained in Richardson's own political career.

On 11 March, Offset Alpine announced that it was discussing a replacement value of $42 million for the old presses in its books at $2.79 million, and claimed the total payout could run as high as $88 million. The final figure still had to be negotiated with the insurance companies, but clearly shareholders were facing a staggering windfall. Four days later Rivkin and Kennedy, the two men with the biggest share of the windfall, celebrated by going into business together—opening a golf driving range on an abandoned building site just a chip shot from the Liberal Party's old Ash Street HQ in the Sydney CBD. It was marvellous timing for Graham Richardson as well, whose name had popped up on 8 March at hearings of the Criminal Justice Commission in Queensland. Two prostitutes claimed they had been with Richardson in a $4000 sex romp the previous August at Hyatt Sanctuary Cove on the Gold Coast, paid for by a US defence contractor. Richardson denied this and it was never proven. However, the knowledge that he was now a Swiss millionaire must have made Richardson's next decision an easier one. On 14 March he told Keating he was leaving politics. He went public with the news ten days later—well before the National Party's Bob Katter broadcast the CJC claims in parliament. Richo made his sentimental speech about the 'dignity of battlers' at his farewell dinner on 31 March before returning to his table with Rivkin.

The good news continued. On 8 April Transport Minister Laurie Brereton appointed his old mate Trevor Kennedy to the Qantas board. Meanwhile, Prime Minister Paul Keating, who had been receiving a caning in Parliament from the Liberal Party over his troubled investment in a piggery, sold his half share in the business on 7 March to wealthy Indonesians. That old Labor numbers man Eddie Obeid now popped up as a director on some of the property companies that had been in the piggery group. It looked like Obeid had come into some money—in late 1993, a number of his companies had been facing wind-up applications but he appears to have secured new backing from Macquarie Bank. Had Obeid earned profits from Offset Alpine shares? There would have been nothing amiss if he had, but Obeid has never talked about it.

Gordon Wood was making his own foray into big business. In March 1994, Gordon and Caroline took a Thai takeaway meal for dinner with Tony Byrne at his apartment in The Connaught on Liverpool Street in the city. Wood carried a share price pager. According to a statutory declaration that Tony Byrne made in March 1998, Wood then said to him: 'Offset Alpine is at $1.37. I've recently bought shares in Offset Alpine. They are going to go up in price—the insurance company is going to pay up.' Byrne said that Wood then told him, 'The fire was a set-up.'

Courier Mail journalist Paul Whittaker subsequently discovered that Offset Alpine's share register showed that Gordon Wood's mother, Brenda Wood, bought 7000 shares for $1.30 on 25 February. However Offset shares were well above $1.30 by then, which suggests that either Mrs Wood received a preferential price, or the shares were bought in January. While it was public knowledge by 18 January that the insurers were paying up, it was not until 11 March that Offset revealed how high the insurance windfall was likely to be. Did Gordon Wood have inside information? During this period, Robert Wainwright reported in the *Sydney Morning Herald* in 2004, Wood approached a businessman with a proposition. Wood told the businessman the fire had been a set-up and that the insurer was going to pay, which created an opportunity to buy a large shareholding in Offset before the share price rose.

Of course, just because Gordon Wood said the fire was a set-up, or even if he believed it was a set-up, it doesn't mean it was. You would never want to bet your house on the Magic Tim Tam. His record suggested he was up for playing all ends against the middle.

Arrangements were now in full swing for Rivkin's fiftieth birthday. It would be a glittering night in the Botanic Gardens held in a huge marquee overlooking Mrs Macquarie's Chair. 'This is conspicuous consumption, absolutely conspicuous,' Rivkin told journalist Tony Stephens at the time. The two hundred and fifty guests, who shared the canapés and vintage champagne while the Little River Band played, included Graham Richardson, Laurie Brereton, Rodney Adler, Ray Martin, Michael Yabsley and Trevor Kennedy. The Packers didn't make it. Caroline and the Tim Tam were there along with George Freris, whose links through the tattoo shop probably helped secure the services of the local chapter of Hells Angels, who cruised through the party on their motorcycles in a salute to Rivkin. Gossip columnist Ros Reines, who was once the officially anointed biographer of the host, costed the affair at $400 000.

Rene told Stephens he had been 'absolutely delighted' to be diagnosed with minor manic depression seven years before: 'I had suspected it but it was a great relief to know for sure.' He was seeing a psychiatrist once a week and had been taking Prozac for years now, without harmful side effects.

How did he feel about turning fifty? As Maurice Chevalier put it, growing old was better than the alternative. 'I'm just waiting to die and having as pleasant a time as possible while waiting,' he told Stephens. He had decided to throw a party but of course now he regretted it. 'One of the things I like about myself is that

I'm frank. There aren't many people like me. Broadly speaking, I am regarded as not an indecent character. My inferiority complex is of major magnitude.'

Then there were the presents. 'Beautiful things, I love beautiful things,' Rivkin told Larry Schwartz. 'I got a 2000-year-old piece of pottery from one of these people. I got a gold watch from another one. I got three sets of gold cufflinks. I got some beautiful books. I got four or five caricatures of me by various cartoonists. I got a beautiful 1910 Lalique decanter which I love . . .'

This is a telling moment for Rivkin. He might be self-obsessed, but he wasn't a bad man. 'Life's been good but I am a caring person,' he told Schwartz. 'I'm not that selfish that I can say to myself, "My life's good, therefore fuck the Rwandans." It actually makes me unhappy that there is so much misery in the world. These things actually bring out tears in me . . . I think the world is a total failure. I lie in bed thinking I'd like to be out of here so at least I don't have to look at it . . . It's no good saying I'm a have. Yes. I am a have. But what about all the have-nots?'

It was one of the reasons his friends loved him. 'I don't believe Rene has an evil thought in his head,' said Richardson.

It was important to Rivkin that his father, Walter, was at the party. Later Rivkin told a fantastic story about that night and its antecedents to Andrew Denton in an interview on ABC's *Enough Rope* in 2003: how his father had criticised him in March 1992 for appearing with Jana Wendt in a television debate over whether Paul Keating had killed the Australian economy. How he called his father's criticism silly and in response his father disinherited him. The other reason for the disinheritance was that ten years before he had neglected to say Happy New Year to his father's friends.

Rivkin said he had negotiated with his aunt to ensure his father came to his fiftieth birthday party: 'I was only willing to issue him an invitation if the sister of his guaranteed that he would come, which he did. Two or three days before the event he withdrew and

I exploded and hit the roof and told the sister to pass on to him that if he didn't come as he promised that I would never speak to him again, and, what's more—that didn't matter much to him, but he adored my five children—and that I would never allow my five children to go and visit him.'

As Rivkin put it to Denton, 'Not everyone is normal like you, Andrew.'

The kindest thing that can be said about this tale is that five months earlier, when the Zurich DA, Dr Nathan Landshut, quizzed him about these matters in Switzerland, Rivkin didn't put it quite like that. He did talk about being estranged from his father, but that was in response to Landshut's questions about the guarantee Rene had signed in September 1990, which pledged his father's Swiss account to cover his own $6 million debt.

'How should I know whether my father was aware of that when I hadn't spoken to him for years?' Rivkin replied. 'Mr Imfeld [Bank Leumi's private client investor in Zurich] actually told me that my father really loved me . . . I only ever had that experience with Mr Imfeld.' Rivkin said that if his father hadn't wanted him to use the account, why had he given him power of attorney? There seems something almost pathological in Rivkin's repeated denials of what he had done, and the transformation of his father into a monster, before retreating into sentimentality with the plaintive cry that Imfeld had told him that his father loved him.

Rene also provided a different account in Zurich of how he made up with his father ahead of his party. It began with Imfeld writing to Walter Rivkin on 21 January 1994, suggesting he invest in certain funds and asking for power of attorney to do this. Ten days later, Walter wrote back to accept the proposal. By 18 April, Walter was complaining to Imfeld of massive losses in his account, which he said were nothing like the investments that Imfeld had described and which had been made before he had given approval. On 29 April, Imfeld faxed back to Walter that 'There is always a solution to a problem and I assure you it will not affect our relationship.' Walter showed the fax to Rene over lunch. On 19 May, Imfeld wrote to Walter to tell him he had made good the loss by transferring US$186 127.51 into Walter's account, two weeks before Rene's party. End of problem.

When questioned about the incident by Landshut, Rene replied airily that he could remember something about a lunch where his father warned him about Imfeld: 'Apparently my father had seen something in his account that shouldn't have been there. Imfeld corrected it but my father said I should be careful. I got the impression that my father might have been imagining a problem.'

What Rene didn't mention was that Imfeld took the money to repay his father out of Rene's own account. 'This is the first I've ever heard of this,' Rene said when Landshut raised it, and claimed the transfer was not authorised. But that seems unlikely.

In the interview on *Enough Rope*, Rivkin was similarly emphatic, continually reassuring Denton that he was telling the truth about his father and about everything else about his life: 'I don't lie . . . I get into trouble by telling the truth.'

Rivkin *was* telling the truth. He just didn't know what it was. Driven by his deepening bipolar disorder, his life had splintered into parallel worlds that he could not reconcile. With the utmost candour he would lie about anything—though they would not be lies because he really believed the things he said. While Walter Rivkin was by many accounts an overbearing and difficult father, the stories of disinheritance and threats to withhold access to grandchildren appear to be attempts to cloak a shabbier exchange. At the heart of a fictitious life, the father–son relationship was the one area where Rene Rivkin was least able to face the truth.

Two weeks after Rivkin's party, on 17 June, Offset Alpine announced that it had reached agreement on its insurance payout. The total would come to $53.2 million. Most of the payout was the $42 million replacement value for the presses. The rest was the value of business lost because of the fire. The insurers had kept the payout from going higher by settling the claim quickly. Fortunately the replacement presses were already on order. The insurers had paid $18 million; Offset would have the rest of the money by the first week of July. Rivkin was already in celebration mode. On 2 June, two days before his party, Rene had bought himself a little present. He settled on a small apartment at 118 Crown Street, opposite the City Gym, for $230 000, which he bought through a shelf company called Romale Pty Ltd. He would use it for afternoon naps. Sometimes the boys could drop over to see him. Now Rivkin decided to treat himself to a little overseas trip.

Tony Byrne remembers his daughter coming to see him with big news. 'Guess what?' she said. 'Rene and George have gone on a world trip together. His wife doesn't know. She thinks he has gone on a business trip on his own.'

Tony Byrne was in the habit of writing up his conversations with Caroline in his diary. The diary notes make it clear that the George to whom Caroline was referring was George Freris, and she was quite clear that Wood saw him as a threat. 'Rene has set George up in business and showered him with gifts,' Caroline told her father. 'It is all for sex of course. Gordon is jealous.' Here Caroline was mistaken. There is no evidence that Rivkin engaged in sex with any of his young men.

On 2 August, Imfeld transferred $935 000 out of the Stilton account to a mystery account at Swiss bank UBS. It was Stilton's biggest cash transfer in five years. Rivkin was settling matters with some unknown party. If there was another Offset Alpine beneficiary, this mystery transfer is the only clue. Six days later, he was sitting in Imfeld's office on Claridenstrasse, writing instructions on a sheet of internal Bank Leumi notepaper. The note said:

Re: George Freris

I wish to leave George Freris $500 000 (five hundred thousand dollars) Australian currency, in the event of my death. I do not wish any member of my family to know about this bequest.

R. Rivkin

Rivkin dated the note and addressed it to Imfeld via his secretary Cahide Ay. Rivkin signed it, then had Imfeld countersign and stamp it. It is tempting, given the cloud of rumour that has dogged Rivkin and his young male friends, together with his reluctance for his family to know anything about it, to see this as some sort of gift for a romantic liaison, or evidence of a romantic attachment. But Rivkin and Freris were not in Zurich on a dirty weekend. This was a business trip and Wood was along too. Offset Alpine had received the final instalment in its $53.2 million payout less than five weeks before. There would be matters to discuss with Ernst Imfeld.

Rivkin had also set up Freris with his own account at Bank Leumi, transferring shares from Stilton as the initial deposit. The bequest was a legal guarantee that more money was coming. Israeli journalist Shraga Elam later discovered that after signing for Freris, Rivkin was about to make a similar provision for Wood when Freris convinced him that it was unwise. Rather than make an identical arrangement at Bank Leumi, Rivkin set up Wood's account and bequest elsewhere, apparently with EBC Zurich. Almost certainly Rivkin transferred Offset Alpine shares to open Wood's account. Wood was now part of the golden circle.

The sheer size of the bequests for Freris and Wood is significant. Rivkin could be extremely generous, showering his favourites with gifts worth thousands of dollars. However, half a million dollars is something more than generous. Even in Rene Rivkin's economy it seems more like something to be given in exchange for exceptional service. The question remains, if Freris and Wood had done something for Rivkin, what was it? Or was it simply Rivkin's affection for them?

Eleven years later, after Rivkin's death, Swiss lawyers would disagree over whether the Freris bequest was a valid will under Swiss law. The consensus was that it wasn't, only because Imfeld filled the date in rather than Rivkin, but lawyers also conceded that some Swiss banks would probably execute such instructions without telling the client's family or Rivkin's executor. It is not known if the Wood bequest survived. But what was it for? Rene Rivkin had become rich from the Offset insurance payout. But at that point he was still only rich on paper. It would not have been easy to pay Freris $500 000 immediately—Rivkin had other spending plans in addition to the mysterious cash payment six days before. It would be simpler to pay Freris the money later, when Rivkin was more liquid. In the meantime, the formal bequest Rivkin signed was an assurance that Freris would get the $500 000.

Freris did not later respond to written questions about the bequest when it came to light in 2005. He certainly knew about Rivkin's Swiss accounts because later he had one himself at Bank Leumi. Rivkin would sometimes buy shares on his behalf through Leumi.

By Wednesday 17 August, Rivkin was back in Australia, where he sold 250 000 Offset Alpine shares from his Australian holding company to his Stilton account. The deal merely transferred $400 000 from Zurich into Rivkin's hands in Sydney. The day after that, Rivkin was spotted lunching with Graham Richardson at Joe's Cafe. It's not surprising that Rivkin would be catching up with Richardson, who had a million-dollar share of the Swiss holdings as well.

The next day, 19 August, saw another piece of unfinished business from the Offset saga resolved. Paul Obeid resigned from the Offset Alpine board. Whatever Eddie Obeid's family interest had been in Offset, it was now over.

Rodney Adler stood to make the most from Offset Alpine. Both FAI and Adler personally had loaned Rivkin $20 million and, with the rise in the Offset share price after the fire, Rivkin was now in a position to pay off the rest of his debt. In addition, FAI was well ahead on its own investment in Offset. FAI now re-entered the market, spending another $3 million in late 1994 to take its shareholding in Offset Alpine to just under 20 per cent. But another of Adler's investments had not turned out so well.

Just after midday on Monday 5 September, the state secretary of the Labor Party, John Della Bosca, sat down for a feed with that estimable fellow, Phuong Ngo. The lunch was a thank you for Ngo's sterling work marshalling votes in the recent election for the Communication Workers Union, the union for which Graham Richardson's father had once worked. Indeed it was Richardson, together with Leo McLeay, who had identified Ngo as an emerging force in Cabramatta the year before and persuaded him to switch over to Labor after he had first dallied with the Liberals. 'Everyone wanted to believe in Ngo,' an ALP source later tried to explain to the *Sunday Telegraph*. 'He has this quiet way of talking and bowing his head—he oozes sincerity.'

When Della Bosca had lunch with Ngo in September 1994, and the two men discussed Ngo's aspirations for a seat in state parliament, Della knew that Ngo was involved in a feud with the sitting member, John Newman. What he didn't know was that, nine hours later, Ngo would drive two men from the Mekong Club to Newman's home; then wait around the corner until the Member for Cabramatta arrived home and the two men shot him.

Subsequently, while the shock waves of this killing rocked Sydney society, the Labor Party held a preselection contest to decide who would take Newman's old seat. Young right-winger Reba Meagher emerged the victor two weeks later with the help of Ngo. He had signed up 185 new members, who all lived in a post box, for the critical Canley Vale branch.

A week later, inspectors from the Liquor Administration Board launched an investigation of the Mekong Club's books. Rodney Adler resigned from the board of Ngo's Asia Press Company the same day. An inquiry by Licensing Court magistrate Denis Collins over the following two years found that Ngo had misappropriated $68 000 from the club's petty cash. FAI had loaned $1 million to the club, but the club secretary could not explain how the loan was to be repaid. FAI put a receiver into the club in May 1996.

Collins eventually cleared FAI and FAI consultant Bruce Rowley of allegations they had an inappropriate involvement in the management of the club between May and August 1994. The $150 000 cheque that Lyndi Adler signed over to the club on Christmas Eve 1993 also came to light—Collins concluded it had been used to help the club meet its liabilities to the Liquor Administration Board.

By October 1994, Gordon Wood was working on a little political deal of his own. With Rivkin's finances improving, he had convinced his boss to put down a deposit on a $270 000 apartment for him in Macleay Street, Potts Point. Wood persuaded Tony Byrne to lend him $150 000 of the $270 000 purchase price, with Rivkin to provide the balance. Unfortunately, Rivkin's understanding was the other way around—that it was Tony Byrne who was providing the balance. The issue was who took the first mortgage. If Wood got behind in the payments, it was the second lender who would lose out. Rivkin was angry about the mix-up, for which he blamed Tony Byrne. Caroline's father no longer wanted anything to do with the deal and neither did Rene. Gordon Wood was disconsolate.

Caroline Byrne was in Manila, representing Australia in the Miss Asia-Pacific Quest. Wood could feel another love letter coming on. He wrote to Caroline on 9 November 1994:

> You are my only love in my whole life—I have never experienced this before I met you and I will never experience it again. I want for nothing . . . I love you my princess, my chicky-babe . . . I am yours forever with passion and deep, deep unbridled love. My Love, My Love, forever. Gordy X.

It wasn't getting any better. He should have stuck with the biscuits.

THIRTEEN

Under surveillance

1995

Two days before Christmas in 1994, Rene Rivkin launched his cunning plan. He had been turning different stratagems over in his mind for a year before he settled on this one and he was comfortable he had hit on quite the little subterfuge. While it had taken a bit of organising, his plan was now running like clockwork so Rivkin decided to celebrate with a little breather in California for two weeks with Gordon Wood and a few friends.

Rivkin had worked out how to raid the cookie jar. He had not had too many choices. The only solution for his money problems was to sell his Offset Alpine shares; however, finding a buyer would be difficult. He decided his best option was to sell his shares back to the company. This would not be a simple affair. The principle of share buybacks is that they must benefit all shareholders equally, which didn't suit Rivkin at all. In addition, at that time, it was illegal for directors of a company to sell their shares into a buyback. Rivkin planned to get around this in a couple of steps. First he would sell parcels of the Offset shares he owned in Australia to his Zurich accounts at Bank Leumi and EBC Zurich. Then, from the anonymity of Switzerland, Rivkin would sell the shares back into Offset Alpine's buyback scheme. It was a long circle from Sydney to Zurich, then back again, to transfer the money from Rene's public company to Rene's Swiss bank account, then to Rene's private pocket. No one would suspect a thing. It was terribly cunning. Unhappily, it was also a little predictable.

Rivkin's plan was similar to all the other cunning plans, with minor variations, that he had been using for years. 'That's the thing about Rene, he always used the same modus operandi, time and time again,' a regulator later commented. Rivkin didn't care. He had been doing this sort of thing for twenty-five years and had grown blasé about the risks of discovery. His position was actually quite precarious; it wouldn't be difficult to uncover, if regulators ever looked seriously at the Bank Leumi shareholding. Remarkably, so far no one had.

ASX Surveillance had reported its suspicions about Rivkin's link to Leumi in 1990 but nothing followed. That was the dreadful secret of share trading in the 1990s—few people ever looked at the offshore cash trail. For much of the decade, regulators put market manipulation cases in the too-hard basket and offshore accounts were a no-go zone. Meanwhile, a whole community of Australian expats had set up shop in Monaco, ready to help Australian investors. Journalist Ali Cromie once asked Richard Weisener why people lived in Monaco. He said, 'It begins with T and ends with X, and it isn't short for tuxedo.'

The first time that regulators had tried to tackle market manipulation involving offshore holdings had been a costly fiasco. In 1987, the National Companies and Securities Commission made an unacceptable conduct finding in regard to trading in Elders IXL during one of John Elliott's trickier manoeuvres. Elders had challenged the finding in the courts and the NCSC had been mauled. The National Crime Authority reopened the case in 1989 and spent the next decade chasing Elliott over a series of Swiss bond deals. The NCA applied for bank documents from the Swiss in 1991, only to find when it got them that it needed to ask for more records. By the time it got this second round of documents from the Swiss in 2000, the case was closed. The NCA had brought charges against Elliott, Weisener, Bob Cowper, Ken Jarrett and the rest of the Elders boys in 1995. Jarrett went to prison after he pleaded guilty and testified against his former colleagues. The cases against the rest of them were dismissed.

When the Australian Securities Commission (today known as the Australian Securities and Investments Commission) came into operation in January 1991, it faced an avalanche of cases pending from the wild days of the 1980s. The ASC's first chairman, Tony Hartnell, issued a list of sixteen priority cases the ASC would focus on. His decision was understandable: the ASC had limited resources and desperately needed some convictions to prove its credentials. The ASC was also restricted by the need to refer all criminal matters to the federal Director of Public Prosecutions office, which took a far more conservative view of ASC cases. The ASC concentrated on black-letter law issues like fraud, breaches of a prospectus or acting dishonestly. Market manipulation cases were far more slippery. In the meantime, senior ASC figures went public with their belief that the Australian share market was almost entirely free from the insider trading and market abuses found on overseas exchanges. One ASC chairman confessed he had never heard of Richard Weisener. The only public figure who talked about widespread insider trading was Rene Rivkin.

At the start of 1995, Sydney society was at a tipping point. The most momentous change began on Macquarie Street. In the weeks before the state election in April, Labor leader Bob Carr did a deal with John Hatton and the independents, who held the balance of power in the Legislative Assembly, to set up a royal commission into the police force, chaired by James Wood. Stories about police corruption have always been endemic to Sydney. It is a truth that politicians rarely say, and never wish to hear. The Wood Royal Commission would change all that, at least for a time, with its regular video footage of policemen caught taking bribes. There was no real comparison with the share traders at the other end of town—there was no suggestion of corruption among corporate regulators and, while a lot of market behaviour might raise eyebrows, it was not necessarily illegal. But the two ends of town did have one thing in common: abuses had flourished in a culture of suspended disbelief. When it came to talking about offshore market scams, as with the more sensational corruption profiled by Wood, few people were listening. Yet this too would change.

Rivkin remained oblivious. In December 1994, he opened a discount broking operation, Rivkin Croll Smith, which would stand in the market to buy Offset Alpine stock as part of the buyback. Rivkin had transferred $500 000 from his EBC Zurich account to fund the new business (when ASC asked him about this later, he said that it was a loan from a Swiss businessman he knew called Marco Baruch, a name which does not appear on any Swiss phone records). The first share trades in the buyback went through on Friday 23 December. Rivkin Croll Smith paid $148 000 to Rivkin's EBC Zurich account for 92 900 shares, with another 30 000 shares from Bank Leumi for $50 000.

It was as easy as that—Rivkin could sell his shares to his company any time he wanted. It was like a private money tap. He didn't even have to be in Sydney for it to work. After Christmas he and Wood flew to Los Angeles to spend a fortnight at the Bel-Air in Beverley Hills with half a dozen of the young men from Joe's Cafe. From there Rivkin instructed other brokers to put a sell order on Offset shares owned by Bank Leumi. He then called Rivkin Croll Smith with instructions to buy the shares that had just come on offer into the buyback. In this way, on 6 January, he sold 400 000 shares from his Stilton account into the buyback for $700 000. Unfortunately, when you're managing things from that far away it's easy to overlook something. One of the rules for a buyback is that a company can't buy shares at a price that is more than 5 per cent above the previous day's closing price. When Rivkin Croll Smith bought the Leumi shares for $1.75, it breached the 5 per cent limit by one cent. It was a tiny mistake but the ASX runs an automated monitoring system that is programmed to catch such errors. The computer picked up the breach of the buyback rules and issued an alert. Rivkin knew nothing of this as he continued to cream money from Offset Alpine. The buybacks continued through January, then on 9 February they stopped. Perhaps Rivkin wanted to take a break. Perhaps he felt the first signs that someone was watching him.

It had all turned out swimmingly for Gordon Wood. The nasty moment back in November, when both Tony Byrne and Rivkin had backed out of the deal to buy the apartment in Macleay Street, had now been turned around through the intervention of that prince of fellows, Graham Richardson. Previously Rivkin had already paid the deposit and, in late November, Wood told Tony Byrne, 'I had lunch with Graham Richardson and Rene today. Graham and I talked Rene into buying it. We said, "Why lose $27 000 plus stamp duty?"'

Rivkin bought the apartment in Wood's name secured by a mortgage, and Gordon was back in favour. When Wood returned from Los Angeles with Rivkin on 14 January, he and Caroline moved into the new apartment and held a house-warming party. Tony Byrne wasn't invited but otherwise all was as before, for January through most of February.

Caroline told her father, 'You know Daddy, Gordon expects that Rene will look after him the way he looks after George with gifts and bonuses.' Tony Byrne had been told repeatedly by Gordon about the huge bonuses and gifts that he would receive from Rivkin. This seems to have been Wood's code for the secret $500 000 bequests Rivkin had made for George Freris at Bank Leumi and for Wood at EBC Zurich.

Wood was playing in a dangerous crowd. A young photographer on the fringe of the group at Joe's Cafe, Brett Cochrane (now known as Basquali), would say later, '[Rivkin] was very, very generous. But I think it was all about control over people. He had half a dozen guys, all at his beck and call. I know a good analogy: it was like a bunch of seagulls, waiting for a chip.'

One day in late February, Caroline told her father of a sudden change: 'Gordon has come home from work very angry. Rene is very depressed and doesn't want Gordon to see him.' The position worsened in the days that followed. 'Rene is still depressed because of me and he is trying to drive a wedge between us,' Caroline told her father. 'Rene believes I know too much about his business and private life and especially his relationship with George. Gordon is really worried. Even if we got married, Rene would not come to the wedding.'

By late March, the position had become critical. Wood came home and spent three days in bed with his head under the sheet. 'Gordon has come home from work—he's absolutely destroyed,' Caroline said. 'Rene has told him he won't be able to give him the home unit, any bonuses or anything else.' Caroline may not have known it, but Wood had much more to lose in Switzerland if Rivkin cancelled his bequest.

Tony Byrne told Caroline he was concerned for her. According to his diary notes, she replied, 'You don't have to worry, Daddy, Gordon loves me, he would not hurt a hair on my head.'

Tony Byrne visited the couple, and asked what had happened to Rivkin. 'What's wrong with the man?' Tony asked of Wood. Gordon Wood said the problem with his boss was all Tony's fault, for the way he had haggled over buying the apartment back in November. 'It's not the money he's depressed about,' Wood said of Rene. 'It's the ego. You've destroyed his ego.'

Later again, Caroline told Tony, 'Daddy, Gordon may not have a loan much longer.' Wood echoed this concern with Caroline's father: 'I'm concerned about my only asset, my motor vehicle. I am considering transferring it into my mother's name.'

It could well be that Rivkin was suddenly overwhelmed by anger and depression about buying an apartment three months before, despite seeming entirely comfortable with it during the intervening time. But, in late February, Rivkin had other worries that Wood didn't mention.

Jim Berry had run the shadow world of ASX Surveillance for eight years. A major part of his job was to educate regulators, ASX officials and journalists about how market scams worked and why surveillance was even necessary. With time had come a grudging realisation by brokers and fund managers that, when Surveillance came knocking on the door, it was best to be helpful. The ASC was also paying more attention. It had begun to second ASC invest-igators to work with Berry's people for training. One of the first of them was Peter Dumas.

When the ASX computer program picked up the mistake in the Offset Alpine share buyback on 6 January, nothing happened immediately. It was, after all, a minor technical breach. However, it had piqued Berry's interest and he now began looking at the Offset Alpine trading. Through February, Berry traced the outlines of what looked like a circular trading pattern in Offset Alpine (OAP) shares between Rivkin, FAI, Bank Leumi and the buyback scheme that Rivkin Croll Smith was operating. Berry had an analyst sort through the trades while he wrote to Philip Croll, the managing director of Rivkin Croll Smith, for some routine details about the trades. Croll replied on Monday 27 February. Three days later, Berry wrote to Croll again, thanking him for his response and asking for copies of all buy and sell orders for OAP stock since 12 December. He also asked for details of 'all clients who have traded in OAP during this period for whom you operate a discretionary account or have acted with any discretion what-soever, irrespective of how limited, in relation to OAP'. The hook here was that Berry was asking a very specific question in the guise of a broader query. It was a simple request for the paper trail that all broking houses must maintain when it comes to discretionary trading.

The following Monday, Croll wrote back:

Dear Jim,

Please find enclosed the information that you have asked for.

Rene Rivkin has authority to operate on the accounts of:
1. EBC Zurich AG A/C 081500 Attention Axel Fundulus, CH 8027 Zurich Switzerland.
2. Bank Leumi A/C 020600 34 Clarendon Strasse [sic] Zurich Switzerland. Attention: Ernst Imfeld.

Croll went on to mention that one of his young children had a small parcel of OAP shares, but the decision to buy was all their own. A little light humour with the regulator. And that was that. Philip Croll is a straight shooter, who had no idea what he had done—he had tied Rivkin to the Swiss shares. Rivkin had authority to operate the accounts, which meant he was an associated party linked to more than 20 per cent of Offset Alpine's share register. It was what Berry had always suspected. Now he had a case to take to the ASC.

Croll would come to regret his lighthearted note to Berry. Three months later, when it all became public, he told me he had got it all mixed up. He concluded: 'I think you'll find that a little bit of knowledge can be a dangerous thing.' Berry, meanwhile, was feeling his way forward carefully, tracing the route of every Offset Alpine share trade in the previous three months.

Change was in the air that month in Sydney. On 25 March Bob Carr defeated Liberal Premier John Fahey in the state election, while on 30 March the Super League war broke out. In motel rooms across the country, lawyers for Super League and for the Australian Rugby League fought each other, armed with chequebooks and seemingly limitless access to Murdoch and Packer money.

The ASX investigation inched forward. On 5 April Berry signed off on a formal referral to the ASC, which suggested that Rivkin had breached the substantial shareholder provisions of the Corporations Law. By chance, the investigator who picked up the brief was Peter Dumas, who had just returned to the Commission from a stint working at ASX Surveillance. Dumas was one of the few ASC staff who was familiar with Berry's way of working. He immediately issued notices to a string of Australia nominee companies that held Offset shares, asking them to identify who owned the shares. The answer came back within days: all of the shares in the nominee companies were owned by Leumi and EBC Zurich. Leumi owned 16.9 per cent of Offset Alpine, while EBC Zurich owned 22.2 per cent. Bingo. A staggering 39 per cent of Offset was secretly controlled through Zurich. Dumas now addressed his inquiries to the two Swiss institutions.

Across at Potts Point, life had suddenly taken a dramatic turn for the better for Gordon Wood. Caroline told her father that 'Gordon has a plan' to handle Rivkin. 'He knows how to get around him,' she said. Indeed, in the first two weeks of April, Wood's relationship with Rivkin improved dramatically. Rivkin gave Wood $1500 to buy a television. Wood ordered a new built-in wardrobe for the apartment, a new lounge and dining room furniture. And then there was the money. They were driving along in the car—Rivkin, Caroline and Gordon—and Rivkin said, 'If you've got an economics degree I'll give you $1000.'

So Wood said, 'I've got an economics degree.'

That was the way it went when you were back in Rene's good books. It was a foreign world to Caroline and Tony Byrne and they had no yardstick to measure it by. Rivkin's abrupt mood switch in February—his depression, his dismissal of Gordon Wood and the references to what Caroline might know—had coincided with the onset of the ASX investigation. Surveillance was contacting people across the market, poking and prodding to tease out the mystery of the OAP share trading. Much of this got back to Rene. By now it was clear that his assistant was highly indiscreet. He had bandied about comments the previous year about the Offset fire being a set-up and had even tried to set up his own insider trading scam. With the spotlight on Rivkin, Wood had become a liability.

The prospect that Rivkin would dump him appalled Gordon Wood. At one stroke the high life, the expensive cars, the apartment, the relationship—everything that he had longed for, and finally achieved a year before—would be gone. He was reduced to planning ways to cheat Rivkin out of reclaiming the car, hiding it in his mother's name. Wood found himself needing to assure Rivkin of his loyalty and of Caroline's, whom he was now calling on her mobile up to ten times a day to reassure himself where she was.

And then the little problem was over and Wood was back in favour. The change of heart coincided with the ASC's discovery of the Swiss shareholdings. Whatever drove the dynamics of the relationship between Rivkin and Wood, with an ASC investigation now inevitable there were pragmatic reasons for Rivkin to keep Wood on side. On Thursday 27 April, Tony Byrne wrote in his diary something Caroline had told him that day: 'Rene and Gordon are going to Europe in about a week's time. It's something to do with a printing company. Zurich and London. To take two weeks.'

On 21 April, Berry at Surveillance had updated his formal referral to the ASC. His team had it all—the trades between Rivkin and Zurich, Zurich and FAI, and Zurich and the buyback. But it would be eight years before their work was vindicated. The day before, Peter Dumas at the ASC had sent by fax and express letter secondary Section 719 notices to Leumi and EBC Zurich, requesting details of their shareholdings. EBC wrote back that under Swiss law it was not able to identify the clients who owned its Offset shares. Leumi ignored the ASC letter. On 26 April, ASC faxed Leumi and EBC Zurich that it was about to begin court action to force the Swiss to reveal the real Offset shareholders. Caroline Byrne learned of the Swiss trip the following day, while Leumi and EBC stalled for time. EBC told ASC that its client manager, Axel Fundulus, was away, then on 3 June Fundulus wrote to the ASC that, 'We are contacting clients from all around the world to get instructions and require another 14 days to get back to you.'

It was too late. That morning I received a tip off from a regulator that someone should be in Federal Court that afternoon. That was how my colleague Kate Bice and I were there to report when ASC lawyer Peter Riordan, who had overall carriage of the Offset matter, made an ex parte application before Justice Hill to freeze the mystery shares. Riordan said the ASC had traced over 38 per cent of Offset Alpine's shares to Bank Leumi and EBC. 'The concern of the ASC in the context of a buyback is that the market cannot be properly informed when such a large shareholding is a black box,' Reardon said.

The newspapers had a field day. Here was a company that was already the butt of Kerry Packer's comment about its 'very good fire'. Now it turned out that the chief beneficiaries of the insurance payout were anonymous investors hiding behind Swiss banks. Rene Rivkin was denying any suggestion that he had discretionary power over the Swiss accounts. In fact, although he had bought the 38 per cent of the company for the Swiss investors, he said he had no idea that they held quite that much of the company for which he was chairman. He had filled the black box, but he didn't know what was in it or who owned it.

With the matter adjourned, Rivkin flew to Zurich on Sunday 7 May. Passport control passed the details to the ASC, along with the details of his travelling companion. By Monday, regulators were making calls, looking for details on someone called Gordon Wood. The only hits in the newspaper databases were a reference to him in Jeni Porter's CBD columns in the *Sydney Morning Herald,* which referred to Wood as some sort of personal assistant to Rivkin; and a more obscure item in September 1994 about the view from the School of Visual Arts at 105 Crown Street, next to the City Gym. One afternoon the previous October, a group of students had spied Rene Rivkin on an apartment balcony on the building opposite, 118 Crown Street, climbing into a jacuzzi for a relaxing bubble bath. 'There was even a man servant to hold the robe and cover the spa—presumably Rivkin's ever present mobile-phone-answering chauffeur Gordon Wood,' Porter wrote. Now the ASC was focusing on black boxes, Swiss shares and jacuzzis. Was Gordon Wood with Rivkin as a personal assistant, or was he there to hold the towel?

With Rivkin out of the country, Peter Riordan began conducting Section 19 examinations of Offset Alpine's directors and major shareholders. The first was Andrew Lakos, who had run Rivkin's back office through the 1970s and '80s. Lakos said he didn't know anything about Swiss bank accounts. Rodney Adler was called in. So was Trevor Kennedy, on 18 May. Eddie Obeid wasn't available, even if Riordan had wanted to speak to him. He had had a cardiac bypass on 12 April.

Rivkin and Wood were in Zurich for only five days before flying out on 12 May. 'I decided to go to London and spend the next ten days there or something,' Rivkin later told the ASC. Wood telephoned Caroline Byrne from Rivkin's palatial apartment, which took up an entire floor in a building at St James. Tony Byrne was with Caroline at the time and remembers her asking Wood why he was whispering. Wood told her he had to be very quiet because it was only a one-bedroom apartment. He had been sleeping on the sofa and Rivkin was asleep in the bedroom. Like much else that Wood said, this too was a fiction.

Rivkin and Wood flew back to Zurich briefly—'They called me back ... they invited me to come back for half a day, sorry, for an overnight,' Rivkin told the ASC—then returned to Sydney on Saturday 27 May. Riordan and his team were waiting.

FOURTEEN
On the clifftop
1995

The newspapers on 6 June 1995 were full of sensational developments the previous day at the Wood Royal Commission. Months before, former detective Trevor Haken had rolled over and become a protected witness for the Commission, taking part in an extensive covert filming exercise. On 5 June, his old mate Detective Inspector Graham Fowler was confronted on the witness stand with film from a hidden camera that showed him sharing a $1500 bribe with Haken in the front seat of a car. 'That was just a fucking drink to keep going as far as I understand it,' Haken told Fowler on the tape. 'Anyway, you're happy with that?'

'Yeah, fuck yeah,' replied Fowler.

The scene would be played and replayed on television bulletins across the country. It was sensational viewing, though Fowler probably wished he hadn't been wearing shorts. Confronted with the footage before Justice Wood he could only pretend that it was a fake. 'You think we got someone to play Graham Fowler?' asked Gary Crooke, senior counsel assisting the Commission.

'Funny things happen, yes,' said Fowler. That Monday was the beginning of a deluge of revelations about police corruption, which would fill the headlines for two years, providing a detailed guide to the economics of drug dealing and protection rackets. It would also illuminate the fine class distinctions between being in on the 'joke', a bribe to be shared among lowly officers, and being part of the 'laugh' or the 'giggle', a bribe pool reserved for sergeants and above. In bribe-taking, as with any Sydney club, there are always better seats for the well-connected. The media sniggered. How very droll it was. At the top end of town, when it came to bending the law, there was nothing quite so down-market as the joke. It was more a mild source of amusement.

The Royal Commission hearings were so much more exciting than the mundane little scene that played out several blocks away on the following day, 6 June. It was Rivkin's birthday. The previous year he had been celebrating at Mrs Macquarie's Chair but this year, at 10.07 a.m. on the Tuesday morning, he was sitting in the ASC offices, flanked by his lawyer, John Landerer, and barrister, Steven Rares SC, facing Peter Riordan, Peter Dumas and another ASC lawyer, Larissa Shafir.

Passport control had flagged to the ASC Rivkin's return to Australia on 27 May. The following day Gordon Wood and Caroline Byrne had gone shopping. Her friend Natalie McCamley remembers, 'Gordon came back about ten days before she died. They went shopping on the Sunday after Gordon came back and he spent about $1000 on clothes for her, for her new job. She seemed very excited about going shopping and Gordon buying her things.'

Caroline went to her father's apartment on 31 May to sign documents that set up a $2 million trust for Tony Byrne's four children and he suggested to his daughter that Gordon join them for dinner. Wood called Caroline on the mobile five minutes later—by this point he was calling to check her whereabouts so frequently that some of her friends likened it to stalking. 'I asked her if Gordon was coming over,' Byrne said. 'She replied, no she would have to go.' Caroline's voice faded as she told her father this. 'He's in a shitty mood,' she said. What Tony Byrne didn't know was that earlier that day, Rivkin and Wood had both received

Section 19 notices from the ASC, requiring them to present themselves for questioning.

The ASC interview on 6 June began with preliminary comments about Leumi and EBC Zurich. 'They were perfect shareholders, exemplary shareholders,' Rivkin said. He described EBC as a funds management company.

'Who makes the decision to buy or sell Offset shares?' Riordan asked.

'Fundulus,' Rivkin replied.

Why had he gone to Switzerland?

'Well you are talking about two very good clients of mine over donkey's years who didn't really understand what was going on and I felt it was the least I owed them, to go over and talk to the various people in what, I mean, I met some of their lawyers, for example a lawyer, trying to explain what it was all about.'

So what did he do in Switzerland, whom did he meet?

'The first day I met my bed,' Rivkin said. Then on the Tuesday he phoned Imfeld and then Fundulus, who suggested lunch. 'We talked about whether, oh yes, sorry, sorry, of course, I tried to convince them to release and issue the names of their customers or their clients as the best way to solve the whole problem.'

He had recommended Offset Alpine shares to Fundulus.

'I knew they had a lot of shares, but I didn't bother tallying it up, whether it was 20 per cent or whatever.'

He said he wasn't aware that any of the nominee companies held shares for EBC or Leumi, even though every year he signed off on the annual report with the Top Twenty shareholders list. 'I knew I had bought a lot of shares for them so they had to be somewhere, so I assumed it was the two nominees. Also, of course, come to think of it, my back office would have known that, because they would have settled it. I am telling you that I suspect it was them, but I didn't go to my back office and ask, "Are they the ones?" if you know what I mean.

'If someone would have said to me, BB Nominees has some

shares in Offset, are they to be EBC's I would have said yes. No one asked me, so I wasn't aware . . . Never turned my mind to it . . . The back office in a stockbrokers' firm has never been my favourite place.'

How had he met Bank Leumi?

'I used to travel the world looking for clients. I can't remember how I first met them but I met thousands of clients in my time, and they would have been among the thousands.' He had originally dealt with Otto Wolff, but for the last four years or so it had been Ernst Imfeld. Leumi also held shares in Hudson Conway.

So it went on.

It was all fiction. Rivkin had spent his time in Zurich instructing EBC and Leumi not to release any information, working out strategies to escape detection by the ASC, and indemnifying them for all their legal costs. Dr Belser, the Leumi lawyer, would be paid directly by Rivkin for his work. Rivkin's performance under oath was hopelessly transparent in the context of the sophisticated trading loop into the buyback that ASX Surveillance had uncovered. But the ASC wasn't looking at the trading. Its focus was purely on the identity of the Swiss shareholders who had failed to issue substantial shareholder notices and who had breached the 20 per cent takeover threshold.

Gordon Wood's interview was over within minutes. He knew nothing about Swiss shares, he said. He verified Rivkin's account of his meetings in Zurich and said nothing about his claims the previous year that the Offset fire had been a set-up.

Caroline had started a new full-time job in sales at the June Dally-Watkins modelling agency on Monday 5 June. She had been working there part-time for several years, giving a modelling class on Saturdays. But the new job meant giving up her work modelling for the Gordon Charles agency. That Monday afternoon she saw her local doctor; she complained of depression over the previous month, worsening in the last week. Dr Cindy Pan arranged a session with a psychiatrist for Wednesday afternoon, but Caroline declined a doctor's certificate for some days off work. Pan said Byrne showed no signs of self-harm. She had decided to give up the new job at June Dally-Watkins and felt some anxiety about that, but nothing seemed out of the ordinary. Caroline was booked for a modelling session on the Tuesday afternoon and a sales promotion for June Dally-Watkins at Parklea. She didn't show up for either appointment. On Tuesday evening Wood phoned Caroline's boss, Carol Clifford, to say that Caroline was ill and he was taking her to a specialist the following day. Gordon would be the last person to see Caroline alive.

More than a decade later, the events of Wednesday 7 June have taken on the antiseptic quality of the inquest that ensued. Wood told police that Caroline was asleep that morning when he went to work. She was still asleep at 1 p.m. when he returned to take her to lunch. When roused, she told him she wanted to sleep more. He said he noticed that five or six Rohypnol sleeping tablets were missing from the bathroom. Caroline said she had taken one and had been taking a quarter each night since he returned. The autopsy would find no trace of Rohypnol in Caroline's body. After ten minutes, Wood left and went to Victoria Road, Darlinghurst, where he met two friends, Nicholas Samartis and Brett Cochrane, at Ditto's restaurant. Cochrane later told police that he had arrived between midday and 1 p.m. and had already ordered when Wood arrived fifteen minutes later. Wood said he was there from 1.15 to 1.45 p.m. He ordered a meal, but never got to eat it.

'As my food arrived at the table, Gordon received a phone call and said that he had to leave to pick up his boss,' Cochrane told police. Nine years later, Cochrane, who now went under the name Basquali, told Caroline Overington at the *Sydney Morning Herald* that Wood appeared perfectly normal when he left to pick up Rivkin, and 'there is just no way, from what I saw, that he was about to go and kill somebody instead.'

Two restaurateurs at Watsons Bay, Craig Martin and Lance Melbourne, would later recognise pictures of Caroline Byrne, which June Dally-Watkins and Caroline's close friend, *Home and Away* actor Kylie Watson, showed around Watsons Bay shortly after her death. They later testified that they had seen Caroline at about 1 p.m., and again at 3 p.m., from the balcony of their restaurant, Bad Dog Cafe, in company with two men whom they later identified as Gordon Wood and Caroline's booking agent, Adam Leigh. Both Wood and Leigh strongly denied being at Watsons Bay that afternoon, though Wood said he might have driven past in Rivkin's green Bentley.

In a police statement he made in July 1995, Wood said that after leaving Ditto's he went to Alife Restaurant in Stanley Street, where he picked up his boss's lunch partner and took him to his office, then drove to Bondi for a hamburger. It would be a year later, under pressure in another police interview, that he dropped the name of Rivkin's alleged lunch partner—Graham Richardson. Wood said he ducked back home briefly at 4 p.m., but Caroline was not there. He came home at 7 p.m. and fell asleep in front of the television. He woke at 12.40 a.m. and was concerned that Caroline was still not home. Their car was gone so he took one of Rivkin's cars and drove past Caroline's father's building, but her car was not there. He drove to Bondi looking for her, then headed towards Watsons Bay, where he saw their car parked in a lane. In one of the surreal moments of that night, the huge blond gym instructor would tell police of running along the clifftop calling out to Caroline: 'I remember running around crying out, "Wait, hang on, baby"—she used to call me Gordy—"Gordy's here to save you. I'll fix everything up."'

Earlier that evening two fishermen had been annoyed to find Caroline's white-top Suzuki parked in the lane beneath the only street light. Their torch was barely working. After an argument about who should go to buy new batteries, they rigged up their lines on the bonnet of the Suzuki. They then fished for some hours before they heard a piercing scream by a woman, between 11 and 11.30 p.m. They said that, soon after, Wood ran out of the darkness and asked if they had seen a young woman. When they told him about the scream, Wood had said, 'Oh no, she's done it, she's done it', and run off.

Wood called Caroline's father and brother to tell them she was missing. Tony Byrne put the time at about 1.30 a.m. Wood drove back to the city to pick them up, and they searched the clifftop for fifteen minutes after borrowing the fishermen's torch. The batteries were on their last legs, but Wood thought he saw shoes at the bottom of the cliff. Police were called but even with a powerful police spotlight they could see only a 'discolouration' at the base of the cliff. Wood, however, insisted: 'That's her, that's the clothes she wore today.' Eventually a police rescue team spotted her body from a helicopter. The night was dark, with clouds hiding the moon and a bitterly cold wind driving in from the sea. Caroline's body was found nine to ten metres out from the thirty-metre drop. She had fallen head first into a rock crevasse. The fall had shattered the top half of her skull. The dawn was breaking by the time the rescue squad winched Caroline's broken body to the top of the cliff and an ambulance took her to the Glebe Morgue. Around the time she arrived at the morgue, Gordon Wood was sitting down for breakfast with Rene at the Lamrock Cafe in Bondi.

Wood had been calling Rivkin all night but the calls didn't get through, Rivkin said later. 'On the night of her death—around 2 a.m.—he called and left a timed message for me on my pager,' Rivkin said. 'He asked me to call him urgently. I called him but his mobile was unreachable and so I went back to bed. At 3 a.m. there was another message to call urgently. Finally at 5.30 a.m. I made contact with him.'

Caroline's death would initially be written down as a suicide. Her mother had killed herself with sleeping tablets in 1991 in the unhappy aftermath of breast surgery that had gone wrong. Caroline had taken an overdose a year later. Wood told police Caroline had once tried to jump off a building, though there had been no other witnesses. On top of all this she had been due to see a psychiatrist that afternoon for her depression. But there were problems with this version of events. First, the timing of events on the clifftop seemed all over the place, though such confusion at a death scene is not uncommon. There was the clash of stories between the two restaurateurs at the Bad Dog Cafe, who saw Gordon at The Gap when he said he was nowhere near it. Other witnesses would also place him at The Gap that evening. Wood's ability to see her body in pitch-darkness with a feeble torch has already been noted. And then there was the question of why, when he was looking for her car, Wood had gone to Watsons Bay. When Detective Sergeant Brian Wyver asked him about it a year later, he turned to the policeman and began, 'This is gunna sound probably odd to you Brian . . .'

Wood told Wyver that he believed there had been some spiritual communication with Caroline that had guided him. This was the first time Wood had mentioned this to police. 'I don't know, I just had this feeling,' is what Wood told Caroline's family about his decision to drive to Watsons Bay, according to Tony Byrne. 'Several days later he said it was Caroline's spirit that told him where to find her,' Byrne said.

Wood initially told friends that Caroline had been run down by a car. He claimed that he did this after a request by her father not to call it a suicide. Byrne denies any such request. In the days after Caroline's death, bank records show Wood made seven withdrawals from her account and attempted to access her sister's account. Within weeks he was making sexual overtures to Caroline's friend, Kylie Watson, and, inevitably, writing her romantic letters.

Gordon Wood does not emerge well from any of this. But all of it is secondary to the basic conundrum of that night: did Caroline jump, or was she thrown? It's conceivable that Wood's story is a complete fabrication, that they spent the afternoon and evening arguing, and in the end she threw herself off the cliff, which is how he came to know where she fell. Wood thought it looked bad for him, so he may have invented a wild tale to cover his feeling of guilt. But none of this indicates that he killed her. Yet there was an issue about where Caroline landed.

The policeman who found her told the coroner he was surprised how far out from the cliff Caroline's body was. He said he normally found suicide victims one or two metres out. It's a gruesome calculation. It takes 2.47 seconds to fall thirty metres. Caroline had travelled nine or ten metres out from the cliff face during her fall. Even if you were to jump *upwards* at the start, you would need to be travelling at 11.6 kilometres per hour horizontally to reach nine metres out in such a leap. But there was a fence on the clifftop, so at most she had a one-step run-up. As a very rough guide, her leap would be equivalent to a long jump of more than 2.5 metres on a flat surface. It's actually harder than that because Caroline fell head first in complete darkness in the face of an onshore wind. She was also flatfooted. In October 2004, Associate Professor Rodney Cross of Sydney University's Physics Department conducted a series of experiments with a dummy and with a policewoman of Caroline's size. He concluded that it was not possible for Caroline Byrne to have jumped that far. He said it was doubtful that one person could have thrown her that far either, though he did not rule out the possibility of summoning extraordinary strength in an act of passion. He found it was likely that she had been thrown by two people.

Rene Rivkin knew none of this when he had breakfast with his driver at Bondi at 7 a.m. on Thursday morning, 8 June. 'His first words to me were, "She's dead,"' Rivkin told Ros Reines in 1998. 'I said, "Who's dead?" He said, "Caroline." And strangely enough, my response was, "Who killed her?" I didn't expect a young person like her to die of natural causes. He said: "No, no, no, no one killed her. She suicided, she jumped over The Gap."'

Three years after the event, Rivkin's memory was crystal clear. 'He did not tell me anything about having a psychic connection with her, which is why he knew to look at The Gap. He also said that Caroline had a history of suicide in her family because her mother had suicided.' He said Wood told him he was going to tell people that Caroline died in a car accident. 'I advised him against it, pointing out that motor car accidents like suicides are written up in the papers, so he might as well tell the truth,' Rivkin said.

This account is in keeping with the description of Rivkin that Wood provided in a police interview, in which he described Rene as 'sort of like a father, if you like, as well as a boss'. There was never any suggestion that Rivkin had been involved in Caroline Byrne's death. At some point, though, whether then or during the years that followed, Rivkin's initial suspicion that someone had killed Caroline must have returned to his mind. If Caroline had been murdered, then Wood was the obvious suspect. The question was what, if anything, Rivkin should do about it.

The police would spend a decade trying to understand the tensions between Caroline and Gordon on the night she died. Their relationship had been showing signs of strain. Had Wood snapped and hit out? Two months earlier the drama over whether Gordon would lose his job and his 'bonus' from Rivkin's huge deals had loomed large in the lives of the young couple. Wood had won his way back into favour only to find Rivkin's world (and indirectly Wood's place in it) under threat again from the ASC investigation. The hurried flight to Zurich and London, followed by the ASC summons for questioning, underlined how high the stakes had become. This did not make Wood a killer. But Wood's financial worries and the links to Zurich were important back-ground information that could help police understand his frame of mind as they struggled to unravel the events of 7 June. However, Rivkin volunteered nothing of this to police.

A year later, Detective Sergeant Brian Wyver, who had been put on the case after pressure from Tony Byrne and family friends, put a remarkable suggestion to Wood in the course of a taped inter-view: 'Now, I have been informed that on the day of Caroline's death she did not in fact attend work, but she made surveillance of you and in the course of this surveillance she caught you and Rene having homosexual intercourse. What can you tell me about that?'

Wood answered: 'Absolute lies.'

There seems no factual basis to Wyver's suggestion. It is possible he threw the suggestion at Wood purely for shock value. In 1998, when the *Sydney Morning Herald* and Channel Seven reported Wyver's question, Rivkin . was outraged and sued, winning $150 000 in damages from Seven in 2002. After a jury dismissed libel imputations against the *Herald* and the *Australian Financial Review* the case ended up on appeal before the High Court, which ordered a partial retrial. Rivkin dropped the action in 2004 after his Swiss accounts were exposed.

On 19 August 1995, ASC investigators stumbled upon another Swiss shareholding. One of the Australian nominee companies involved in the Offset Alpine investigation also held just over 5 per cent of two mining stocks, Alliance Mining and Dome Resources, on behalf of EBC Zurich. The ASC froze those shares as well. Rivkin was called in again for questioning, though there was no sign that the shares were his. A search warrant was executed on Rivkin's office at Offset Alpine. Riordan and his team were aware of the talk across town that Graham Richardson was tied up with the Swiss shares. Unlike Kennedy, Richardson was not on the Top Twenty list of shareholders so there appeared to be no legitimate reason to question him. Another name had surfaced in the welter of information the ASC received: Colin Cunningham. It seemed to be some sort of codename.

In October, Rivkin's luck changed. Another printing company, Kalamazoo Holdings, made a takeover bid for Offset Alpine at $2.20 a share. On Friday 27 October, the Offset Alpine board—

Rivkin, Corlett and Henty—recommended that shareholders accept the bid. Then Rivkin disappeared. On the Saturday, he had been due to host a charity function at his and Trevor Kennedy's city driving range. Rene didn't show. The story was that he had had to go to the dentist. The following week, the Hannan Printing Group and the John B. Fairfax family announced a joint bid that topped Kalamazoo's offer for Offset. By mid-November, Kalamazoo and Hannan/Fairfax were in the middle of a fierce bidding war for Rivkin's company, but Rivkin was nowhere to be seen.

Graham Richardson was also overseas, attending to some business for the Australian Rugby League in Britain as part of the Super League war that had kept him so busy since April. Trevor Kennedy was also reported to be in Britain on business in early November. But behind these stories—the ARL mission, the business trip and the dentist appointment—all three men were secretly making their way to Zurich. In late 2005, Israeli journalist Shraga Elam confirmed that Rivkin and Richardson booked into the Eden Au Lac Hotel in Zurich on Monday 30 October. Richardson booked out on the Tuesday, while Rivkin stayed until the Thursday. A well-informed source told Elam that Kennedy accompanied the other two men. The hotel computer does not show Kennedy booking in but the hotel staff told Elam that guests were not always recorded on the computer file. The source saw the three men walk into the offices of Zurich lawyer Benno Hafner, who worked with many Bank Leumi clients. The takeover bid meant that the Offset Alpine shares frozen by the ASC would be sold and converted into money. It is believed the Zurich meeting was needed to authorise Hafner to handle the matter for the three men. In any case, the three were back in Sydney by 18 November.

The regulators' smooth run was about to end. In December, Justice Ron Sackville lowered the boom on the ASC. He made it clear, when the Federal Court case began to determine what to do with the Swiss Offset Alpine shares, that it was not the mystery shareholders who were on trial.

'I am not in a position to assess the motives of the beneficial owners of the shares held by Leumi and EBC, since there is no evidence as to who the beneficial owners are or what prompted them to acquire their shares,' he ruled. In a similar vein: 'I do not know what motivated those shareholders to refuse to waive the secrecy requirements of Swiss law. I am not prepared to find that their refusal stems from any desire to avoid Australian laws.'

The Bank Leumi and EBC Zurich executives, Ernst Imfeld and Axel Fundulus, emerged well from the case.

'I did not understand [ASC Counsel] Mr Lindsay to suggest that either Leumi or EBC was party to a deliberate attempt to circumvent Australian laws,' Justice Sackville found. 'In any event I would reject such a suggestion . . . This is not a case where the evidence suggests that either Leumi or EBC has courted legal impediments to the production of the information.'

Four years later, Fundulus would be convicted of fraud. Two years after that, Imfeld would be found to be at the centre of a $300 million embezzlement scandal. Fundulus's assurance to the ASC in April 1995 that EBC was 'contacting clients from all around the world to get instructions' was true only if you believe (as some would) by that he meant EBC was contacting clients all around Sydney. Imfeld told the court that the bank had been acting in its own right when it bought Offset shares from Rivkin in early 1995. Yet Leumi records show that at least some of the Offset shares bought by Leumi during this period went to Rivkin's Stilton account. Rivkin had instructed Leumi and EBC to contest the Australian court action and was paying for all of their legal costs. Stilton records show that Rivkin paid $166 430 to Leumi's Australian lawyers, Atanaskovic Hartnell, in 1996. EBC Zurich is believed to have made similar payments to Freehill Hollingdale & Page. Rivkin paid a further $16 549 directly to Leumi's Swiss lawyer, Peter Belser. In addition, Leumi appears to have retained another $200 000 from the payout for its own costs in 1995.

EBC Zurich and Bank Leumi claimed that Swiss law banned them from releasing client information, that in fact their officers could be imprisoned merely for reading the correspondence from the ASC. Sackville dismissed these defences. EBC and Leumi should have responded to the ASC notices to identify their clients, he found. The problem for Sackville lay with Australian laws.

By December, the Hannan Group and the Fairfax family had won the takeover battle with Kalamazoo Holdings after bidding $65 million for Offset Alpine, at $2.72 a share. Sackville ordered the Swiss shares be sold into the market. Including dividend payments, the shares were worth $26.2 million, which was paid into a Credit Suisse account operated by a Zurich lawyer who was acting for both Bank Leumi and the ASC. It was Benno Hafner. Sackville concluded that the Corporations Law focused on keeping the market informed. The mystery Swiss investors had breached their duty of disclosure. But with the shares sold, the issue had been resolved. He ruled that the Substantial Shareholder provisions of the law were not there to punish shareholders who had breached the disclosure provisions. Once the market was informed, the ASC's role was over. He denied the ASC's request to hold on to the $26 million until the Swiss banks came clean with the name of their clients. That would smack of punishment, Sackville said, and he ordered the money be released. Rivkin and his pals were free and clear.

On the same day, 20 December, Sackville handed the ASC a consolation prize when he ruled on the Dome Resources and Alliance Mining shares that had been frozen in August. EBC Zurich had not contested the case and, in the absence of a defence, Sackville ordered the shares to be vested with the ASC for two months; if, at the end of that time, EBC Zurich still had not disclosed the owner, the shares should be sold and the proceeds go to pay the ASC's costs, and then to general revenue. The shares were worth $1.5 million. From Rivkin's share trading records at Bank Leumi, it seems unlikely that the Dome and Alliance shares were his. But whoever the owners were, they were prepared to lose $1.5 million worth of shares rather than disclose their identity.

It turned out happily, however. The ASC released the Dome and Alliance shares to EBC in return for an assurance that EBC would sell them. Perhaps the ASC feared that Sackville's Offset decision would leave them vulnerable to an appeal if they tried to sell the shares themselves. Perhaps they had taken Sackville's comments about not seeking to punish errant investors to heart. The sweet thing for the EBC clients was that the Dome and Alliance share prices surged in early 1996. By March–April, when the shares were sold, their value had doubled. Rather than losing $1.5 million, EBC's anonymous clients ended up gaining $3 million.

These were far from the only Swiss shares held in the Australian nominee companies investigated by the ASC. What singled these shares out was that the Dome and Alliance shareholdings had breached the 5 per cent limit, which entitled the ASC to ask who owned them. Smaller shareholdings did not attract such scrutiny.

On 29 December 1995, the frozen Offset funds were released and $10 723 306 was credited to Rivkin's Stilton account. The rest of the $26.2 million went to EBC. The money itself was still restricted, held in a Societe Generale term account in Australia while the ASC appealed Sackville's decision, but Rivkin was ready to celebrate. On Friday 22 December, George Freris was appointed sole director and shareholder of Romale Pty Ltd, the company that owned the apartment on Crown Street opposite City Gym. Rivkin was finally making good on the bequest he had signed in Zurich sixteen months before.

PART FIVE

The rise of the suits

GENERAL: No Englishman unmoved that statement hears,
          Because, with all our faults, we love our House of Peers.

                                        Pirates of Penzance

FIFTEEN

The friends of Machiavelli

1996–97

On a fine spring day in 1997, Katerina Toppi was having one of those moments that give restaurateurs nightmares. It had begun, as most bad news does, with a little too much success. The steady flow of lunch customers into Machiavelli on this day had become an urgent, unruly crowd. Toppi had been settling down a table of almost-VIPs on one side of the restaurant. Angelo Italiani, the floor manager since Machiavelli opened in 1988, was busy elsewhere. Toppi turned back and was appalled. There in Machiavelli's front room a harried waiter was seating a party of businessmen around a large table. It was a complete disaster. This feckless group of diners had wandered on to Table 31. They had pinched Packer's seat.

Neither Kerry nor James had shown up that day, and there was no indication that they were planning an appearance later. That only made the slip-up worse. The presence or otherwise of the Packers that day wasn't the point. The point was Table 31. That was where the damage was being done. This was a power table—in restaurant politics in 1997 it was arguably *the* power table in Sydney. And, in an act of reckless profligacy, that power and cachet had been squandered heedlessly on a bunch of mere suits—undistinguished executive types who, oblivious, were settling down to look at their menus.

The fallout affected the entire restaurant. Machiavelli had not become one of the power centres of Sydney on its culinary credentials alone. The heart of an haute cuisine restaurant—any haute cuisine restaurant—is not really about food. It is about an idea. It's about something that is not there. Machiavelli operated as an entire social and political ecosystem. The world supervised by Katerina Toppi had its own natural order, a system of social and power rankings that determined who got to sit near the pictures of Graham Richardson, Bob Carr and John Laws (or, at an earlier time, Nick Greiner, Paul Keating and Gough Whitlam) in the front room, and who would be banished to uttermost darkness down the corridor, in the room they called Queensland. Even in the front room, among the very elect, there were infinite degrees and gradations of favour—Robert Hughes, on his visit from the US a few months before this, had only made it to Table 24, the fringe of power.

The idea behind this, as behind any system of exclusivity, is the need for absence. It's an us-and-them thing, a belief system that has been practised ruthlessly by headwaiters since the dawn of time. Maître d's have always had the keenest grasp on the spiky end of postmodernism. There is an *in* and there is an *out*. One defines the other. It is not just that John Laws or Laurie Brereton, or Nick Whitlam or Malcolm Turnbull, dines at Machiavelli, but that Arthur Dogsbody and all the other cohorts of the great unwashed do not. Ditto for anyone named Bozo. Just how much of a drawcard the celebrity factor is for Machiavelli could be measured in each day's takings. A brief mention in the CBD column of the *Sydney Morning Herald* that James Packer had been dining there would see a flood of extra custom in the following days.

This is the genius that lay behind Table 31, because it flipped the whole absence/presence thing. It was the Packer table. Everyone knew this. When one of the Packers was there, that is where they would lunch. It was still the Packer table even when they didn't show up, in which case no one sat there. Table 31 could seat ten people. The simple act of setting it with just four, or even two, places in a crowded restaurant each day was an exquisite power moment. On any particular day the Packers might not be there. But diners need only look as far as Table 31 to be assured that they were still with us. Their absence confirmed their presence.

This whole system, the very fabric that made up Machiavelli itself, was now under threat from a group of insufferable suits— suits, moreover, who gave no indication that they even knew what Table 31 meant or were conscious of the enormity of the social largesse that had been bestowed upon their unworthy persons. These philistines were so new to the power circle that they even needed to peer at the menu. It was appalling. What was next— anarchy in the streets?

It was just one day's embarrassment. Toppi followed the only course of action possible, which was to carry on regardless, pretend that the unsavoury incident had never happened, and never speak of it again. Nonetheless, something *was* happening on a wider scale in Sydney's power structure. An emerging new force was infiltrating the power circle. The town was being taken over by nobodies.

There had been a telling incident a year earlier. In early September 1996, a social nonentity called Simon Gautier Hannes decided to make a little quick money on the side. Hannes at that time was best known for the fact that he had a brain the size of several small buildings. There was no doubt about it, Simon Gautier was chockful of grey matter and his employer, Macquarie Bank, cherished him for it. When Macquarie found itself in a jam, a financial conundrum that required a solution of bewildering complexity, Hannes was the cerebral pointy-head they directed at the problem. Sooner or later, out would pop the solution. And they paid him well for it, even when he took some time off in late 1995 to study at a Buddhist monastery in Nepal. If there is one thing that Macquarie excels at, it is giving its star performers that warm all-over feeling. Which makes it all the harder to understand the debacle that followed.

The question of why someone who earned $30 000 a week would find himself short of money was never resolved. Whatever the reason, by September 1996 and after eleven years at Macquarie, Hannes had decided to try a spot of insider trading. There was no question that financial crime was eminently feasible for a man of his undoubted abilities. It was only a matter of calculating the best way of doing it. As luck would have it, his quick mind told him that the world's best practice for insider trading should involve a woman's wig and huge false glasses—which was not bad for a first effort. With a little more time he would probably have worked up to a rubber nose and a hump.

When the news broke in January 1997 that Hannes had been charged with insider trading, and in such bizarre circumstances, the first theory that did the rounds was that all Macquarie bankers dress like that. Up in their eyrie in Martin Place each morning, when no outsiders were around to see, they would whip out their wigs and false noses and go straight into their Inspector Clouseau routine, with chief executive Allan Moss leading them from the front. All it took was someone in the dealing room to whisper, 'Does your doag bate?' and they would be off. What wags. This theory, while obviously appealing, was eventually dropped because the thought of Allan Moss in a wig was just too scary.

The next theory was that the problem was Hannes' school. Who had ever heard of a successful criminal who went to Sydney Grammar? Any better class of GPS school would have taught their students that, if a job is worth doing, it is worth doing well. And a school with a stronger rugby tradition would have helped its students work through any lingering desire to wear funny clothes and behave in a sexually indeterminate manner.

What actually happened was that Hannes, alone and unaided, came up with a scheme to buy $100 000 worth of share options on Sir Peter Abeles's old transport group, TNT. Hannes knew the shares were about to soar because Macquarie was advising on a friendly takeover scheme by Dutch group KLN. As one of the seven directors in Macquarie's corporate advisory section, he was privy to all the details of the scheme, including the most important detail, the takeover price. So he knew exactly where the TNT share price would go after the bid was announced.

Hannes' first move was to set up a false identity, as Englishman Mark Booth, in a trading account at broker Ord Minnett. That was easy. But funding the insider trade was a little harder. How was he going to get the hundred gorillas into the Ords account without being traced? Hannes knew that every time $10 000 or more is moved in or out of a bank account, the bank informs the Australian Transaction Reports and Analysis Centre. (It was AUSTRAC that killed off the Cook Islands as a money-laundering destination. The Cook Islands is too obvious. 'If you're going to move money offshore, then you need to send it through somewhere like Singapore or Hong Kong, where it gets lost in the volume going through,' one financial advisor urges.) If ever the Australian Securities and Investments Commisssion (as the ASC had been renamed) grew suspicious about Mark Booth and his option play, its first move would be to try to trace where the money had come from. They would ask AUSTRAC to check who had taken $100 000 out of their bank account close to the time the money went into the Booth account at Ord Minnett. Hannes decided he could get around that by making a lot of cash withdrawals from his bank account, each just under $10 000, from a lot of different branches. So Hannes bought himself a train ticket and spent a day on the Parramatta line, stopping at each station to make a withdrawal of $9900 at the nearest Commonwealth Bank branch. He didn't want anyone to remember the man who made each withdrawal. To help ensure this, he wore a disguise.

Hannes was way too clever. He had worked out a brilliant way of buying share options that would turn his $100 000 kitty into a $2.16 million payout. The one-month investment would give him a return of more than 2000 per cent. The reason the return was so high was that it was the sort of option play you only make when you haven't been taking your injections. With the kind of options he bought, unless the TNT share price shot up 50 per cent in a month—which, given TNT's previously sluggish share trading history, was highly unlikely to happen—then Hannes would receive nothing and would lose all of his $100 000. Hannes knew, however, that he was betting on a certainty.

The windfall Hannes engineered was so spectacular—and the chances of it happening by accident so incredibly remote—that, when the takeover was announced in October 1996 and TNT shares shot up, alarm bells rang all over the Ords dealing room, all the way across to ASX Surveillance. So the hunt was on for the mysterious Mr Booth. With enough computers crunching through transactions in every bank account in Australia at the period, it was only a matter of time before Hannes's name came up, with or without the funny wig. And then the business world was agog with the spectacular fall from grace of Macquarie's star strategist.

The truth is: cardigans and pointy-heads should stay out of crime, because—let's face it—they suck at it. They obviously read too many trashy novels. Macquarie tried its best to manage the media fallout after Hannes was arrested. Each day for a week they stuck by their man and put up a different senior executive to handle press calls, to answer media questions fully and freely.

'There was never any suggestion of any blemish on his professional behaviour, never any suggestion that he behaved anything other than properly. It is completely astounding that this allegation should be made,' Allan Moss told the media on the first day.

'Simon has been one of the most outstanding employees Macquarie has had in its history,' the bank's deputy managing director, John Caldon, said on the evening of the second day.

Each morning after these little efforts the bank would be absolutely mauled in the press coverage, leaving the hapless senior executive thoroughly rattled, so they would find another one to be cannon fodder for the press for another day. And so on. They were like fish in a barrel. On the seventh day, whether because the bank grew short of senior execs with a suicide wish or they changed their media strategy, they decided it was time to rest. They stopped talking to the press completely.

Somewhere in the absurdity of all this was the tragedy of a bright young man destroying his life. The sad truth is that Simon Hannes had no idea how to be dishonest, no understanding that major crime involves something a little more ambitious than an all-day rover ticket on the Parramatta line. He really needed to get out more. If Hannes was truly corrupt, he could have made the insider trade through his banker in the Dutch Antilles and he would never have been traced. One would have to be remarkably bright to be so outstandingly stupid.

Hannes's TNT play was one of three options deals that ASIC investigated after the TNT takeover bid was announced. Two other investors with links to Macquarie made substantial profits. One of them invested $2 million in options five days before the TNT bid was announced and made a $7 million profit—dwarfing Hannes's payout. But these were professional investors with more cautious option strategies and ASIC judged that no further investigation was warranted. The investors involved had made windfall profits on sharp share movements before this, which convinced ASIC that it was less likely that they were acting on insider information.

Increasingly, however, it was the pointy-heads and the traders who were ending up in court charged with financial crime. Nick Leeson made the term 'rogue trader' a buzzword of the 1990s, when his unauthorised currency deals brought down his employer, Barings Bank. Barings was the august institution that put up the prize money in Jules Verne's *Around the World in 80 Days*. With their rude introduction to the split-second world of modern derivatives trading, if they survived a Leeson fiasco today, they would more likely back the film *Gone in 60 Seconds*.

Then there were the 'barrow boys' who ran Nomura Securities' global options desk in London. In March 1996, they faced a tricky options position in Australia. Nomura stood to lose several million dollars. To get out of it, they decided on a wild strategy of dumping $900 million of shares onto the Australian market in the last three minutes of trading on the last day of the March quarter. They expected the selling would wipe $40 billion off the value of the Australian market in those minutes. Causing the market to crash was intended as the key to their strategy. While it would devastate returns for Australian fund managers, the crash would allow Nomura to get out of its options position and provide it with extra profits of up to $35 million. It was 'good fun—quite a giggle actually,' said Nomura's head of equities in London, Robert Mapstone, whom the *Financial Times* regularly described as 'the best stockbroker in the City'. Mapstone's comment was one of many references that Nomura traders made to their private jokes, jests and merry japes when the matter came up in the Federal Court in 1998 before Justice Sackville. In Sydney, a city which had endured two years of corrupt policemen in completely unrelated circumstances explaining a different sort of joke, this really wasn't the note that Nomura wanted to hit.

The strategy had been dreamed up by Duncan Moss, a British Nomura trader working out of Hong Kong. If the plan worked, Moss was in line for a million-dollar bonus. He was only twenty-four years old, so that was still quite a lot to him. In the cold light of the Federal Court two years later, Justice Sackville didn't have a lot of time for the maestros of mirth and ruled that Nomura had engaged in market manipulation.

Two features stood out about the scam. The first was its breath-taking scope. Here was a twenty-four-year-old in Hong Kong, reporting to London for a Japanese trading house, ready to rain death and destruction on the Australian market just to tweak up his end-of-month trading figures. The other feature was that Nomura's cunning plan didn't actually work. The Australian broking houses that Moss was working through from Hong Kong bungled his selling orders. Some brokers got it wrong. Some realised what was going on and didn't want any part of it. And some preferred to support other, longer-standing clients who were pushing the market up, rather than down. The Nomura boys were just a passing shower.

The Australian market dipped only twenty-six points, not the 230 points that Moss and the boys were counting on. Nomura ended up losing $900 000. While this was disappointing, it was less than the loss it had otherwise been facing. Then they moved on to another market to *play with*. The Nomura team went on to stage similar stunts in Johannesburg, London and Rome. This was a new kind of jetsetting: Today is Tuesday, therefore I am mugging . . . the Italian market.

Behind all this colour and movement, a more profound power shift was taking shape as a new power class took over Sydney. New institutional powers were emerging. This was the day of the suits, the fund managers, the index watchers, the aspirational professionals. They had money but not a lot of taste or time, so there was a whole new growth industry in telling the new rich what to wear, where to eat, and how to decorate.

The way that business was done was changing. One of Paul Keating's enduring legacies has been the superannuation guarantee, which forces employers to pay 9 per cent of their workers' wages into a super fund. The introduction of the superannuation guarantee has diverted enormous amounts of money into forced savings, which is controlled by the super fund managers. Every year, more than $50 billion of new contributions is channelled towards the super funds to be invested, creating a pool of $750 billion of superannuation money. The superannuation guarantee has become the biggest money pump that Australia has ever seen. It has shifted the balance of business power to the people who run the pump. Many of the fund managers and bank executives who comprise the new elites are former public servants who took golden parachutes into the private sector in the early 1990s, again as a result of Keating initiatives. The funds they pilot are leviathans in the market, disinterested in the penny stocks and minor companies that have been the basis for traditional Australian market manipulation plays. Their investment strategy revolves around matching the market index. They are the new *uber* managers. Frankly, they're a boring lot, for the most part. Many of these people are seriously dull. As previously noted, they have absolutely no aptitude for crime. And they certainly don't know much about lunch. But they do know about power.

In early 1996, when John Howard wanted a quiet meeting with the Deputy Governor of the Reserve Bank, Ian Macfarlane, Bankers Trust offered its private dining room. A year later when the Melbourne Establishment, along with the ANZ Bank and Don Argus at National Australia Bank, were pressing for Peter Jonson, the then head of Norwich Union, to replace Bernie Fraser as RBA Governor, BT and the Sydney banks persuaded Howard to go with Macfarlane.

The most spectacular powerplay came from Elizabeth Bryan, who was head of the old NSW State Super when the $19 billion funds management operation was renamed Axiom and put up for sale. Don Argus at the NAB thought he had sewn up the deal with a bid for Axiom that was $25 million more than the closest rival offer. It looked a pretty good deal until Bryan threatened to walk out, with her top-performing team, if NAB won. Argus was toast. That's the smell of power—a management wobbly that cost Axiom's government owner $25 million.

There was another change. Fortunes in Sydney traditionally have been made by insiders who win special favours or concessions from the state government. These can be land sales or monopolies, or deals like the Lotto licence, which has made so much money for Packer and Murdoch. But in the 1990s, the privatisation process became the biggest driver of corporate deals. There was great wealth to be made from advising and assisting the federal and state governments as they sold assets in public floats. The winners here became the merchant bankers, like those at Macquarie, who structured the deals in highly profitable ways.

Of course they got a lot of media coverage. As Rivkin and Adler had already demonstrated, media is a force multiplier. Fund managers and investment bankers became iconic figures. Their skirmishes and rivalries would have far-reaching effects, but none of these would compare with the titanic fight to control AMP.

It began in 1992, when AMP hired Andrew Threadgold, the head of Britain's fourth largest pension fund, PosTel Investment Management, to be its investment manager. Threadgold had been managing $66 billion in investments funds in his old job. It seemed unlikely he would have given this up without the promise that he would become head of AMP when Ian Salmon retired. Whatever assurances Threadgold had received were to founder when AMP's strategic partnership with Westpac subsequently became an embarrassing failure and the Provident Society descended into a crisis of confidence. AMP's investment returns were down but, as a mutual association, it was limited in its ability to raise new capital. So its board decided to demutualise and to float the new company on the share market. To head this dramatic transformation, directors decided to look outside AMP for a replacement when Salmon retired in 1994. Their choice was burly American insurance executive, George Trumbull.

'Let me tell you something about me,' Trumbull said at his first meeting with AMP's top agents and partners. 'In the US I played pro football. I'm an ex-marine, I'm tough . . . Don't fuck with me and don't fuck with the AMP.' That was George. He had a genius for annoying the wrong people. But he never let that faze him. Early on he had a lunch with ten senior male AMP executives, and asked them what they thought were AMP's biggest problems. 'It's funny you should say that,' he said when the answers had subsided, 'because I had a group of women executives in recently and they said one of the biggest problems at AMP is sexual harassment and sexual discrimination. And five of the biggest offenders are sitting at this table.' As lunch conversation goes, it was pretty much a show stopper.

Trumbull put AMP's corporate culture through the blender. By 1997, he recounted, he had moved or replaced all but four of the top eighty-seven AMP executives. The one part of AMP on which he had yet to put his stamp was the funds management division. That was the domain of Andrew Threadgold, who ran it with Trumbull-like tightness. Threadgold's motto was FIFO—Fit In or Fuck Off. With $114 billion of funds under his management, Andrew produced 60 per cent of AMP's earnings, which really made him more important to AMP than George. The two men bickered on a range of subjects, from asset allocation to corporate governance.

As the AMP privatisation and float approached in early 1998, Trumbull took to bemoaning at executive meetings about the intense pressures he was under. The demutualisation process was a nightmare, the demands on him were overwhelming, and now the media were giving him a hard time over his $20 million incentive share package over his regular $3.9 million salary package. Really, would anyone in the room want to take such an awful job as his? There was a little pause of silence after this rhetorical question . . . then Threadgold put up his hand.

While it was no doubt fun to play with George's blood pressure, at the end of the day Threadgold's position depended on getting the investment returns that would ensure the continuing support of the board. He had bet his future on a belief that world equity markets were heading for a fall, as Asia pushed Australia and eventually Wall Street off balance. He would have been a hero if it had happened, but it didn't. Trumbull soon saw his opportunity. On Friday 30 January 1998, two weeks after Trumbull had confirmed Threadgold as global head of AMP investment, UK funds management group Henderson announced it was in talks with AMP financial officer Paul Batchelor that were expected to lead to its acquisition.

Threadgold was due to fly in to London the next day. By Monday it was a done deal. AMP would pay £382 million for Hendersons, which managed £14.3 billion in assets. AMP already managed $114.6 billion in assets worldwide, including £6 billion in Britain. A major part of Henderson's appeal was its high-profile CEO, Dugald Eadie, who was known as the Tartan Spartan. It was a condition of the deal that Eadie would run AMP's $102 billion of international funds, reporting directly to Trumbull. Threadgold's empire would be slashed back to managing the $54 billion of Australian and New Zealand investments. Trumbull had slashed Threadgold's power base.

On 3 July, two weeks after the AMP float, Trumbull walked into Threadgold's office and told him he had come to discuss his resignation.

'But I have no intention of resigning,' Threadgold said.

'Then I've come to discuss your sacking,' Trumbull said.

And that was that. Andrew Mohl replaced Threadgold in Australia. A year later the Tartan Spartan resigned as well, which meant that most of the rationale for Trumbull's manoeuvre had disappeared. Trumbull had merely transferred control of most of Australia's biggest pension fund to a British investment team of middling ability. The move tilted the investment decision-making that would determine the retirement payouts for a large slab of Australia towards Britain. British institutions allocate far more of their assets to equities than Australian funds tend to. As AMP's position in the UK grew more precarious, its dependence on the British share market grew greater and greater, guided by a financial strategy that reflected the judgments of its British managers. Trumbull was long gone, replaced by Batchelor, when it hit the fan three years later. The crippling losses from its UK investments almost broke AMP. It cost Batchelor his job, with Andrew Mohl taking the helm of a desperately battered AMP in late 2002.

Trumbull had survived little longer than Threadgold, being forced out months later after he posed for a Pamela Williams story for the *Australian Financial Review* wearing an American Indian headdress. The board was already deeply unhappy with Trumbull over the disastrous takeover of GIO and other issues, and this was the last straw. The beleaguered AMP board called in the head-hunters immediately. There was wistful talk of a scalping.

Meanwhile, a wave of industry consolidation among the big fund managers had seen the rise of operators like Greg Perry (the fund manager whose track record in the tech boom was so good they called him The Freak) and Chris Cuffe at Colonial First State, who both earned more than $30 million in bonuses and in exit payments when they left. As corporate payouts go, this was rivalled only by BT Australia chief Rob Ferguson, who was paid more than $35 million when he cashed out stock in the US parent, Bankers Trust. However, these were insignificant figures compared with the tens of billions of dollars they managed. It's also a drop in the bucket when compared to the $900 million that Alan Bond was able to extract from Bell Resources in 1988. The big players of the 1990s were not playing in the same league as Bond, Robert Holmes à Court, John Spalvins or John Elliott. But the evolution from figures such as Elliott and Holmes à Court as Australia's major corporate players to Chris Cuffe was a profound one.

SIXTEEN
The secret pilgrims
1996–97

It is a truth, universally acknowledged, that an Australian in possession of a good fortune must be in want of a Swiss banker. It's a spiritual thing. In the postmodern world, the unconditional regard and trust that once characterised relations with a priest, and in later times with a psychiatrist, for many can now be expressed only through close communion with their offshore financial advisor. A banking relationship goes so much further than discussing mere money. In the banking confessional, anything can be said. Ernst Imfeld—'Dear Earnest', as some of his clients called him—understood this. It was Imfeld who told Rene Rivkin that his father really loved him; who assured Walter Rivkin that 'there is always a solution to a problem'; who handled the sensitive matter of Rivkin's secret $500 000 bequest to George Freris; and who, in 1997, was helping Rivkin and his fellow investors set up a better way to hide their activities from Australian authorities.

Ernst Imfeld is one of those people born to smile. Two of the most famous pictures of him show him with a table of ten in an upmarket Zurich restaurant in December 2000, sitting next to Swiss Attorney-General Dr Valentin Roschacher. Imfeld is a picture of solid respectability—distinguished greying hair, white shirt and tie, square features and the rounded cheeks of the professional luncher.

The stilted poses in the first picture suggest a mild awkwardness between the two key figures: Imfeld seemingly genial but looking off into the middle distance, while the Attorney-General shows a hint of stiffness—a politician mixing in an unfamiliar crowd. The second shot, taken several hours later, captures the quintessence of conviviality. Imfeld is grinning broadly, his tie undone and his collar open, his body turned to share something with Roschacher. The Attorney-General is turned to Imfeld, his tie a little askew and his face full of amusement as he enjoys the joke, hanging on what Imfeld is saying. Later Roschacher would wish he had remained uptight. Weeks after the picture was taken, Imfeld and two others at the table would be under arrest while the pictures of the Attorney-General at play were splashed across the Swiss dailies.

'Ernst Imfeld was an important man in the bank and he was an important man in Switzerland,' was all Leumi spokesman, Yona Fogel, would say of the picture. Imfeld could charm the birds out of the trees. He had been fired by the Union Bank of Switzerland (UBS) in 1989, after he rushed through two transactions without doing the paperwork. He did it as a favour for clients who wanted a quick investment, only to see them renege when the deal went bad. At least that's the way the story went. His appointment as private client manager at Bank Leumi in Zurich galvanised this little Israeli outpost. He became widely recognised as a share-market genius and he pushed Leumi to the top of the Swiss currency trading table. But it was his manner that won clients.

'I found him the most colourful banker in Zurich,' Rivkin said later. 'I must say we all liked Mr Imfeld. Richardson liked him, Kennedy liked him, and I did too . . . We always agreed with each other. I had the impression that he liked me. I liked him very much.'

There was a ritual to seeing Ernst. It began, Brent Potts told Zurich DA Nathan Landshut, with a phone call to Imfeld's secretary to set up an appointment. For such visits Potts liked to stay in the swanky Bauer au Lac. Rivkin favoured the picturesque Eden au Lac or the more discreet Neues Schloss. Just a short stroll away from either hotel squats the Leumi building on Claridenstrasse, like a white concrete bunker. Its entrance is through two armoured glass doors.

'Right at the entrance was a lady behind a glass partition,' Potts said. 'I had to identify myself and she would then admit me to the reception room.' Imfeld's secretary would bring clients into his office. A view of the Uetliberg peak beckoned through the window on the left. A Hebrew poster—a verse from Ecclesiastes, 'A time to every purpose under heaven'—hung high on the right. Between them would be the portly figure of the great man himself: informed, witty, scathingly wry.

'I would arrive at the bank at 11.30 a.m.,' Potts said. 'That was the time Mr Imfeld always preferred. I would spend about twenty minutes in his office and then we would go out for lunch.'

It was a natural progression; clients were ushered out of the bank with minimal delay and were then tying on the bibs at the exclusive Bauer au Lac Club for a little culinary bonding at Leumi's expense. If Potts needed travellers cheques or cash, one of the Leumi people would hand it to him while Imfeld lectured Potts on the danger of discovery from using his Leumi credit card. Imfeld understood the finer points of schmoozing. For Potts and Rivkin there would be the courtesy Mercedes limousine.

Despite all the joviality and fine dining, Potts told Landshut, he never actually got any statements for his account. After doing this for twenty years he didn't feel he needed them. And where would he keep his Swiss bank statements? 'Clearly I wouldn't want to take them back to my country,' he said. Imfeld would merely pass him three or four pages that listed how much money Potts had in his account, then detailed all the shares he held in alphabetical order. Potts traded regularly through his brokerage, PG Intercapital, on behalf of Leumi and other clients. When the shares were for his account, Potts would add his codename,

LAC, to the sale documents and Imfeld would know they were for him. Potts carried the details of all this around with him in his laptop. When he rolled back into his hotel room after lunch with Imfeld he would check Leumi's list of his shareholdings with his own record. 'If I found a discrepancy, when for instance shares were listed that did not belong to me, I called Ernst from my hotel, he then checked it out and called me back to say I was right, and eliminated it from my portfolio,' Potts said. 'It was always just a tiny discrepancy, in 99.9 per cent of the time his and my lists corresponded.'

According to Potts, Imfeld was a stickler for procedure and forms:

> I remember well how often Mr Imfeld asked me for my signature. The thing is that occasionally I would want to have money transferred, for example to the university where my sons studied. Mr Imfeld would ask me to sign certain forms—I mean when I called him from Australia to ask him to transfer money to my sons, he would tell me it was no problem but that, on my next visit, I would have to sign an order for it. He went to great lengths to explain to me that such written orders were important in order to prevent unauthorised transfers, that he needed them for internal audits. Sometimes he would tell me to send a fax when I asked for a transfer. Oddly enough Mr Imfeld wanted the fax sent to his home address . . . As I recall, I never signed a blank sheet.

How do you account for the way hard-headed businessmen all over the world walk into an offshore banking office and lose all sense of caution? When does hard-headed become bone-headed? 'These guys have no idea what they are getting into,' commented one advisor who regularly sets up offshore facilities. 'They go offshore and they think everything is rosy. It goes wrong, and they are devastated.'

Maybe it's the intimacy that comes from sharing a secret. One of the comforting aspects for Australians as they walked into Swiss banks in the 1990s was the assurance they were not alone. All through the Rivkin saga there were hints, allusions and suggestions of other accounts, other account-holders, a solid rank of Australians—probably in the thousands—making their annual pilgrimage to Zurich to check up on their nest eggs. It's not that everyone who has a Swiss account is a tax evader or involved in anything illegal. There are legitimate reasons to hold such accounts. But most clients don't want the account to be known. And discretion is the better part of Swiss banking; never more so than when something goes wrong.

'When my husband dumped me, he took the British bank accounts, I kept what was in the Australian accounts, and he kept the Swiss accounts,' the ex-wife of a senior Australian executive said. The Swiss accounts? 'The bank was very unhelpful when my lawyer contacted it during the divorce.'

The Silence of the Clams. Then there was the high-profile Sydney family who were drawn together in grief after the death of their father—until the siblings discovered several years later that the eldest son had taken over their father's Swiss accounts. He hadn't told them about this money and neither had the bank.

It didn't take Rene Rivkin long to adjust to the world after Offset Alpine. On 29 December 1995, his Stilton and EBC Zurich accounts were credited with $26.6 million from the sale of the Offset shares, after Justice Sackville's order to release the money. This was just a nominal entry; in reality the money remained frozen in two Credit Suisse accounts, jointly administered by the ASC, EBC and Leumi, while the case went to appeal. Rivkin, however, was already in spending mode.

On 2 January, Rivkin began buying shares in a little miner called Coolawin Resources, which had just received a takeover bid from Plutonic Resources. By February, Rivkin had spent $2.4 million and owned 13 per cent of Coolawin. All the old crowd of Rivkin supporters at Offset Alpine had piled in to buy stock—Trevor Kennedy, FAI, Bruce Corlett, Ray Martin, Nora Goodridge and Bart and Ronald Doff—in the expectation that Plutonic would be forced to raise its takeover bid and give them a quick profit. Instead Plutonic dropped its bid, leaving Rivkin and his friends stuck with their stock. Coolawin Resources would be renamed Morgans Gold and later Abednego Nickel. Despite these transformations it sat on Rivkin's books like lard. It would take him four years and $12 million to get out of this hole.

At last it seemed that Rivkin was about to get his money from Offset Alpine. On 18 September 1996, the Court of Appeal upheld Sackville's judgment and the funds were about to be released. Rivkin celebrated by transferring $433 000 from his Stilton account to UK yacht broker Cavendish White as a deposit for a new boat. But what happened next was like the last-minute twist in a horror movie—the beast has been slain, the heroine is safe in the arms of the hero and the credits are ready to roll when, suddenly, skeleton hands reach out from the grave to grip her ankles. Yes, it was the tax man.

Counsel for the Australian Tax Office bobbed up at the final hearing, saying that the plan to ship the money off to Switzerland was 'a little bit cute'. 'Transmitting it to Zurich to invest in Australian dollars is a curious thing to do,' he said, and—ahem, ahem—when were they thinking of paying income tax on this splendid windfall?

After some haggling, the ATO released $13.9 million to Leumi and EBC on 25 October and froze the rest while negotiations continued. For the moment, the tax office was keeping 48 cents in the dollar.

In his December 2002 interview with Zurich DA Nathan

Landshut, Rivkin described the Offset position as follows: 'The shares of Offset Alpine, which this was originally all about, were for the most part, let's say 81 per cent mine, and about 7 per cent Richardson's. Twelve per cent were held by Kennedy. The numbers don't square exactly.' In practice that meant Rivkin kept all of the money paid to Leumi, and two thirds of the payout to EBC. True to form, Rivkin began spending the money even before it reached him. On 24 October 1996, Rivkin's Stilton account paid $625 000 to buy 2.5 million more shares in Morgans Gold from his Australian holdings. Once again Rivkin was using share trading to launder money from overseas back to Australia.

In December, Rivkin took delivery of a 31-metre motor cruiser registered in the British Virgin Islands that he named *Dajoshadita* (a combination of the names of his four children). Rivkin's Stilton account shows a $2 million transfer on 17 December, half of the purchase price for the boat. The rest of the money presumably came from his EBC account. Next Rivkin set up a new trading account using an entity in the Channel Islands called Mallard Holdings: 'That's a business . . . [that] was established for me by a bank in Holland by the name of Insinger,' Rivkin told Landshut. 'That bank also has an office in London and my representative there is a lady called Amanda Chon. The business belongs to me and trades in shares.'

As his offshore share trading took off, however, Rivkin faced bad news at home. Walter Rivkin was diagnosed with terminal cancer; he died on 5 April 1997. Walter had reconciled with his son before his death, but Rene was in the United States when the end came. 'I wasn't here for his death,' Rivkin later told Andrew Denton:

I decided not to be here intentionally. It wasn't a very pretty death. It was a thing called multiple myeloma, which is basically cancer of everything . . . I felt that I could add nothing to the disastrous state he was in. He'd lost basically all his faculties, functions and what else have you and it was very sad to see, and I . . . if I can avoid sadness, I will. And I did.

Rivkin told Landshut that his father took his own life. Despite Rene's brave words, the loss of this powerful figure in his life must have affected him. He dealt with the loss as he had with other personal crises: he went shopping. On 11 April, Imfeld transferred US$325 000 to cover bills that Rene had run up in the US buying furniture, antiques, carpet and a BMW, which he charged to his father's account. Rene now ordered Imfeld to liquidate the shares and bonds in Walter's 8405 account and transfer them to Stilton. After probate was granted on his father's will on 4 July, Rivkin set about selling his father's extensive Sydney property holdings.

Across town, Trevor Kennedy was breaking out the champagne. Ozemail listed on the American Nasdaq exchange at US$1.50 on 29 May, raising US$46.9 million in new capital. Sean Howard's shares were now worth US$49 million, while the twin investments of $450 000 that Kennedy and Turnbull had made nineteen months before were each now worth US$24.5 million. It dwarfed Kennedy's $4.5 million payout from Offset Alpine, half of which was still tied up in the courts. Aglow with moral virtue, Kennedy used his chairman's address at the Oil Search annual meeting in Port Moresby on 7 May to thunder at the 'growing levels of corruption' in the Papua New Guinea government. If they could only be more like Kennedy's company, which practised only 'the highest levels of corporate governance and ethics'.

Rivkin was on the brink of one of his most successful ventures. On 6 May 1997, the great and mighty were summoned to a cocktail party on the *Dajoshadita* to launch Rivkin's new subscriber tipsheet, the *Rivkin Report*. While Rivkin was away in the US the previous month, Bruce Corlett had used Rivkin's power of attorney to sign a $6 million mortgage over Rivkin's house at Bellevue Hill, perhaps to help fund the new venture. It was a fabulous affair on the boat, captained by Rivkin's favourite tattooist, George Freris. All Rivkin's friends were there, most particularly the names that featured in the share registers of Offset Alpine and what was now called Morgans Gold—Trevor Kennedy, Graham Richardson, Rodney Adler, Ray Martin and the usual media crowd. It was a triumph. Thousands of Australians would subscribe to the tipsheet because they believed in Rene Rivkin.

'My business is very much show business,' Rivkin later told Kerry-Anne Kennerley on the *Midday Show*. 'It is because of the show business aspects of my life that I am successful at what I do, partially. I also have brains and a lot of luck.'

He had made the name Rivkin synonymous with success and high living. 'If I lost my wealth tomorrow I would feel suicidal,' Rivkin told the *Financial Review* that year. 'There is no question of that. Because I would have lost most of what is me.'

Rivkin now had the perfect combination for the 1990s. He was his own brand name. The different parts of his public life were all meshing—his discount broking business, his tipsheet and his carefully orchestrated media profile. Rivkin was all over the gossip pages. While he was a great media performer, his ubiquity also reflected the lengths to which he went to court journalists. In 1998, *BRW* journalist Ali Cromie was contacted by a public relations firm who offered her a free weekend at Hamilton Island. The only proviso was that she write that she had seen Rivkin there.

In his weekly column in the *Sun-Herald*, Rivkin joked about Swiss gnomes that he knew. He used the column and his tipsheet to talk up Morgans Gold, which had been proving up its nickel reserves at its Abednego deposit in Western Australia. With Rivkin's support, the stock rocketed from 40 cents in May to $1.70 in September. Rivkin's buy-in price was 30 cents and he was sitting on another $10 million windfall.

Everything Rivkin touched was turning to gold. On 12 August 1997, $3 million was transferred into his Stilton account. Another $2.48 million was received on 3 September. The first appears to have been a transfer from his father's account. The second may have been a settlement that EBC Zurich had made with the Australian Tax Office (Leumi's negotiations with the ATO would drag on until December). On 15 August, Rivkin set up Rejoleer, the company which would run the Cave Nightclub at Star City Casino, in partnership with Joe Elcham, who had long since sold Joe's Cafe. The plan hit a snag later that year, however, when the Casino Control Authority found Elcham was not a fit and proper person to be licensed to run the casino nightclub. Rivkin felt for his friend. He bought Elcham a $327 000 new yellow Ferrari, while in Zurich he transferred assets worth $550 000 to a Leumi account he set up for Elcham.

'I gave him the car to cheer him up because through no fault of his own he failed probity at Star City—which means he could not run my new nightclub there,' Rivkin told Ros Reines at the *Sunday Telegraph*.

Ernst Imfeld at Leumi and the lawyer Benno Hafner now believed they had solved the problem of hiding the tracks of their Australian clients, if the ASC came calling again. Graham Richardson would be the first to test their strategy. Rivkin testified to Landshut:

> I have explained to you that Mr Richardson had a specific slice of the [Offset Alpine] shares. He held those via the bank August Roth within his own account. I remember I gave Mr Richardson one of my inactive accounts at the bank August Roth . . . Graham Richardson . . . didn't want to open an official account in his own

name and for that reason we had a portfolio opened within my [Leumi] account labelled Cheshire.

EBC Zurich had run into problems with Swiss authorities in 1996 for providing banking services without a licence. It was agreed that Bank August Roth would take over the EBC business. This made little immediate difference—the accounts continued to be administered by the same people in the same building. What the clients didn't know was that, by April 1997, EBC's private client manager, Axel Fundulus, had begun embezzling funds. It was purely fortuitous that Richardson's share of the Offset proceeds were being transferred out of EBC. His money followed a tortuous path, first to an account at the ANZ Bank in Melbourne, which was operated by Credit Suisse for Leumi, then back to Zurich.

Richardson had $1.44 million in cash in the Swiss funds. The EBC accounts also held 2.27 million Morgans Gold shares that Rivkin had bought the previous year, for about $700 000. They too would end up in the new Bank Leumi account that was being set up for Richardson. By late September 1997, when the Morgans Gold share price touched $1.70, this packet of shares in the EBC account was worth $3.9 million. When Richardson hosted Bob Carr's fiftieth birthday celebrations on 28 September at the Hotel Intercontinental, his Swiss holdings in cash and shares were worth $5.9 million.

Hafner had convinced Imfeld that the best way to shroud the identity of clients was to set up accounts in the name of Scottish partnerships. These strange corporate structures have a limited partner, who is a front man, and a general partner, who owns and controls the assets. If the general partner is offshore, the partnership escapes British tax. Edsaco, a tax advisory service on the Isle of Man originally owned by the Union Bank of Switzerland, was selling Scottish partnerships, which all had the same business address in Lothian Road, Edinburgh. The addresses for the limited and general partners were in two adjoining buildings in Regent Street, London.

In the offshore tax world, older is better. The price for an offshore shelf company goes up US$1000 for every year since they were set up. The reason is that when an offshore investor buys an already established company it becomes harder for authorities to trace when the offshore investor became involved. But there's a trap for unwary players here. Most people like to put their own name on their companies. It defeats the purpose when you buy a pre-aged tax haven company to rename it. The name change gives regulators a date to track you from. Richardson and Trevor Kennedy would both make this mistake.

In September 1997, Edsaco reactivated a Scottish partnership called Laira Consulting Company, which had lain dormant since it was set up four years before. Its general partner was listed as Cedargrove Ltd, care of 169/173 Regent Street, London. Cedargrove's real address appears to have been in the Cayman Islands. On 30 September, two days after Bob Carr's fiftieth birthday bash, Edsaco filed an application at Companies House in Edinburgh to change Laira's name to Laira Investment Company. The change was approved on Thursday 9 October. The following Monday, Imfeld opened a Leumi account in Laira's name. A new Swiss law had been passed that month, designed to clamp down on money laundering and prevent bank clients from hiding behind obscure companies and trusts—which was the very thing Rivkin and co. were anxious to do. Under the new law, Imfeld was required to fill in a Form A, which listed the individual person, as opposed to an entity, who was the beneficial owner of the account. But this didn't happen with the Laira account, which listed the beneficial owner only as Cedargrove Ltd. This was illegal. When Swiss authorities later questioned Imfeld and Hafner about it, each man blamed the other. Then they blamed Edsaco.

'We had sent Form A and the other papers to England and they came back signed,' Hafner testified to Landshut. Landshut didn't believe him:

You know as well as I do, that limited or general partnerships in England and Scotland have absolutely no idea what the real intention is but they make available their services and structure and all the decisions that their boards take only have the status of recommendations. You cannot push the responsibility for what happened on to those people.

This would be the pattern for the Scottish partnerships that Imfeld and Hafner set up. But Laira had a twist. Within this account, which had no real owner, were two sub-accounts. One was operated by Rivkin and, behind that, was the second sub-account called Cheshire, which had been set up to hold Richardson's money. In reality, Rivkin later testified, 'Laira was Richardson.'

A minor hiatus followed while Rivkin had yet another financial windfall. Canadian securities house Toronto Dominion had opened negotiations to buy Rivkin Croll Smith. The deal was announced Thursday 23 October, for $24 million, half an hour before the Asian share crash paralysed world markets. Rivkin's share of the money was $15 million. It really was his year. The irony in Rivkin's story is that he would make more money from legitimate business—from his broking businesses and the Rivkin Report—than from all his dodgy dealing. But that never seemed to offer Rivkin the same thrill.

Arrangements in Switzerland were now complete. On Wednesday 5 November, Bank August Roth issued a cheque for $1.44 million from the Credit Suisse account with the ANZ Bank in Melbourne, sending the money to Switzerland where it was deposited in the Cheshire sub-account at Leumi. What happened next is detailed in a substantial shareholder notice that Laira filed with the Australian Stock Exchange on 11 December 1997, which was signed by Benno Hafner. As we have already seen, in addition to the $1.44 million, Richardson's EBC account also held 2.27 million Morgans Gold shares. The company had changed its name by this time to Abednego Nickel. The 2.27 million Abednego

Nickel shares were also transferred to Laira. Rivkin now proceeded to spend all of Richardson's money.

The cheque from Bank August Roth was cleared in the Laira account on Friday 7 November. On the following Monday, Rivkin began an eight-day $1.4 million spending spree, buying more Abednego Nickel shares. The shares were all Rene's idea. 'Richardson knows nothing about shares, not even their names,' Rivkin later told Zurich DA Nathan Landshut. In fact, it's not even clear if Richardson knew what his very good friend Rene was doing. Richardson's money was supposed to be invested in bonds, and that is what his accounts showed. However, Rivkin had used the bonds as security to borrow money for the new shares. It was a little like the way Rivkin had ripped off his father's account in 1990.

Whether or not Richardson knew about it, by 11 December, when Hafner filed the substantial shareholder notice, Laira owned 3.8 million Abednego Nickel shares. Richardson also held shares through his family company in Australia, Erinrose Enterprises. Together with the Laira parcel he now owned 8.3 per cent of Abednego. He was the second largest shareholder after Rivkin. It's the sort of stake that buys you a seat on the board. And indeed, eleven days later, on 22 December, Richardson's long-time best friend, former Hawke advisor and now Packer lobbyist Peter Barron, was appointed a director of Abednego. Barron has since denied categorically any knowledge that Richardson was the second largest shareholder in Abednego, a stake then worth $4.2 million.

For Richardson it must have seemed the perfect cover. If ASIC ever tried to trace the Bank Leumi account, the trail led only to the Scottish partnership and behind that to the mysterious Cedargrove. If anyone pushed further, the account ostensibly belonged to Rivkin. Richardson would say, 'I never owned the account, I never owned the shares.' Richardson was invisible and took care to stay that way. When he withdrew cash from Laira, he would first transfer it from his Cheshire sub-account across to

Rivkin's Portfolio 1 and then withdraw the money from there. If challenged, he would say that the money was a loan from Rivkin.

If Richardson had been dealing with anyone other than Ernst Imfeld and Rene Rivkin, this system would have been foolproof. As it was, Rivkin began transferring money out of Cheshire almost immediately. Imfeld, meanwhile, embarked on a series of foreign currency trades that saw a quarter of a billion dollars flow in and out of Laira. Even Kennedy would casually mention Richardson's link to the Zurich District Attorney's office in March 2002: 'Mr Graham Richardson, yes. I can remember that I once knew that Mr Richardson possessed an account by Bank Leumi.' Richardson was the very picture of the innocent abroad. All of his careful attention to secrecy had been overturned. But no one was telling him that.

While Richardson was trying to stay invisible and Rivkin was openly joking about his Swiss connections, their friend Trevor Kennedy had taken a different tack.

When ASIC investigators questioned him during a Section 19 examination on 1 and 2 December 2003, Kennedy was emphatic that he had known nothing about Offset Alpine shares. He recalled that in the 1980s he had set up an entity—a trust or company, he couldn't remember which—called Brampton. It was set up by 'some supposedly smart accountants and lawyers in London on the basis that I—what I was doing was strictly legal and that I had no ownership or—or authority over it. Beyond that I have no knowledge, and I don't believe I ever had, of what it was.'

Someone had suggested that the Brampton structure might be useful, but he had forgotten who. He didn't remember which country it was in, though he appeared to narrow it down to somewhere in 'the Turks and Caicos and Netherlands BVs, Liechtenstein, Switzerland etc. What specifically I don't recall.' It was managed without reference to him. He didn't remember why it was set up, or if he had ever received a payout from it. 'I have an appalling memory, and always have had. I can't remember what happened last Wednesday, let alone what happened eighteen months ago,' he said. Some of Brampton's money had ended up with EBC Zurich. It might be, he told ASIC, that Brampton held some Offset Alpine shares, but he didn't think so: 'I am—I don't— as far as I know, Brampton had never held shares in—in—in Offset, if that's—as far as I'm aware it—it—it wasn't a—it wasn't a shareholder in—in Offset Alpine.'

Did Rivkin have anything to do with Brampton?

'Certainly not,' Kennedy said.

Why not?

'Privilege. Because I just know that he has never been involved in my—in anything like that with me. I mean, that's, I would have thought, crazy stuff. Why do you ask that question?' And again: 'I am absolutely sure that Mr Rivkin was not involved . . . I don't believe he would have even known about it . . . Because it was a very private piece of my own affairs.'

When ASIC searched Rivkin's offices two weeks earlier, on 13 November 2003, they had found documents referring to an EBC account called Brampton holding Stroika shares in 1992 and 1993. Kennedy's lawyers have since argued that the Brampton trading was conducted entirely by Rivkin. Kennedy knew nothing about it. Kennedy and Rivkin were working in adjoining offices at the time, with Kennedy unaware that his offshore entity was being managed by his next-door neighbour.

Justice Roger Gyles found in the Federal Court in March 2004 that Kennedy's testimony before ASIC four months before was not believable:

It is not credible that any person, let alone an experienced business person, would set up a series of entities to manage investments overseas without having any idea as to the ultimate fate of the investments or their proceeds, which is the picture that Kennedy sought to convey in the answers to the questions asked to him during the examination.

What Kennedy did remember at his ASIC hearing was that there was more than one Brampton. In 1997 or 1998—he couldn't recall when—some 'smart lawyers and accountants in Switzerland' had set up a new entity, which was also called Brampton:

> The two companies are completely different in the—sorry, I withdraw the word companies. I don't know what the actual status of the—the—of the entities are. But I can assure the Commission that the first Brampton has absolutely nothing to do with the second Brampton.

He didn't remember anything about the second Brampton either, except that unlike Brampton 1, he had had some sort of management input into Brampton 2: 'Whether and what the nature of my interest is after '98 I am unclear, but I certainly had an influence over things like its choice of investment managers, etc.'

Kennedy had pioneered the 'Bananas in Pyjamas' approach to Swiss banking. The subtle distinction here is that it was the first Brampton, B1, that might have held Offset Alpine shares. Kennedy had no control or knowledge of B1 and when he told the ASC in 1995 that he knew nothing about Offset Alpine shares he was telling the truth. Kennedy did know something about B2, but that second entity had no connection with Offset Alpine. As Kennedy's lawyer Tony Hartnell pointed out, that meant that ASIC was not allowed to ask anything about B2, because it was Kennedy's private business and was unconnected with the terms of the ASIC investigation into the Offset Alpine affair.

Kennedy was already on record talking about his Swiss bank accounts. Like Rivkin he had been called into the Zurich district attorney's office, fronting up on 11 March 2002. Assistant DA Bruno Stochli questioned Kennedy about an account he had opened with another Swiss bank, Maerki Baumann, on 11 March 1997. Kennedy said both he and his wife Christina held signing rights over the Maerki Baumann account, as did a Swiss banker called Hans Rudi Moser. Kennedy held a stake in a small invest-ment bank in Basel run by Moser, who was a regular investor in Australian speculative mining companies with Kennedy.

None of this was out of the ordinary. What brought Kennedy to the DA's attention was that, on 7 July 1997, Ernst Imfeld trans-ferred US$500 000 into Kennedy's Maerki Baumann account. The money came from a Leumi account that wasn't supposed to exist. Imfeld operated the secret account as a slush fund for his dodgy deals. So why was Imfeld sending money to Kennedy? Kennedy said he thought the money was from Rivkin, but he couldn't remember why. 'I engaged in many transactions of this magnitude, mainly in Australia, with a group of my associates,' he wrote to the DA. 'It was not unusual for us to lend each other money or to have part or all of the loan and/or interest paid offshore.'

Rivkin denied any link to the money, though there was a matching payment between two of his Leumi accounts on the same day. Kennedy sued Bank Leumi in 2002 after the bank tried to reclaim the US$500 000—ultimately Kennedy got his money. ASIC raised the matter with Kennedy after the *Australian Finan-cial Review* published his correspondence in October 2003. Kennedy said: 'I have a recollection of writing a letter to the Swiss authorities.'

Did he write these words?

'I may have. I have no clear recollection of writing those words.'

ASIC asked: 'Were you or any person, company, entity, struc-ture, trust, partnership associated with yourself, connected with Bank Maerki Baumann as at July or August 1997?'

'Privilege. I cannot attest to the date, but I believe the new entity, the new Brampton, had an association with Bank Maerki Baumann,' Kennedy replied.

This was the heart of the Bananas in Pyjamas defence. Kennedy had no role in B1 and couldn't remember anything about it to help ASIC. He did have some sort of role in B2—but B2 had nothing to do with Offset Alpine, so ASIC wasn't allowed to ask about it. Such a defence stands or falls on the timing. But Kennedy's Bramptons seemed to overlap. The Maerki Baumann account, which he did have control over, was opened on 11 March 1997. On Kennedy's account, B2 must have been set up before then. He described for ASIC how he came to set up the second Brampton: 'Following a fraud at EBC where money was stolen from the—the—the entity, or misused or defrauded, or whatever, I had Swiss lawyers examine how I might get them to try and ensure that this didn't happen further.'

In 2002, Kennedy told Stochli in Zurich: 'I was a client of Bank August Roth when Mr Alexander Fundulus defrauded my account about three years ago, a substantial amount of which I was unable to recover.'

In 2000, Fundulus was convicted for embezzling client funds. The embezzlement, which began in early 1997, was uncovered in the northern summer of 1998. Thus the embezzlement which Kennedy told ASIC had led him to set up B2 had not been detected by the time he opened the Maerki Baumann account. If the embezzlement was what convinced Kennedy to set up the second Brampton, the earliest date you would expect him to be doing it would be late 1998. Kennedy's comment to Stochli suggests an even later date.

In February 1999, Benno Hafner opened a new account at Bank Leumi. It was a Scottish partnership operating out of the same adjoining addresses in Regent Street, London, as Rivkin's two other Leumi accounts, with its forms filled out in the same handwriting. The general partner was listed as Crabtree Enterprises Ltd. But the most significant fact was the date. Edsaco had set the partnership up in 1994 under the name Gazella Enterprises & Co. On 21 January 1999, the name was changed from Gazella to Brampton International & Co. This appears to mark the start of the second Brampton. It suggests that until this point, B2 didn't exist.

What does that mean for the Maerki Baumann account opened in 1997, which Kennedy claimed was owned by the second Brampton? In his interview with Stochli, Kennedy referred to the account as 'my money' and claimed that he and Christina had signing rights over it. But if Brampton International didn't exist as a name until 1999, it suggests that Maerki Baumann was Brampton 1, and Kennedy's role in it was more active than he admitted. Kennedy's lawyers declined to comment on the issue and it is not clear what his position on this has been with ASIC.

Kennedy has not commented publicly about Rivkin's claim that Kennedy owned Offset Alpine shares. In mid-2004 he wrote to me via his public relations agent. 'As you know, I am the subject of an ASIC investigation which has received extraordinary and dispro-portionate media coverage in which I have been unfairly vilified,' he said. He had at the time begun legal proceedings against the regulators which had themselves 'led to further unfair and derogatory media coverage of me and my affairs'. With these legal cases continuing, he said:

> I have been advised that it would be improper and inappropriate for me to comment publicly, let alone to do so in the form of the question-and-answer scenario you contemplate, or to expand on what I have said. In addition, I do not intend to answer any ques-tions from the media on an ad hoc basis, particularly when they have no factual basis supporting them or contain assumptions or inferences which are simply wrong.

Back in 1997, such concerns seemed a world away. This was the golden summer of the Sydney networks. Five years before, everyone had been stony broke. Now it was payday for everybody. It had begun with the US Ozemail float in May. On 10 October, St George launched a takeover bid for Advance Bank. Robert Whyte sold out with a profit of more than $62 million (including his earlier sales). His old friend Rene Rivkin had a little happiness as well, spending $649 000 on Advance Bank shares and options in the three days before the bid was announced. Two weeks later he had cashed out for a $200 000 profit. Whyte made it clear he had not discussed the bid with Rivkin. Whyte and John Singleton were about to sell shares in the Ten Network, which they had bought in 1992. Ultimately they walked away with $133 million profit between them, but by early 1998 strains had appeared in their friendship.

John Desmond Singleton is a one-man variety show. He plays front man, straight man, funny man, audience, ticket seller and the fat lady singing, all in the one conversation. Gerry Harvey only makes him worse. I met them together in 2003, when Harvey arranged to meet for an interview in Singleton's office after a board meeting of their Magic Millions horse auction business. Harvey had set up an elaborate practical joke on me with the receptionist. Then Harvey couldn't come out because Singo had hidden his shoes. When Harvey did come out, Singo came out behind him to grab him, because Harvey had pinched Singo's wallet. Oh these guys.

Singleton cultivates laid-back relationships with sharp-edged humour as a lubricant. With Robert Whyte, for example: 'When I think of Robert Whyte, I think of a lifestyle of which I'm very jealous: one of basically cigar smoke, conversation, golf and massive amounts of delegation.' Shortly after April 1994, when he turned fifty, Whyte had announced he was taking a twelve-month sabbatical to study comparative religions at Oxford University. It was either that or international relations—and really, what's to tell the difference? He came back slimmed down and with a shorter haircut. Whyte's relations with Rivkin were a little distant by 1996, but he was as close as ever to Kerry Packer, with whom he had endless wagers on card games and golf. One story has Whyte and Packer bogged down in a bunker on the back nine of the Australian course. God created sandtraps to separate male golfers from their money. 'I'll bet you $10 000 that you can't get down in two,' Packer said. Whyte proceeded to do just that, chipping his ball out of the bunker on to the green, then holing out with his second shot. Packer wasn't happy. 'I'll bet you $10 000 you can't do it again,' he growled. It's the sort of thing that makes comparative religion seem attractive.

When Singleton was looking to sell out of Ten, it was late 1996. On 10 October, the day St George announced the Advance takeover, Singleton told his fellow shareholders he was ready to sell at $13 a share. Izzy Asper, the head of CanWest Global Communications Corp, was the obvious buyer, but he was offering only $11.40. However, by 8 November, Singleton had had his way and was paid out for $59 million. Two weeks later Whyte and Jack Cowin put their Ten shares on the market at $15 a share. The Canadians said the price was outrageous, but Whyte also got his money. He had already sold a third of his stake in 1994 and the sale of the rest to CanWest brought his total profit from his four-year investment in Ten to $74 million. If you added together his returns from Ten, Advance Bank, and Manboom's billboard business, Whyte had made more than $200 million. As an investor, he was in a league of his own.

Singleton and Whyte had sold the same number of shares to CanWest, but Whyte had got $10 million more from the higher price. Had Singleton discussed his plans to sell his Ten shares with Whyte? Neither of the two men commented on the deal. Whatever the reason, there seemed a growing coolness between them. When Andrew Griffin, Whyte's long-time property chief, resigned in April 1997, he showed up a week later working for Singleton.

In June 1997, Whyte set up a new company, which would later be renamed Manboom 2, as a vehicle for his investments with Kerry Packer but not with Singleton. In the meantime, the main Manboom partnership with all three men continued, albeit a little subdued. There were no reports of high jinks at the Manboom board meetings—directors hiding each other's shoes or stealing each other's wallets or that kind of merry jape. But then Robert Whyte was never a shoe-hiding kind of guy. It's hard to imagine him even in slippers.

It was still a triumph, a triumph upon triumph, as the pre-Boomers cashed out. Offset Alpine, Ozemail, Advance Bank, Ten and Manboom generated more than half a billion dollars profit for these refugees from the 1980s. They were Masters of the Universe again. They were back. And so was another nightmare from the 1980s called Jodee Rich.

SEVENTEEN

Death by Double Bay
1998–2000

Sydney is a wonderfully forgiving town. In the early weeks of 1998, Brent Potts, that finely attuned reader of Sydney society, began to pick up signals that the city was ready to embrace once more that bad boy of the 1980s, John David Rich. Jodee Rich has always presented as some sort of bizarre accident from the overheated Bellevue Hill gene pool. In a suburb renowned for its freakiness, Rich's family stands out as truly weird. From his mother Gayl, who split her time between a spiritual advisory business selling chakra crystals and sitting on the board of a key operating subsidiary of Jodee's software company, to his sister, who held her nude wedding ceremony in the family swimming pool, the Rich clan has always been a group that screamed out: Made In The Eastern Suburbs. Jodee Rich is the quintessential creature of the network—after his spectacular personal failure in his twenties, he fashioned in his thirties a multi-billion-dollar phone company based largely on illusion. Rich's achievement was the signature deal for Sydney society at the close of the twentieth century. He managed what countless others had tried and failed. He latched on to the biggest honey pots in the country—James Packer and Lachlan Murdoch—and relieved them of close to a billion dollars. In hindsight, it was so simple.

Jodee Rich has a charm zone of about half a metre. Beyond that range, he's a gawky, geeky marketing type with receding hair and chinos. In the zone, he turns his body in to you, *mano a mano*, and he becomes the most compelling figure you have ever come across. It is intoxicating. All he needs is proximity. And that's what he gets from the network. He has been part of it since his Cranbrook days, when he launched a business renting fish tanks. His Cranbrook classmates included Rodney Adler and his Monaco friend, Paul Brown. James Packer was eight years behind—his school friends included John Ryan, Ben Tilley and Chris Hancock—but he knew Rodney and Jodee as part of the network. Later Jodee would marry Maxine Brenner, whose cousin was married to Robert Whyte. Maxine's brother Phillip once dated Gretel Packer.

The Richheimers had been cigar makers in Germany when the Nazis came to power. Jodee's father, Steven Rich, was just five when his father, Hugo, moved the family to London in 1933. During the Blitz they moved to New York. They also changed their name in their travels. Steven came to Australia in 1953 to run the local arm of the family company, Hunter Douglas, which produced window blinds. He was thirty-seven when he was appointed chairman of the Australia–New Guinea Corporation; then in 1968 he founded the Traveland International group, which he sold to Sir Peter Abeles at Ansett Airlines in 1986.

After the fish tanks, Jodee started a financial software business in 1979 with Rodney Adler while both were at university. 'Even then Jodee [then 20] wanted to do things in a big way,' Rodney Adler told *Business Review Weekly*'s Sandy Plunkett in 1991. 'He is extremely driven and highly intelligent, and he wanted to go for it.' Rodney had bowed out by 1981, when Rich relaunched the business as Imagineering with $20 000 of Jodee's savings and an $80 000 family loan. After four years and another $500 000 of family funds and bank loans guaranteed by the family, Rich floated Imagineering, and he was a millionaire. Two years later he was worth $85 million.

Rich tapped his father's contacts for his three heavyweight Imagineering directors—the late Kevin Kirby AO (ACI International, Wormald International, Barclays Bank), Dr Brian Scott (ACI, ANZ Bank) and McDonalds chief Peter Ritchie. But the group's key operating subsidiary, Imagineering Australia, was still controlled directly by the Rich family. Its board comprised Jodee Rich, his father, his mother, his sister (Nicolet Long) and two executive directors. While Steven Rich denied any day-to-day role in the company, geographically they could not have been closer. Jodee and Maxine lived in a house next to Steven and Gayl in Bulkara Road, Bellevue Hill, while Nicolet and her husband lived in a cottage in her parents' grounds. By December 1989, Imagineering Australia had assets of $64 million and liabilities of $88 million, which must have made for a lot of colourful family conversation.

'Jodee's vision built Imagineering, and he deserves credit for that,' Adler said in 1991. 'But when the economy went bad, perhaps his experience didn't balance his gall and vision.' There is a less charitable interpretation. By 1989, as the economy hit the wall, Imagineering's management structure had collapsed. Jodee Rich persuaded Hong Kong firm First Pacific to invest $27 million. Instead of using the money to save the company, Rich immediately funnelled a third of it to shareholders. The chief beneficiary was himself. Imagineering had to keep rewriting its accounts as more and more undisclosed losses appeared and eventually First Pacific discovered its investment was worth very little—though First Pacific later was able to rebuild the business.

This was the Jodee Rich modus operandi. He burnt fund managers and investors across the country. By early 1991, he was taking an extended overseas vacation—*BRW* caught up with him while he was heli-skiing in Canada. In Sydney the lesson was clear: he was never going to do business in this town again. This principled stand lasted as long as three years, but life moves on. Jodee Rich had too many friends, too many contacts and too many good ideas to ignore. So, in March 1995, just as ASX was tracking Rivkin's Swiss share trades and the Wood Royal Commission was limbering up, Rich found himself back in business again.

It was a modest effort. Jodee Rich reached an agreement with Bob Mansfield at Optus to resell telephone time. One.Tel was a marginal business, where the profits would come from a subsidy Optus paid for every mobile phone handset that was sold. Optus invested \$750 000. Rich put in \$1.3 million in time and money. His old Cranbrook classmate, Rodney Adler at FAI, plonked down \$950 000. Rich brought in some of his old Imagineering alumni—Brad Keeling as co-chief executive and company secretary Kevin Beck. Several former staff of One.Tel's auditor, BDO Nelson Parkhill, were on the payroll, including the former Imagineering audit partner, who now worked privately for the family.

It all went like a bomb as the handset subsidy turned One.Tel into a money spinner. There was one rule—no one mentioned Imagineering. When outsiders did, they were greeted with sorrow rather than anger. 'It gets thrown in his face all the time,' John Greaves told me mournfully in 1999. Greaves was the Optus finance director, who went on to work for Fairfax before becoming One.Tel chairman. The Imagineering comparison was so unfair, said Greaves: 'You go forward, you learn from your experiences, and don't look back.'

Rich and Keeling racked up extraordinary growth. But One.Tel was never really about what anyone did. It was about the people they knew. Rodney Adler would claim credit for the whole affair, from the seed money to Rich's introduction to James Packer. 'I actually introduced James Packer to the investment, six to nine months after Jodee and Brad first started it,' he said in December 1998.

Packer saw it a little differently when he was questioned by the One.Tel receiver in 2002: 'I was in what could be loosely described as a business partnership with a gentleman by the name of Theo Onisforou. We decided—or came to a view—that telephony reselling was a potential opportunity.'

Onisforou and Packer were in business with Adler on a number of fronts, from property to burglar alarms. In 1994, Adler had convinced James to invest $200 000 to buy 19 per cent of a Sydney business called Ness Security Products, which made burglar alarms that were sold door to door by Brad Cooper's Home Security International. A year later, Adler's school friend Paul Brown, who was now helping John Elliott's old mate Richard Weisener run his Alliance Investments in Monaco, bought out the Packer interest through a company in the British Virgin Islands. With all these convivial exchanges, it's not hard to imagine Adler having a little word to Packer and Onisforou about his old mate Jodee.

But in a network the shortest distance between two points is never the shortest path. According to James Packer, in his testimony to the One.Tel receiver in 2002, it all began with an accidental meeting with Bob Mansfield. 'I remember running into him at an airport one day and asking him what he thought the best way for me to explore the opportunity [in telephony reselling] would be,' Packer said. Mansfield told him, 'You should go and speak to Jodee Rich.' Packer testified:

> Clearly Jodee Rich had been involved with Imagineering, and that had been a bad outcome for people involved in that company, but I completely and fully believed, as he assured me on a regular basis, that he had learnt all of his lessons from that experience and that he was never going to let anything like that happen again.

When did Rich say this?

'I can't recall the exact date, but probably a hundred times, in different conversations,' Packer testified. While he could not recall when he first spoke to Rich about Imagineering, he thought it was 'at a guess, 1998'.

If Packer's date is right, he had been in the Rich charm zone nearly two years by then without the subject of Imagineering coming up. On 16 May 1996, Packer's company Dorigad invested

$500 000 in One.Tel. Within fifteen months Dorigad received $558 000 in dividends. That was the pattern. Every time Packer advanced money to One.Tel he received a spectacular return. Every time Jodee Rich asked Packer to trust him, it turned out well—and Packer was prepared to invest a little bit more money. In August 1997, after receiving its second One.Tel dividend, Dorigad put another $5 million into One.Tel at $1.50 a share. Two months later, Rich floated One.Tel at $2. Packer's investment was now worth $16.6 million. It would get a lot better.

A year earlier, Optus had sold out of One.Tel for $4 million. It also made a one-off payment to end the handset subsidy. One.Tel spread the payment over several years in its accounts, so that it looked like it still had an ongoing, viable business. Most of the 1997 profit came from chasing up bad debts from the previous year. Underneath it all, One.Tel was a dubious investment proposition. The public float involved selling just 500 000 shares to raise $1 million. It didn't matter where the shares went—One.Tel just needed five hundred individual shareholders to call itself a public listed company. The largest holding outside the four founders was 9000 shares. Brent Potts's family held twelve separate parcels— presumably to get the numbers up—though he makes it clear he had nothing to do with the float. With another 103 million shares held by Rich, FAI and Dorigad, One.Tel was now valued at $206 million. The net tangible assets came to $5 million. The rest of the valuation was high hopes and eastern suburbs networking.

The turnover of One.Tel shares was minuscule. The key to One.Tel's fortunes was that almost all the shares were locked up in escrow. Only a little more than two million of its shares could be traded. Half of the tradable shares were owned by FAI director Peter O'Connell, who had been paid in shares for his consulting working in One.Tel two years before (O'Connell's shares were not in escrow as he no longer had ties with the company). The effect of the tight One.Tel share registry was that any increase in the daily turnover and share price was multiplied by one hundred in the value of the total company. One. Tel was now primed for a spectacular rise. But in the early months of 1998, the network had found something else to talk about.

The year had ended well. On Christmas Eve 1997, Malcolm Turnbull, the new head of Goldman Sachs Australia, dropped by to see Rodney Adler. He was full of ideas for FAI deals, which by early January had become a plan for Goldman to fund a management buyout for either FAI Insurances, or FAI Life. Adler was receptive. Turnbull called the plan Operation Firelight.

On 10 December, the Australian Tax Office had released $2.87 million to Rene Rivkin's Stilton account as the settlement for the last of the frozen Offset Alpine funds. Rivkin's lawyers challenged the payout and on 24 December, while Turnbull was bending Adler's ear, the ATO was shelling out another $205 000 to Stilton. In the end, the ATO had settled for 20 cents in the dollar, a compromise between the 10 per cent retaining tax for foreign companies and the 35 per cent Australian company tax. The tax bill was $5 million for the Leumi and EBC accounts, leaving Rivkin, Richardson and Kennedy with $21 million.

Rivkin was ready to draw the curtain on the Offset Alpine saga. On 26 January, Ernst Imfeld closed Rene Rivkin's Stilton account and transferred the funds to 8405, Walter Rivkin's old account. Benno Hafner now contacted the obliging fellows at Edsaco to buy another Scottish partnership, World International Constructors & Co. The general partner was Storrington Services Limited, another offshore entity. On 6 February, Rivkin opened an account for World International at Bank Leumi and days later Imfeld transferred 8405 (which now held the Offset money that had come from Stilton) into World. Rene now had no live Swiss accounts that could link him to Offset Alpine. He had covered his tracks just three days before controversy erupted again.

On Monday 9 February, the NSW Senior Deputy State Coroner, John Abernethy, reopened the inquest into the death of Caroline Byrne three years before. He had held a preliminary hearing in November 1997, now the full story emerged. Gordon Wood was the star witness, appearing in white shirt and slacks to describe again the spiritual communication that had led him to The Gap on the fatal night, and his job driving Rivkin and Graham Richardson to and from lunch earlier in the day, when other witnesses put him at The Gap. Abernethy returned an open verdict on 13 February, finding that Byrne either jumped, slipped or was pushed from the top of the cliff on the night of 7 June 1995. He described Wood's testimony as 'bizarre', with a number of 'glaring inconsistencies'. At the same time, he noted that Wood kept to his version of events in a lengthy record of interview with police. 'Much of what Wood said has been independently corroborated by others,' he said. The 'most telling inconsistency' was the evidence of the two restaurateurs who gave 'convincing evidence' that they saw Byrne with Wood at The Gap at various times during Wednesday afternoon, as well as a green Bentley. 'It would be totally against the weight of evidence not to accept that evidence of identification,' Abernethy said.

At that point I had never heard of Caroline Byrne. But the reports of Wood driving Rivkin and Richardson—two of the chief suspects over the Offset Alpine Swiss shares—led me to re-examine the Offset court file. There in the appeal documents was a transcript of Rivkin's Section 19 examination by the ASC's Peter Riordan—and the date. It was the first sign that there had been two parallel investigations involving Wood's actions in the first week of May 1995. Neither Peter Riordan's investigators at the ASC nor the police team knew of each other's existence. The timing coincidence was revealed in an article in the *Weekend Australian Financial Review* titled, 'It's a Bad Business', a week after

Abernethy's finding. My story reported that Byrne had died the day after Wood and Rivkin had been questioned by the ASC over a $40 million slush fund that was suspected to be linked to politicians. The article did not suggest Rivkin or anyone else was linked to Caroline's death but suggested the Offset saga could have affected Caroline's state of mind. It had to be at least considered as a factor in the events leading up to her fall from the cliff. With the cause of her death uncertain, the article argued the ASC investigation 'may have contributed to her depression'.

Four days later, Ben Hills at the *Sydney Morning Herald* revealed Detective Sergeant Brian Wyver's questioning of Wood in 1996, over whether he had had a gay affair with Rivkin. Hills canvassed several theories about her death, including the possibility that she had been murdered by a contract killer because of what she knew about a financial deal. A week later, Paul Barry interviewed Gordon Wood on Channel Seven's 'Witness' program. Barry raised the homosexual query by Wyver and asked Wood if he had killed Caroline. Wood strenuously denied both matters.

The story had all the elements for compulsive cafe conversation: the mysterious death of a beautiful model; an alibi involving two celebrity names; a $53 million insurance payout from a factory fire; and $26 million in shares in a black box in Zurich. No one who knew Rivkin could really think he was involved in Byrne's death. But gossip could make connections that never had to be proven. Rivkin sued the *SMH* and Channel Seven over the homosexual allegations and the murder theory; and the *AFR* for imputations that he was involved in Byrnes' death, that the Offset Alpine affair had damaged his reputation, and that the ASC suspected he was involved in something dodgy at Offset Alpine. Rivkin's damages claim was Death by the Eastern Suburbs. You couldn't really understand what Rivkin had endured, his lawyers argued, unless you knew the Sydney social scene.

'It's cafe tittle-tattle—for years this city has been bedevilled by rumours about prominent people . . . all of which have been found to be false,' Rivkin's counsel, Bruce McClintock SC, told the Supreme Court when arguing for aggravated damages in the Seven case four years later.

Trevor Kennedy also weighed in: 'Everyone who knows the eastern suburbs of Sydney knows it is a constant maelstrom of gossip, and something like this, with someone as high-profile as Rene, tends to get booted about quite widely.'

Former state government minister Michael Yabsley testified to a 'substantial whispering campaign' against Rivkin, which included innuendo that 'Mr Rivkin was seeking the company of young boys around town.'

'It was just appalling for us to deal with that,' Gayle Rivkin later told *Australian Story*. She testified in the Seven case how she had confronted a group of strangers in a Double Bay cafe gossiping about her husband: 'I approached the man and told him who I was. He was very uncomfortable—he said everyone saw the 'Witness' program, and I said, "You shouldn't repeat things unless you know they're true."'

The only kind words for the eastern suburbs came from Acting Justice Gerald Cripps. In May 2002, he awarded Rivkin $150 000 damages against Seven on the homosexuality allegation (juries had earlier rejected claims that the *AFR*, *SMH* and Seven linked Rivkin with Byrne's murder) but threw out the argument that 'people who live in the eastern suburbs are more prone to absorb salacious gossip and translate imputations' than for someone who 'happened to live in, say, Bankstown'.

'I can't tell you how awful it's been,' Rivkin told Radio 2UE later that day. He felt the damages award was woefully inadequate.

In February 1998, however, with such vindication four years away, Rivkin was forced to take matters into his own hands. On 21 February, the day the story broke in the *AFR*, he attacked Caroline Byrne's character in interviews he gave with journalists for the Sunday papers. Caroline was 'not a little angel', he told *Sun-Herald* business editor David Potts. Caroline had been having an affair with someone else at the time of her death, he claimed. But Rivkin declined to name the man involved. The *AFR* story was 'fairy tales', 'just inaccurate' and 'the most convoluted connection between the death of a girl and a share trade you could imagine'. There was 'more than meets the eye' in the case, 'but that doesn't make [Wood] a killer'.

Rivkin told Ros Reines in a longer interview for the *Sunday Telegraph* that he could barely recall the sequence of events on the day Byrne died. 'Can you remember where you had lunch three years ago?' he said. He then gave a detailed description of Wood's attempts to contact him through that night, his conversation with him at breakfast in Bondi after Byrne's body had been recovered ('He did not tell me anything about a psychic connection with her—which is why he knew to look at The Gap') and his decision six months later to sack him: 'He had the loan of the [Macleay Street] apartment—he couldn't service the mortgage because he spent all of his salary funding his lifestyle. He kept hassling me for money although I helped him make money off the stock market, I had given him a gold watch and a second-hand Suzuki Vitara worth about $18 000. In the end I got sick of the constant demands.'

Rivkin didn't approach the police to tell them any of this— though one might equally say that the police did not ask him about it. Wyver had approached Rivkin briefly at Joe's Cafe in 1996, but Rivkin brushed him aside. No formal approach was made. When the police did interview Rivkin in August 2000, two years later, he had a different view of events. He told *60 Minutes* in June 2001 that he now thought that Wood had been on the clifftop with Caroline. 'My gut feeling is that he was there but he didn't do it,' Rivkin said. 'They might have been strolling, they might have had an argument and she might have jumped to her death.'

For Caroline Byrne's family, Rivkin's claims in the *Sun-Herald* seem incomprehensible. There was never any evidence that Caroline was having an affair and police quickly dismissed the suggestion. For Tony Byrne, who would spend more than a decade working tirelessly to discover what happened to his daughter, Rivkin's claim to have information about events surrounding her death and his failure to volunteer this immediately to police is hard to excuse. It was particularly unfortunate that Rivkin was not able to shed light on the one key area that might have helped the investigation—whether Wood had been driving Rivkin and Richardson to lunch that day. When police interviewed the two men in August 2001, Richardson said that he had not been to lunch with Rivkin on the day Byrne died. According to Richardson's diary, he had been having lunch that day with Peter Moore, the head of the Canterbury Bulldogs. 'Diaries can be wrong, but I believe I lunched with Peter, and I think it is unlikely I was driven to Alife's by Gordon Wood, as he stated on that day,' Richardson said.

He had not realised this before because 'I did not think to look in my diary. I didn't until the police asked me [in 2000],' Richardson said. He didn't believe it was important where Wood was at lunch time, because Caroline Byrne had not died until that evening. As Rivkin told *60 Minutes*, even if Wood was with Caroline that night, it didn't mean that he killed her. The police rescue team had raised doubts about whether Caroline could have jumped from the cliff, but in 1998 this critical point remained far from clear. If she *had* been thrown, then the bizarre elements in Wood's story, and his claim that he was driving Rivkin and Richardson to and from lunch when he was seen at The Gap, all made Wood the prime suspect in her murder.

There was another way that Rivkin could have helped police. If Caroline died in a crime of passion involving Wood, as police came to believe, then the details of Wood's trip to Zurich with Rivkin, Rivkin's link to the Leumi shares, and any promises made to Wood, would seem to be critical information for the investigation. Police were struggling to build a picture of the relationship between Wood and Caroline—what was going through Gordon

Wood's mind at that time. The Swiss money link and the personal stress it caused is an important factor in building that picture. Whether in the final analysis it was relevant or not, this seems to be information that the police needed to know.

Rivkin and Richardson were under no obligation to consult their diaries or to approach police with whatever they knew or suspected. They didn't believe that Wood was guilty, and saw no need to be part of any attempt to build a case against him. There was nothing improper or illegal about this. Richardson knew nothing about the case; however, there seems precious little moral virtue in Rivkin's silence. In hindsight it looks self-serving, at a time when Rivkin had much to lose if Wood ended up facing charges over Caroline's death. If Rivkin told police the background of Wood's financial worries and about his own Swiss interests, he could end up facing a perjury charge over his false evidence to the ASC in 1995. Rivkin was in similar danger if Wood ever revealed the identity of the secret Offset Alpine shareholders. There is no evidence that Rivkin's actions were motivated by anything other than his belief in Gordon Wood's innocence. That, though, doesn't stop Tony Byrne from agonising over why Rivkin did so little to shed light on his daughter's death.

A lot of other people in Sydney could have filled the police in about Rivkin's Swiss links. In the 1980s, Axel Fundulus had operated many EBC accounts for Australian businessmen, including Rivkin clients. Others knew about Rivkin's Bank Leumi holdings. When the secret EBC and Leumi accounts came to light in 1995, there can have been little doubt among the Swiss banking set that Rivkin was involved. Double Bay cafes were alive with speculation about Rivkin's Zurich link and Wood's indirect involvement in it. But when it came to providing the police or the ASC with information, the network was entirely silent. Frankly, how could anyone tell the authorities about Rivkin without exposing their own financial dealings? Their whole way of life was based upon secrecy, hidden channels and rewards for insiders.

And what was wrong with that? For the tax avoiders, Swiss banking had always been a victimless crime. Now, no one could be so sure. Their silence spoke volumes. One could find many names for such moral equivalence. But one would never mistake it for decency.

~~~

Seven's program about Wood had prompted a new witness to approach police. Irish artist John Doherty had seen a blonde woman, who he believed was Byrne, on the night she died arguing loudly with a tall blond man in a leather jacket on Military Road at The Gap. The man was shouting at the blonde woman, who was weeping, while a second shorter man with dark hair stood in the shadows nearby, he said. Police interviewed Doherty on 9 April. Gordon Wood had left the country the day before. *Sun-Herald* journalist Jamie Fawcett, who had befriended Wood, gave him a lift to the airport where he boarded Qantas flight QF11, flying out at 1.55 p.m. bound for Los Angeles on the way to Barbados. Wood told him that, with all the media pressure, he needed to get away for a while. He spent the next months bouncing around the Caribbean and Europe from a base in Florida.

'He said he'd made a bundle of money acting in a TV commercial, spent $6000 on [a Brietling] watch and used the rest of the money to have an extended holiday in Florida and Cuba,' said an executive who later worked with Wood in Britain.

'He mentioned that he had a place in Cuba,' another former colleague said. 'He would go to Florida—he had friends there. He had a pad in Havana.'

There had been no television commercial. Wood sold the Suzuki Vitara before he left. He was paid $20 000 for the Channel Seven interview. NSW police also investigated allegations that

Wood had misappropriated cheques for more than $50 000 from Rivkin, but no evidence was found. The strangest account came from Ernst Imfeld, who later testified that he thought Wood was paid US$25 000 out of the Laira account. On 26 January, the day that Rivkin closed his Stilton account and transferred the balance to his father's old 8405 account, Imfeld transferred US$25 000 ($41 500) to an account in Florida. He told Zurich District Attorney Nathan Landshut that the money went to pay for work done on Imfeld's holiday home there, as a repayment for an earlier advance Imfeld had made:

> I had sent some money to somebody on the instructions from Herr Rivkin. My memory tells me I must have given this amount in cash, and no signature for a cash drawdown was available. Rene, you instructed me to hand over this sum to a person, who would come past where I was. But I had no right to sign for it. I would have advanced this person the money from my own pocket. And for this reason, this transaction appears to be a balancing item. That person may be Gordon Wood.

Rivkin, who was present during this exchange, strenuously denied ever paying money to Wood.

'Where should I know Gordon Wood from?' said Imfeld.

'Because I was with him in Zurich, but I never gave you the instruction to give him US$25 000,' Rivkin replied.

On 30 April, the coroner, Abernethy, briefed the Homicide and Violent Serial Offenders Agency to reopen the Byrne investigation in what became Task Force Irondale headed by Detective Senior Sergeant Paul Jacob. Abernethy had marked the Byrne case closed after the inquest on 13 April. His new referral cited media coverage as one of the principal reasons for further investigation.

Wood's sudden departure had thrown Rivkin's property plans into disarray. On 9 April, George Freris signed papers for The Highflying Company Pty Ltd, an apartment project he was developing with Rivkin in the inner west. The day before, Joe Elcham had lodged a development application for 186 Victoria Street, the building next to Joe's Cafe, which now houses the fashionable Jimmy Liks restaurant. Rivkin had bought the site two years before and had registered in Gordon Wood's name an accompanying liquor licence that lasted through to 3 a.m. What Elcham didn't know was that while he was submitting the DA on 8 April, Wood was boarding his Qantas flight for the US. On 20 April, Rivkin as property owner moved to compulsorily transfer the liquor licence to Elcham. But a *BRW* article by Ali Cromie about Elcham's previous probity problems at Star City prompted the Licensing Enforcement Agency to interview the applicant licensee about his own activities and his relationship to Rivkin. Rivkin hired a barrister, Anthony Whealy QC, to sort out the licence problem.

Five years later Rivkin would run into Whealy once more. This time the former silk was a Supreme Court judge, who would sentence Rivkin for insider trading. Rivkin's lawyers would argue unsuccessfully in the Court of Appeal that Whealy could have been biased—that what Whealy learned while working for Rivkin might have reflected on Rivkin's character and credibility.

Back in 1998, the pressure was taking its toll. 'I have a minor manic depression so I'm on Prozac every day,' Rivkin told Elle McFeast in May. 'I've lost 13.5 kilograms in the last two months.' He said he had been taking an extra Prozac tablet each night. By this time he was self-medicating.

His secret life had become even stranger, for while Rivkin was saying nothing to police in Australia, he was doing the exact opposite in Switzerland. In the northern summer of 1998, EBC Zurich was gripped by controversy when Axel Fundulus's embezzlement was discovered. Fundulus was convicted two years later when the case came to trial, but Swiss court records offer no detail on how the scam worked, how much clients lost or even what Fundulus was charged with. In fact it was Rivkin who blew the whistle on Fundulus. In mid-1998, while Rivkin's liquor licencing problems unfolded in Sydney, he approached Zurich police to report some irregularities in his EBC Zurich account. He had noticed some Canadian shares there that he hadn't ordered. An investigation revealed that this was just the tip of the iceberg. Scores of clients lost substantial sums, including Rivkin, Kennedy and Brent Potts.

When bad things happen in the offshore world, few people can share your pain. In this hour of need Ernst Imfeld offered a sympathetic ear. Potts already had a Leumi account through a Liechtenstein trust company called Remgus Establishment, but like Rivkin he had used EBC for much of his share trading. Imfeld suggested he move the remaining EBC funds over to Leumi. 'Mr Imfeld assured me that something like this could never happen at Bank Leumi, that no bank officer would carry out unauthorised transactions,' Potts later told DA Landshut.

It was such a cunning stroke. Imfeld had been embezzling from Potts's account since 1991, as part of his wild reshufflings between client accounts to produce the profits that he was so famous for, and to hide the mounting losses. Now Potts was entrusting him with more money. Imfeld won a lot of grateful new clients as he helped to clear up the EBC mess—and in the process he ended up with an even larger pool of money to steal from. His activities over the next three years would feature deception upon deception, dwarfing Fundulus's more modest efforts.

The trigger for this new wave of money had been Rivkin's decision to inform on Fundulus. Imfeld had forged a singular relationship with Rene. This had taken a peculiar turn on 6 February, the day Rivkin opened the World International account at Bank Leumi, when Imfeld began a spectacular series of currency trades in Rivkin's portfolio in the Laira account. In the course of twenty-three currency trades in the next four months, over a quarter of a billion US dollars passed through Laira. All but one of the trades was profitable and, when they stopped on 19 June,

Rivkin had been credited with profits of more than $1.5 million. While Rivkin's sharp eye caught the mistake with the unauthorised Canadian shares in his EBC account, he said he never picked up on the currency trades in Laira until they were pointed out in 2002. 'I had no idea until the moment when I first saw them in the accounts,' he told DA Landshut.

Rivkin came out ahead in another deal late in April 1999, when Rivkin needed a quick US$1 million to pay to UK soccer club Manchester United for an Australian tour. With Rivkin's Leumi accounts already overstretched from share purchases, Imfeld took the money out of the account of an unsuspecting Leumi client in Britain. It was never repaid. As Imfeld later put it to Swiss authorities, this was a small favour for a friend—so small that he didn't even tell Rivkin about it. While Imfeld's other clients would lose more than 300 million Swiss francs, Rivkin's account was now at least $3 million ahead.

EIGHTEEN

A tale of two networks

1998–99

The 1998–99 summer saw two network sagas which said every-thing about what Sydney was, and what it was becoming. They were both tales of insiders and secret agreements. While one was about the future, the other represented the past. One was about access, technology, media and sex appeal. It was so 1990s, which is perhaps the biggest reason that it failed. This was One.Tel, the Generation-X debacle. The other deal was insignificant, overcomplicated and irredeemably retro. The Murrin Murrin wheeze worked because that dinosaur Rene Rivkin had stumbled upon the future of marketing. Across Australia the pre-Boomers—refugees from the 1980s, that generation of frantic forty-year-olds who had peaked early and were now pushing sixty—were still firmly in control. In Canberra, the biggest pre-Boomer of them all, John Howard, was looking set for another decade. But the ground was moving.

In early 1998, other stories held the headlines. The BHP board was in meltdown while the AMP Society was struggling through a public float. In April, Goldman Sachs in New York quietly canned the idea of privatising FAI, though Malcolm Turnbull continued to press it. Without Goldman's help, FAI's future was looking very bleak to those who knew the real state of the company's accounts.

In May, Rodney Adler was in the US, meeting Mafia figure Jeffrey Pokross who, unbeknown to Adler, had become an FBI informant.

'He wanted to figure out if I could assist him secretly parking stock in the US so he can get some money and try to drive the [share] price up in Australia to attract a higher takeover bid than apparently he was getting,' Pokross later testified in US court proceedings against an American stockbroker. When questioned about this at the HIH Royal Commission in 2002, Adler denied asking Pokross to manipulate the FAI share price.

Gerard Farley's appeal in the Administrative Appeals Tribunal, against the four-year ban on him from acting as a broker because of the Bendigo Mining affair, was heard in early May. On 22 May, Theo Onisforou resigned from the boards of all Consolidated Press companies, apparently after a row with Kerry Packer. One estimate suggests that Consolidated Press paid Onisforou $20 million to buy him out of his partnerships with James Packer.

Meanwhile, the eastern suburbs were hearing exciting stories about shares in a new local telephone company, which was winning support from canny US investors. On 26 March, One.Tel announced it had placed 7.5 million shares with Coldstream Capital LLC, a Los Angeles-based investment partnership. Brent Potts handled the deal. 'The new issue was initiated and organised by P.G. Intercapital Ltd,' One.Tel said. In a second placement another half a million shares had been issued to institutional investors, the company said. Potts's Bank Leumi records show another story, though Potts says the trading details noted here are incorrect and the conclusions drawn from them are wrong.

According to Bank Leumi records, Potts had begun buying One.Tel shares through his Swiss account in early February. When he organised the Coldstream deal, the secondary placement did not go to institutions as was announced. Instead, 450 000 shares went straight to his Leumi account. His fee for handling Coldstream paid for half of his new shares. The One.Tel stock that Potts now held would soon be worth a fortune. If only he had known. Instead, in August, he began selling out. By October, he had sold more than $1 million of stock. While this provided him with a profit of several hundred thousand dollars, if he had held on for a few months more, he would have walked away with $7 million. It's not clear why Potts began selling in August 1998. It's possible that he was short of funds and needed to liquidate some assets after the discovery of the losses in his EBC Zurich account from Axel Fundulus's embezzlement, which had just come to light.

Or it might have been simply that Potts didn't believe in One.Tel. FAI director Peter O'Connell had sold his shares for $2.6 million in February, while Lachlan Murdoch's next-door neighbour, property developer Philip Wolanski, who had invested more than $350 000, sold out by August. The rollcall of people who might have made a killing in One.Tel makes sad reading. Through much of 1998, the only consistent buyer for One.Tel shares was Rodney Adler. He made the market. FAI spent $3 million buying One.Tel shares between April and October. Adler accounted for two thirds of the turnover in those six months, standing in the market day after day, pushing the share price from $2.22 up to $2.80. The sheer volume of FAI trades in a thin market suggests Adler was manipulating the stock.

Adler's support was critical for One.Tel because in October the founder shareholdings of the company came out of escrow and James Packer faced the decision whether to invest more money or to walk away. The high share price made the decision easy. Packer signed up to a new share agreement, while Rich raised another $10 million in convertible notes from Packer and Westfield's David Lowy.

Jodee Rich had just made his most audacious—and absurd—move yet. The Australian Communications Authority had held an auction of spectrum for mobile phone companies. At the end of the auction, it was left with a ragbag collection of frequencies that no one wanted. On 15 September, Rich bought this spectrum for

$9.49 million. He then announced dramatically that One.Tel would be building its own mobile telephone network.

It was an intoxicating concept and Rich had shown he was a superb marketer. There was no end to what he could achieve with his own network. This was an idea tailor-made for the dotcom boom, and the Murdochs and the Packers would bet a billion dollars on it. However, right from the start, there was a technical problem.

Running a wireless network is a complex business that needs a certain amount of spectrum to handle the traffic. Some channels must be set aside for managing interference, leaving fewer channels for control and subscriber traffic. The bottom line is that running a mobile phone network takes eight to ten megahertz of spectrum and One.Tel didn't have nearly enough. Despite all the hype and bright promises, Rich had bought a tiny sliver of spectrum that was too small to do much with. It was technically impossible to run a telephone network with the 2.5 megahertz of spectrum that he had bought for Sydney. In fact One.Tel was based on an illusion.

As the dotcom boom began, technical concerns took a back seat while the whole tech stock sector, including One.Tel, simply took off. On 14 December, Worldcom bid $530 million for Ozemail. Malcolm Turnbull and Trevor Kennedy would walk away with $59 million apiece and Sean Howard $118 million. Another venture called LibertyOne had part-ownership of an Internet search engine; it turned a $1 investment by its chief executive, Graham Bristow, into a $52 million fortune.

Jodee Rich had now lured James Packer away from his most senior advisors. In 1997, the then Consolidated Press Holdings chief, Brian Powers, had warned James against putting money into One.Tel. Powers' successor, Ashok Jacob, would repeat the warnings, as would Nick Falloon, CEO at Publishing and Broadcasting Ltd.

'Nick Falloon told me to be cautious about everything,' James Packer scoffed later at the One.Tel receiver's hearing. Falloon had expressed negative sentiments about One.Tel management 'just as he expressed at some times negative views about buying Crown Casino'. However, 'at the end of 1999 for example I think he said to me something along the lines of, "James, you were right and I was wrong."'

On 11 December, Packer made his biggest commitment yet to One.Tel, paying $47.3 million for One.Tel shares acquired from FAI and from director John Greaves. One.Tel's share price doubled and Packer was a winner again. The shares in his company Dorigad were now worth $150 million, a profit of $65 million. Packer's judgement was confirmed five days later when US fund manager Gilbert Global Equity Partners, run by George Soros's associate Steven Gilbert, agreed to invest US$30 million in One.Tel (Gilbert was a regular visitor to Sydney, where he sat on the board of Star City Casino with One.Tel shareholders Dick Warburton and Neil Gamble). By the end of December, One.Tel's share price had zoomed to $6.

One.Tel's trajectory was determined by personal relationships between a small group of people. Behind the slick talk, Jodee Rich and his followers really believed in the product. The soap opera they spun off was not a trick. It was a generational debacle: a product of the total disaster zone that characterises the Australian alpha male and his progeny. Jodee Rich may have moved away from the Rich compound on Bulkara Road since the Imagineering days, but the shadow of his father never seemed far off. Jodee's One.Tel shareholding was held through a family trust linked to his parents.

'We [eldest sons] all feel a special pressure to prove ourselves, and Jodee is no exception,' Adler told Sandy Plunkett in 1991. 'He [Rich] didn't do it for any material gain; he grew up in a wealthy family. He admires his father's business skills.' Adler himself would never be free of his father's legacy. James Packer skirted the same issue in a 1994 interview: 'I want to be able to look at my father in ten years' time and say, "I'm proud of you, and you should be proud of me."'

Father–son tensions are standard issue for Australia's richest postcode. Bellevue Hill is awash with Oedipal angst. With the possible exception of the Lowys and the Pratts, Australia's wave of post-World War II fortunes has arguably never seen a successful family succession (the Smorgons would be contenders as well, but only after the third generation split up). It was perhaps only a matter of time before James Packer and Jodee Rich got together with that other victim of an over-achieving father, Lachlan Murdoch. It began with James Packer hosting a dinner for Lachlan at his home on 20 January 1999. The two young heirs had become friends of sorts during the Super League battle in 1995, despite their different styles and interests. At the end of a wide-ranging discussion, Packer raised the potential returns if News Corporation and Publishing and Broadcasting Ltd (PBL) ever got together in a telecommunications venture. Lachlan agreed. Packer then suggested they could do it through One.Tel.

Several days later, Packer called Murdoch and suggested he meet Jodee Rich. The meeting took place during the last days of January at the News Ltd offices in Holt Street, Surry Hills. At some point after that meeting, the 'I' word came up.

'He (Packer) described Imagineering and put his opinion that it was a company that had grown too quickly, which was the cause of its ultimate downfall,' Murdoch said.

A week later Jodee, James, Lachlan and Brad Keeling were in New York putting a proposal to Rupert Murdoch. On Monday 16 February, News and PBL signed off on a $754 million investment in One.Tel. It wasn't just money that Murdoch and Packer were offering—it was also the political muscle to convince the government to release more spectrum for One.Tel.

The Tuesday newspapers ran variations of the same photo op— Jodee and James and Lachlan and Brad arm in arm, three of them beaming varying shades of morose, while Keeling flashed that billion-dollar grin, all of them clinging together like drunken sailors. The shares were at $6.40 when Packer first broached the idea on 20 January, but within days they had risen sharply. The morning after the deal was announced the stock hit $13. Overnight One.Tel had become a $3 billion company, and the Murdoch and Packer interests together were sitting on a $900 million profit. It was another roaring success. This was the deal of the decade, the highwater point of the network, and all Bellevue Hill wanted a piece of it.

Jodee Rich was following the same game plan he had with Imagineering. He had hyped up a marginally viable business to a rich investor. And as with Imagineering, a third of the new cash he raised was paid straight to shareholders as a share buyback, which left the company without enough money to fund its expansion plan. This was payday. Jodee Rich trousered $52 million that year, part of more than $75 million he extracted from One.Tel. James Packer's share of the stock buyback came to $26 million.

There was now a new eastern suburbs parlour game called Who Made Money on One.Tel? By 29 January, poor old Brent Potts had cashed total profits of $737 000 through his Swiss account—too early to make real money. He now held only 25 000 shares, worth $325 000. The One.Tel family connections had done well. As of 3 March 1999, the share register showed that Gayl Rich had two share parcels worth $234 000 at the $13 share price. Her son-in-law, Adam Long, held $221 000 of shares. Maxine Rich's brother, Philip, held $58 000, while Dr Leonard Brenner held an $86 000 stake. Brad Keeling's father, William, held a $104 000 stake, while Ashley Keeling's stake was worth $130 000.

Rodney Adler was one of the biggest winners after he guided One.Tel options, which arguably should have gone to FAI, into his own family trust. Their sale eventually raised $15 million. David Lowy also ended up $15 million ahead from his convertible notes. John Greaves, the One.Tel chairman, raised $3.77 million. Neil Gamble had sold his 40 000 shares. Brad Keeling's old boss at Strathfield Car Radio, Andrew Kelly, had sold a third of his stake, but still held another 20 000 shares worth $260 000.

The lucky winners included plastics manufacturer John Hill, who held shares worth $782 000, Gresham Partners ($650 000), Toorak socialite Dianne Allen ($520 000), Julie Trethowan of the Hyde Park Club ($117 000), Michael Rennie of the McKinsey group ($121 000), Dianne Jagelman ($65 000), James Packer's friend Ben Tilley ($65 000) and Alec Shand QC ($50 000). Other investors included the Sarich family, Andrew Kroger, Bryan Frost, Bruce Corlett and the family of FAI executive Tim Mainprize. Tessa Philips, the mother of Lachlan Murdoch's friend and Ecorp executive Jeremy Philips, held a modest $32 000 parcel.

Like any list, what is most interesting are the names that are not on it. There were no major fund managers. For all the hype and excitement, Jodee Rich had managed to keep 98 per cent of the shares locked up with shareholder agreements. Only a handful of people made serious money from One.Tel. Everyone else had tiny holdings. One.Tel was like a club with a line of people outside who weren't allowed in. Long ago God made Sydney restaurants to show us there is nothing so appealing as exclusivity. By June 1999, Theo Onisforou's company Angreb had amassed a $3.6 million stake. But the windfall profits were over.

By late 1998, the different threads of the network were falling over each other. Adler had gone to New York in July to lobby Goldman Sachs to save Operation Firelight, but on Thursday 3 September, Goldman Sachs formally canned the deal. An internal memo at Goldman in Sydney after certain assumptions put FAI's net tangible assets at only $20 million. (Goldman executives told the HIH Royal Commission that this was an opinion held by one executive which was not generally circulated.) Turnbull told Adlerthe deal was off the following Tuesday. While it was well disguised, FAI was next to insolvent. Adler was fighting with his board over a deal to pay $25 million for a Sydney fire alarm manufacturer, Ness Systems. It was owned by Adler's former school friend Paul Brown, who had paid $781 000 for his stake four years before via the British Virgin Islands. The FAI board minutes, later tabled in the HIH Royal Commission, show that chairman John Landerer openly doubted Adler's claim that he was not connected with Brown. With the last hope of a Goldman Sachs rescue dashed, Adler began takeover talks with Ray Williams at HIH Insurance. On 23 September, Adler sold half his family stake on-market at 75 cents a share to HIH, which announced a $300 million takeover bid for FAI.

A week before the bid, Brent Potts was having lunch in the south of France with Robert Pittorino, the former head of broking house County NatWest, when he was phoned by Ernst Imfeld at Bank Leumi. Imfeld placed an order to buy FAI shares. The conversation was detailed in a formal referral that ASX Surveillance made to ASIC two weeks later, quoting Potts. Leumi had been buying GIO Insurance 'for some months' and Imfeld was buying FAI in the expectation that it would be taken over as part of industry rationalisation, Potts told Jim Berry at Surveillance on 28 September. 'Adler had been rumoured as a seller for ten years, but always wanted too much, even $1.50,' Potts continued. Pittorino had also ordered some FAI shares, he said, and there was some buying by Cantrade Private Bank, Switzerland.

If Potts really said all this, he was pulling Berry's leg. P.G. Intercapital did buy FAI shares for Leumi on 17 September, but they went straight to Potts's Remgus account. He sold them on 29 September—the day after he talked to Berry—and booked a $54 000 profit. The GIO buying that Potts mentioned was also for himself. Remgus sold into the AMP takeover bid for GIO in January 1999 for a $158 000 profit.

Rivkin had lunch with Adler the day before the FAI bid, along with Gary Gray, the ALP national campaign director, and Labor senators John Faulkner and Bob McMullan. After lunch the subject turned to FAI's future plans. Rivkin bought FAI shares that day for his son Jordan and his company Tarfaya Nominee. The next day, before the bid was announced, Rivkin bought 200 000 FAI shares through his World account at Leumi, which he sold three weeks later for a modest $16 000 profit. The day after the FAI bid was announced he made a superb judgment call to buy FAI Life shares through Zurich. This was Rivkin at his best—realising before anyone else did that if FAI was facing a takeover then FAI Life was also in play and notching up a quick $86 000 profit.

That kind of shrewd trade was more like the Rene of old. In fact, while the rest of the world was delirious over tech stocks, Rivkin was working on an old chestnut of a deal that would have sounded passé in the 1950s. It was the old story—a hole in the ground and lots of paper. Rivkin's finest moment would be his escape act from Abednego Nickel.

It had been a difficult year for Rivkin, what with the scandal of Axel Fundulus's unmasking in Zurich, Joe Elcham's probity problems at Star City Casino and the media coverage of the Caroline Byrne inquest. He later told Andrew Denton that the speculation about him ran so high that at a dinner, where he was to have sat at the prime minister's table, federal police had warned that associating with Rivkin might embarrass the PM. The eastern suburbs had dropped him. Most of his old friends had moved on. He was never part of the One.Tel rush. But Rivkin didn't need the old network links—he had created his own private network with the *Rivkin Report.* In April 1998, it had 1900 subscribers paying $600 a year for Rivkin's weekly views. By June 1999, it was up to 5800. At its peak, Rivkin would claim to have 17 000 subscribers, collectively paying $13 million a year in fees, all drawn by the Rivkin brand name. The most successful thing Rivkin had ever done was himself. He had become a franchise, spinning off a string of ventures from legal services to insurance products based on his name. This was the future of networking. It was now a question of how to squeeze the most money out of it.

In late October, the *Rivkin Report* once again began urging subscribers to buy Abednego Nickel shares 'if you have not already . . . the stock is 82 cents and under takeover by Anaconda at $1.' Andrew Forrest at Anaconda Nickel had launched a takeover bid for Abednego at the start of the month, after circling the company for years. Anaconda had a nickel project in Western Australia called Murrin Murrin. The nickel deposit ran into the lease next door, which was owned by Abednego, which was why Forrest wanted Rivkin's company.

Rivkin was desperate to sell. Abednego was a $5 million dud investment that had sat on his books for almost three years. On 1 October, Anaconda agreed to buy 20 per cent of Abednego from Rivkin and his circle of friends as prelude to a full takeover bid. The sellers included Trevor Kennedy, Joe Elcham, George Freris, Laira Investment Company and Rivkin's former butler, Thomas Mann. Anaconda was offering $1 a share, but only 15 cents of that would be cash. The rest of the payment would be in the form of convertible notes in a subsidiary of Anaconda, which was called Murrin Murrin Investments. The Murrin Murrin notes would be paid out in cash in 2000 and 2001.

This delayed payment did not suit Abednego's other major shareholder, Dominion Mining, which wanted cash upfront for its 20 per cent stake. On 27 October, it sold its shares for 75 cents. It is a measure of Rivkin's desperation that he bought a large portion of the Dominion shares himself, shelling out $3.7 million in Switzerland and Australia. As he shuttled stock back and forth between Sydney and Zurich, his total outlay on Abednego grew to $12 million. Rivkin needed to find buyers for his shares, which is where the *Rivkin Report* became so useful.

Rivkin issued a strong 'Buy' recommendation to his subscribers the day before he did the Dominion deal. He followed it up a week later: 'I strongly urge you not to sell at these levels since you will be delivering the buyer of the stock returns of over 100 per cent over a two-year period. This is one to buy [around 85¢]

and just put away for the next two years, if you do you will end up loving me for it.'

Rivkin's faithful fans—the Mum and Dad investors, the aspirational share traders, the true believers—dutifully bought Abednego shares and later Murrin Murrin notes, while Rivkin sold and sold and sold. By July 2000, $12.6 million had flown through Rivkin's World account. It was showing a $1 million profit.

Amid all the excitement, Graham Richardson was taking a European holiday. On Friday 11 December, he slipped into Bank Leumi's London office with his old friend Peter Barron. Barron presented his passport (Number E510–4496) and withdrew $30 000 from the Laira account. Barron later told the *Australian* that it was a gift from Richardson. Laira's records show that a month before, Richardson had transferred $30 000 from Portfolio 2 (Richardson's sub-account called Cheshire) to Portfolio 1, which held Rivkin's money. This way, Richardson could claim that the payment from Laira was actually a loan from Rivkin.

Life was good for Richo. On 16 December, Anaconda raised the cash component of its Abednego bid from 15 cents to 40 cents. The Abednego board, which included Rivkin, Barron and chairman Bruce Corlett, unanimously recommended the revised bid. The cash payout for Laira's 3.8 million Abednego shares had just gone up by $1 million.

Richardson's route onward from London was marked by a series of bank transfers and withdrawals—in Spain at the end of December, then Zermatt in Switzerland on New Year's Eve (Corlett was skiing across the Austrian border in Zürs am Arlberg, staying at the luxurious Thurnhers Alpenhof). On Friday 8 January, Richardson slipped down Claridenstrasse in Zurich to knock on the armoured glass doors of Bank Leumi. Ernst Imfeld, charming as ever, helped Richardson fill in the forms for four withdrawals from Portfolio 2 totalling $41 540. Leumi's records state: 'Cash withdrawal, client signed the receipt.' Despite all his precautions, Richardson had now signed his name to the Cheshire account he wasn't supposed to own.

A week later, Richardson was back at Bank Leumi in London, showing his passport (Number L5264526) to withdraw US$3355. Richardson didn't know it, but he was now only a taxi ride away from an old acquaintance, that inveterate networker Gordon Wood.

The Gordon Wood saga just refused to die away. On 25 October, as Nigel Littlewood was writing his recommendation to buy Abednego shares in the *Rivkin Report*, Jamie Fawcett in the *Sun-Herald* reported a sensational new development in the Caroline Byrne murder investigation. The coroner had made a suppression order in relation to new evidence that Fawcett had given to police about another witness in the Caroline Byrne case now in hiding abroad. The witness's mother expressed fears for her safety. 'My child doesn't want to go over The Gap too,' the mother said.

Interpol records show that Wood took a plane flight the next day, 26 October. It is believed he flew from Florida to London. Once there, Wood experienced a stunning transformation in his fortunes. A mystery figure had arranged a new life for him. Wood, at thirty-six years of age, had no professional qualifications and little training beyond his stint looking after Rivkin's cars in the mid-1990s—in fact, he had never worked in an office. Yet within days of his arrival in Britain, Wood's unknown benefactor had arranged a $400 000 a year job for him, and a fictitious work history to match.

Wood's advancement was due to a Welsh-born investigating accountant called Glyn Harris. Harris worked for BP in the 1980s as vice president corporate finance at BP Finance International, then went on to become finance director for Man Financial, a major commodities broker, fund manager and later discount broker. By 1993, he was a director of Graig Shipping and managing director of Europe Energy Group before it was taken over. By the mid-1990s, Harris was on the NatWest panel of corporate turnaround specialists. In late 1998, NatWest called him to fix a management buyout that had run into problems.

For fifty years, PressTech Controls had provided technical expertise for publishers around the world who required high-calibration printing—for example, in printing bank notes, securities and lotto forms. NatWest Bank had part-funded a £9.2 million ($24 million) management buyout in 1996, but the Asian economic crisis and the surging British pound had decimated the value of PressTech's foreign contracts. The venture capital partners, 3i Group and Barclays Private Investors, wrote off their £4.2 million investment and NatWest called for a corporate doctor.

It was a part-time job for Harris, who would delegate the day-to-day work. He knew just the man for the job . . . which is how Harris came to be introducing Gordon Wood to NatWest Bank and PressTech management. He told them that Wood was a senior financial controller and an experienced turnaround expert. Harris knew how good Wood was, he said, because he had worked with him previously.

Six years later, Harris conceded that this was not true. He had invented Wood's work history. In reality, he said, he engineered Wood's appointment after someone recommended Wood to him. But Harris refused to say who the recommendation came from. A former NatWest executive said:

Gordon Wood was someone not known to NatWest at all, but we had 100 per cent faith in Glyn Harris. He was described to us as a financial controller who had worked in a number of turnaround situations in the past. That's how Glyn introduced Gordon to us. There's no doubt about that. Gordon was introduced to us as someone who had worked with him before.

Wood told colleagues that he lived with Harris and his wife in their Hertfordshire house when he first arrived in Britain. At Harris's urging, Wood's appointment was written into his contract with NatWest. The bank restructuring agreement for PressTech explicitly stated: 'Gordon Wood shall be employed for three months at £500 a day.' None of Wood's workmates at PressTech questioned his qualifications.

Chris Male, the outgoing executive chairman of PressTech, who in ten years had doubled the firm's sales, said Harris described Wood as an 'excellent chap', 'excellent on collecting debts' and 'dealing with debtors and creditors'; 'Harris said he'd worked with [Wood] in a turnaround situation before.' Male said that Harris had been given a mandate that allowed him to employ whoever he wanted. 'I know that Glyn had been involved in some venture in Australia in the mid-90s . . . I believe he did have some project in Australia,' he said.

When asked about Gordon Wood in late 2004, Harris told me, 'I really have no comment, it was really a very long time ago,' before hanging up the phone. In a subsequent call he made a brief response to written questions about why he employed Wood.

'He was recommended to us by someone who knew him, who had nothing to do with Australia,' Harris said.

Who recommended Wood?

'I could tell you, but he would not want to be pestered by you. I'm aware of the people who recommended him and they had nothing to do with Australia or NatWest.'

So why did he tell PressTech and NatWest executives that he had worked with Wood previously, and that Wood was an experienced financial controller?

'I think that's probably as far as we'd like to go. As you know we have been pestered by reporters and so forth over this affair. There are no further comments to make,' he said, and hung up again.

PART SIX

A change of cutlery

Qu'à la minceur des épeluchures, on voit la grandeur des nations.

It is the thinness of the potato slices that defines the greatness of a nation.

Jacques Brel

NINETEEN

To dine for

On a balmy day in the Sydney autumn, a decent interval after elevenses, Hyde Park offers welcome relief for weary city dwellers. A century ago, wise city planners conceived the park around an avenue of overarching trees, a canopy of green under which the traffic hum of the city would be hushed to a murmur. Under the boughs of the soaring Moreton Bay figs there is peace and solace for jaded city nerves. True, it is not a very large park. One might call it compact. And later city planners' decision to split the park in two by running William Street, the major route to the eastern suburbs, slap through the middle has made it that little bit more compact. That's all right. There's nothing wrong with compact, or small, or dwarfish. Admittedly, the traffic noise on four sides is a little more intrusive than the original city planners envisaged, so it is important, as you wander down the shaded walk that leads to the Archibald Fountain along with several hundred others, to fix clearly in your mind how tranquil and relaxing you are finding the sylvan setting. And it will be so.

If you amble north, say from Kerry Packer's headquarters in Park Street, the gentle whisper of wind in the trees—and it is important to ignore *completely* some of the other noises—will usher you gently towards the Archibald Fountain. From there, it is a simple stretch across College Street, past St Mary's Cathedral and on to the lush, grassy slopes of the Domain. Past the Art Gallery of New South Wales on your left as you descend to Sir John Young Crescent, then you merely work your way through a screen of laneways and houses. And there you are, on the waterfront: primed, dangerous, and ready for a whole lot of lunching.

Not that any of the power-lunching crowd actually walks to Woolloomooloo. They prefer to arrive by various combinations of yacht, motorised launch, ship's tender, water taxi, seaplane or helicopter; by Roller, Ferrari, Aston, company car, limousine, hire car, cab, Harley-Davidson, or private vehicles of lesser pedigree. There is no ugly talk of public transport.

The outlook on the waterfront, once you get there, is non-descript. Overwhelming tiny Woolloomooloo Bay, with the Naval Dockyards on the right, and the Botanic Gardens on the left, stands the monstrous Finger Wharf. At three hundred metres it is the city's longest edifice of unfinished wood, a class of construction known to architects as rude timber. (It is listed in Sydney's Rude Building Index.) It is the Rude Finger Wharf. This is the spot where Anzacs piled on to the transport ships in 1915; where Australian troops, heading off to World War II, Korea and later Vietnam, waved goodbye to their loved ones. It's a national treasure. Inevitably this meant that in Sydney, in the early 1990s, it became ground zero for the vigorous discussions between the city's great and good over who should be entrusted with the sacred task of developing the exciting commercial potential of this priceless piece of the past. When the smoke cleared in 1994, after almost a decade of wrangling—involving community groups, politicians from the prime minister down, endless planning authorities and some nifty elbow work among the lobbyists—property developer Lang Walker emerged from the scrum with a piece of paper that made him king of the boardwalk.

Sydney loves its own. The city lives and breathes around a harbour that is a property developer's dream—from the bleak cliffs of the Heads to the nooks and crannies of Pittwater; from Watsons Bay through Vaucluse to the 'low swampy land' (as referred to in early Admiralty charts) that is now trendy Double Bay; from Sydney Cove and the city up into the reaches of the Parramatta River. When the weather is fine, the harbour is a glistening jewel, and now and then the city's favourite sons are entrusted with historic parts of it, highlights on that larger gem. Like John Roberts at Multiplex taking up the mantle to save Luna Park—we know the future of the historic fun park is *completely safe*. Or Franco Belgiorno-Nettis and Paul Salteri, slugging out the bitterest of corporate divorces after four decades running the Transfield group—they divvied up almost everything but hung on to their joint half-share in the Harbour Tunnel. It's a sentimental touch—two former friends who now can't stand each other, bound together by a hole in the ground—that and the $77 million in dividends they and their partner Kumugai Gumi took out of the Tunnel company in 2003 and 2004.

Above the jewel runs that other fabulous money stream, from which Paul Cave's company, Ottto Holdings, extracts $32 million a year by allowing Sydneysiders (and, of course, tourists) to walk over their own Harbour Bridge. An eighth of that money goes to the state government to help with the paintwork, according to the company's 2004 accounts. Half the revenue ends up as pre-tax profit. It's a wonderful tribute to private enterprise, the way in which Cave, then an unknown entrepreneur and after years of trying, finally persuaded the state government in 1998 to give his company an operating lease on the bridge. One of the more colourful public service tales that does the rounds is that the government was so concerned about liability claims from falling climbers it set up a hybrid lease arrangement that in effect transferred ownership of the bridge to Ottto for twenty-five years, then immediately leased it back again so the trains could still run across it. But that can't be right. Selling the Harbour Bridge would be like subdividing Luna Park.

Business in Sydney is personal. So when Lang Walker won the redevelopment rights for the Woolloomooloo Finger Wharf, you knew he would leave his own style all over it. Walker is a one-off. The four decades since he began work with his father's earth-moving business have shown that you can take the boy out of the bulldozer, but you can't take the bulldozer out of the boy. Walker understands that when it comes to being a billionaire there are no short cuts. He maintains five yachts—any less would smack of meanness. He has the obligatory mutiple residences around the world. And he does a bit of flying. It's said that Walker celebrated his wife Suzanne's fiftieth birthday by 'buying her' a corporate jet. It's not the sort of thing he would talk about, but it does look as if birthday presents at chez Walker are a little more substantial than just another Nana Mouskouri CD. Check the paper trail: in 1994, three days before Suzanne Walker turned forty-eight, Walker's companies were filing documents to buy a Beechjet 400A, to replace the former plane, a Grumman; two years later, three days before Suzanne turned fifty, the Beechjet was replaced by a Hawker 800XP, registration VH-LAW; then in 2003, five days before Suzanne's birthday again, Wells Fargo Bank bought a Falcon 900C in Sao Paolo for the Walkers. As a male gesture, surprising the little woman every other birthday with a private jet with your initials painted all over it really is in a league of its own. Another birthday, another chapter in aviation. Of course it may be that these were all corporate purchases and the aircraft had nothing to do with Mrs Walker. But then that's the point about giving electric drills to the missus as well.

This is a long way from the Finger Wharf. Back in 1994, Walker had been cogitating over the possibilities at Wool-loomooloo and decided he needed to make the rude Finger Wharf a little ruder still, by adding another thirty metres to its tip to allow for the penthouse apartments that would eventually house himself, radio announcer John Laws and film star Russell Crowe. Walker filled the rest of the wharf with minor apartments and a

W hotel, then threw in a handful of restaurants. Which is why the Finger Wharf is famous today.

Restaurants are everywhere in Sydney. They cluster most densely less than fifty metres above the highwater mark around the harbour, like barnacles on the hull of a great sea beast (which is what the harbour resembles when the weather turns grey). Every decade or so a recession leaves Sydney hard up and the hull is scraped clean as restaurateurs by the hundreds go out of business. But they come back. It's a Sydney thing. Paris has romance. New York is the place for parties. Melbourne is absolutely marvellous for gangland killings. Adelaide has cornered the market for wine and bizarre serial killers. Brisbane has an enviable record for producing political wackos. Sydney has the lunch trade.

Decades ago, the Sydney psyche figured there was more to life than money and sex. There was also food. You can understand much that is otherwise incomprehensible about Sydney's culture by replacing the word *love*, wherever it appears, with the word *lunch*. As in, all we need is lunch. Lunch is a many splendoured thing. That lunch is all we know, is all we know of lunch. There is a culinary philosophy for every occasion: lunch of my life; my long-lost lunch; he lunched not wisely but too well. Lunch's labours lost. My lunch it is a red, red rosé.

Graham Richardson, that wizened servant of the city, put the lure of political power into perspective, by comparing it with the draw of the dining room. He said his first taste of political power in the Hawke Labor Government in the 1980s was 'better than sex and almost as exciting as a good feed'.

By the end of the 1990s, however, a strange thing had happened to Sydney's restaurants. In June 2003, David Dale wrote in the *Sydney Morning Herald* about the way that Otto Ristorante on the Finger Wharf (which is nothing to do with Ottto Holdings, the bridge-walkers' outfit with three t's) had come to have a social and celebrity cachet akin to Romano's and Beppi's, the killer restaurants of the 1950s and '60s. Four decades ago, one lunched at Romano's on Wednesdays to be seen, to be photographed, to fill the social space. But in the 1970s and '80s a plethora of new eating places sprang up. Every tribe in Sydney had its favoured waterhole, with half a dozen superior establishments frequented by the A-list of Sydney socialites. Dale argued that by the end of the 1990s, this diaspora had reversed: '. . . in 1999, all the tribes seemed to coalesce at Otto, on the newly developed Finger Wharf . . . You can see them there most Fridays, table-hopping and boldly lingering till 3.30 p.m.' According to Dale's rough census, Otto was now the only place to be seen. Sydney still had many fine eating places, despite Dale's references to the 'gastronomic bleakness' and 'alarming moderation' of the new century. But in an age of unmatched choice and variation, the social range was back where it was in the '50s.

The amusing aspect of this was that Maurizio Terzini, the man who had transformed Sydney's eating protocols from his post on the Finger Wharf, had come from Melbourne. Not that there's anything wrong with that. Terzini had run Caffe e Cucina and Il Bacaro on the Yarra before coming to his senses in 1999 and heading north. 'Sydney was a dream come true for me, I love this city,' he confided. By early 2004, Terzini had moved on to open Icebergs at Bondi, but he remained a consultant at Wool-loomooloo. It was Terzini's influence that filled Otto chockful of ambience, transformed it into a Sydney institution. Walker had been one of his original backers along with a group of investors headed by Neil Wild and James Burkitt. By the time John Laws bought into it two years later, the Finger Wharf had been established as A-list territory. For the very rich and the very indebted, for actors, television presenters, fashion designers, ageing cultural icons and social lions, for bright young things, property developers, upmarket flaks, merchant bankers, celebrity doctors and socialite psychiatrists, organisers of charity balls, sports heroes of the moment, international celebrities, major music acts, reality television identities and soap stars, Otto was the place to be seen. This, after all, is the age of appearances.

Something more was going on here, though, than just a change of restaurant. To look at Otto is to confront a deeper question of what has happened to Sydney, and to Australia. Where did the parties and the lunches, the diversity and confidence, the wild times and blithe spirits of the 1980s go? How did the twenty-first century get to be so straitlaced and dull? How did the zeitgeist for a new millennium get to be so boring? More simply, when did the 1990s turn out to be such a bad idea? Part of the answer is a survival story.

There was the generational thing going on. John Winston Howard had become the number one ticketholder for the pre-Boomers. He represented that cohort of Australians who were born just before or during World War II, who came into their prime in the late 1970s. Almost thirty years later, Howard, like the rest of them, was still clinging to power, shrugging off the lightweight challenges by the Baby Boomers. Mark Latham, Peter Costello and the rest of the generation that followed Howard had yet to lay a glove on him. But globalisation was also changing Australia.

The pressure of globalisation and the tyranny of the market had been ratcheting its way through every part of Australian culture. The 1990s had been a story of failing resistance. In place of the entrepreneurs of the 1980s, corporate power had accumulated around a new breed of institutions—the Macquarie Banks, the fund managers and the rocket scientists in the infrastructure bonds set. This is what was so threatening for Sydney, a town that had always been run by and for insiders. It still was. But increasingly now it was a different kind of insider. Rene Rivkin, Trevor Kennedy and Graham Richardson had put together some remarkable deals. They ended the 1990s wealthy, powerful and successful. But their power was waning. Few could have seen how dramatically their fortunes would change. But their story was only a chapter in a wider saga, the fall of the old network . . . and the end of the long lunchers.

TWENTY

Many unhappy discoveries

2001

Ernst Imfeld had warned Brent Potts many times of the danger of discovery from using his Bank Leumi credit card. It was quite alarming then when the card suddenly stopped working. It was 10 January 2001, and he was settling the hotel bill at a Colorado ski resort when the concierge began making those embarrassed gestures that mean your card has been rejected. Potts immediately called Leumi in Switzerland and asked to speak to Imfeld. He was told that was impossible because Imfeld didn't work there any more.

'I said, "What do you mean he doesn't work for the bank any more? I talked to him three weeks ago,"' Brent later told the Zurich District Attorney's office. It was pure Hitchcock: The Banker Vanishes. Imfeld had gone and no one would tell him why. 'I was told that one can't say anything about it,' Potts said. 'I wanted to know what happened, and a Mr Wolman called and said that he couldn't give me any further information, but that he would arrange that I would be able to use my credit card again.'

This call was so much worse than Potts was expecting, beginning with the moment that Potts asked for the balance of his Leumi account. 'He told me that Portfolio 1 . . . contained $10 million and that portfolio 2 was $7 million in deficit. I asked,

"What is this Portfolio 2?" and was informed that Portfolio 2 was my "trading account".'

Potts said he had never heard of any trading account. When he was up $10 million from trading Australian shares, why would he allow Imfeld to run a foreign exchange and US portfolio that frittered it all away?

> Do you really believe that I would tolerate that my portfolio traded normally and showed real profits, while a portfolio allegedly under Mr Imfeld (where I had given him full power of attorney, which is absolutely absurd) accumulated million of dollars of losses over the years? You would have to have me committed . . . That just doesn't make sense.

The Swiss audit firm Beret later calculated for Potts that he had lost $9 million through Portfolio 2 since 1991. In the previous year alone, Imfeld had run $35 million in foreign exchange trading through the account, losing $500 000. The position was so dire that the previous October Leumi had issued a $1.3 million margin call on the Parkes account, via Potts's lawyer Benno Hafner, before Imfeld fudged it. Potts hadn't heard about that either.

The avalanche that buried Ernst Imfeld was triggered by a telephone call from Munich a week before Potts's unhappy adventure après ski. The head of a German film distribution company called the Leumi office in Zurich on Thursday 4 January to check his account. Imfeld was on vacation at his house in Florida, so the call was put through to the head of Bank Leumi (Switzerland), Meir Grosz, who read off the cash balance as US$1.8 million. The client said the balance was supposed to be US$6 million. That would be because of the US$4.2 million losses from currency trading and the share portfolio, Grosz told him. What currency trading and what share portfolio, the client asked. The account was just supposed to hold cash. The questions uncovered a string of unauthorised transactions by Imfeld, which in turn revealed a mountain of other unauthorised transactions in other accounts, and a lot of missing money. Leumi called Imfeld in Florida for an explanation. Imfeld gave the answer Leumi least wanted to hear, that he had been trading without authorisation from clients. He insisted he had made no personal gain from it, but the increasingly desperate shuffling of accounts to cover up his huge losses had exhausted Imfeld. If anything, he seemed relieved to be discovered. In Florida he broke open the champagne.

In Zurich Meir Grosz was facing a catastrophe. Imfeld was a legend at the bank. Leumi's Swiss operation had been built on his investing prowess. Listening to Imfeld 'analyse and dissect the state of the global marketplace was like hearing the prophecies of Jeremiah, Isaiah and Ezekiel all at once in a span of twenty minutes,' the *Jerusalem Post* wrote in 1998. At the time, Grosz had agreed: 'He is always right.'

Shraga Elam, a Zurich-based Israeli journalist, broke the story on 17 January. Leumi confirmed that it had 'recently identified a number of customer accounts in which it suspects unauthorised transactions ...' But it was a small, local affair, a spokesman insisted. 'He embezzled about 21.9 million Swiss francs [then about $24.8 million],' Bank Leumi's head of marketing and strategic development in Israel, Jona Fogel, told me in late February 2001. 'Mr Imfeld will get, I hope, what he deserves.' However the investigation soon led to International Investments NV, a Netherlands Antilles-based subsidiary of Bank Leumi, which announced that auditors were checking a small number of accounts totalling 180 million Swiss francs ($206 million) 'to clarify whether damage was actually caused to any of these accounts'. A year later, total losses would reach 300 million Swiss francs.

A PriceWaterhouseCoopers report on 31 January focused on Imfeld's money laundering, where money was switched between accounts to hide money movements from tax authorities. In a section headed, 'Allegations of EI (Imfeld) with respect to money laundering and incorrect Form A's', the PriceWaterhouseCoopers report said Imfeld had said he falsified the names of account holders on the Form A documents:

> He indicated that he had three clients who had a surplus of cash (in the US, the UK and Australia), as well as clients who had a need for cash in these countries. EI stated that he would arrange for the surplus of cash from respective customers to be delivered to the client in need, and would then have the transaction recorded in the respective client accounts at the Bank ('clearing').

None of this was clear on Thursday 4 January when the embezzlement was discovered.

Imfeld flew back to Zurich and was assisting the bank as a frantic investigation continued through the weekend. The immediate issue was how much money was missing, and who at Bank Leumi had been helping Imfeld. It was in this scene of total confusion at 11 o'clock on Monday morning, 7 January, that the world's happiest Swiss investor, Graham Richardson, ambled along the icy Claridenstrasse and knocked on the Leumi door. He had an appointment to see Herr Imfeld.

When he eventually got past the armoured glass entry, Leumi staff photocopied Richardson's driver's licence before he was allowed to see Grosz and Imfeld's secretary, Cahide Ay. Richardson explained that he owned Portfolio 2, Cheshire, in the Laira account. But there was no paperwork to show it. According to handwritten notes in the Laira file, Richardson 'was here in January and spoke to Ay and Grosz who were also surprised'. Three months before, Richardson had been in the international limelight as mayor of the Olympic Village in Sydney. Now no one would admit they knew him. There was good reason for this reticence. The failure to identify the beneficial owners of Laira in the Form A was a serious offence, and anyone who acknowledged knowing that Richardson was linked to the account risked criminal prosecution. The bank itself could face sanctions.

Richardson made a second visit to Claridenstrasse on 10 April. A handwritten note in the bank files records what he told Leumi staff:

> I deposited a check [sic] three years ago. Rivkin had authority on the account. Rivkin was trading shares. I knew this.
> Check for 1.4 million AUD. Bank check.
> No deposits—only withdrawals.
> 340 K out plus cash received from Rivkin (matching).
> I visited 3–4 times with Imfeld. I think last time Jan '99.
> Rivkin will know about the transfers and deposits.
> Please check transactions with Rivkin—I rely on him.

In an email written later that day, Leumi's portfolio manager, Orlando Alessandro, said that Richardson had identified himself explicitly as the beneficial owner of Portfolio 2, Cheshire, of Laira. Benno Hafner claimed not to have heard of Richardson's interest before that morning. On 17 April, he signed a Form A for Laira showing Rivkin as the beneficial owner for the account and for Richardson for the Cheshire and Junior sub-accounts. In 2004, Richardson said he had not authorised Zurich lawyer Benno Hafner to name him as an owner of the account and said withdrawals he had made from the account were loans from Rivkin.

Imfeld had been sacked on Friday 5 January. On Tuesday 9 January, the day after Richardson's visit, he went to the Zurich police and turned himself in. He admitted making unauthorised transactions but insisted that he received no personal gain. By Wednesday, Potts was wanting to know what had happened to his credit card. In Australia, Rene Rivkin was organising a panic trip to Zurich, accompanied by George Freris. Only two weeks before, Hafner had closed Rivkin's World account and transferred the funds to two new sub-accounts within Laira, called Junior and Senior. Hafner made an appointment for Rivkin to see Grosz at 11 a.m. on Monday 15 January. Early on the Monday morning,

Rivkin and Freris met Imfeld in Hafner's first-floor office in Genferstrasse, around the corner from Leumi, 'to find what the devil has gone on', as Rivkin later put it. Imfeld was 'very distraught' but he told Rivkin he had made more money for him than he had lost. Imfeld gave Rivkin the pragmatic line that bankers have been giving unhappy clients since time immemorial. 'It's the way it is,' he told his old friend.

In Australia, the great deals of the 1990s were now collapsing. One.Tel, HIH Insurance and its newly acquired subsidiary FAI were all teetering on collapse. On 21 September 1999, I wrote a story detailing the way that One.Tel had covered up $48 million in operating losses by changing its accounting policy three times in twelve months. In a court examination three years later, Michael Slattery QC revealed that the *Australian Financial Review* story was the trigger for an ASIC investigation into One.Tel's accounts.

The accounts were Jodee Rich's Achilles heel. Despite the profits that One.Tel had been reporting, in reality its business was haemorrhaging money well before Rich struck his deal with James Packer and Lachlan Murdoch in February 1999. The terms of that deal had made it vital that One.Tel continued to report healthy profits. On paper the total News and PBL investment came to a massive $754 million, but One.Tel ended up with only $174 million of this in cash. News and PBL would pay for some of their shares by providing advertising while the share buyback would consume another $105 million (more than half of which went to Rich). The bulk of the investment, however, was in the form of share options that News and PBL did not have to exercise for another two years, and then only if they wanted to. While One.Tel was burning through cash, Jodee Rich needed to keep reporting good news to keep the share price high, to ensure News and PBL would come through with the money from the options. Rich's juggling act became harder as a result of the ASIC investigation, which forced One.Tel to write off $190 million in 'deferred expenses' in 2000 for the previous two years. While One.Tel denied that its accounting approach was illegal, disciplinary action against the auditor who signed the accounts cost him his audit licence in 2002.

Jodee Rich had a more basic problem: he couldn't deliver what he had promised. One.Tel did not have the spectrum that it needed to run the mobile telephone network that had been the core of Rich's sales pitch since 1998. On 9 June 1999, the communications minister, Richard Alston, came to the rescue with an announcement that the government would auction off more telephone spectrum. Three weeks later, Rich made his bravest decision yet, signing a $1.1 billion contract with American technology giant Lucent to build and set up a mobile network. Rich signed the deal and construction began even though One.Tel still did not yet have the spectrum to run the network on. This made it absolutely imperative, when the auction for the new Australian spectrum began in early 2000, that One.Tel emerged a winner. It meant that, no matter how high the price went, One.Tel had to get spectrum.

To the market's surprise, One.Tel faced fierce competition in the auction. In their worst nightmares, analysts had feared that One.Tel would have to pay up to $200 million for its Australian frequencies. By the time the bidding closed, One.Tel had been forced to pay $523 million to secure its spectrum. One.Tel raised the funds to pay for this from News and PBL, which pumped in more money by cashing their share options, and from a $340 million share placement to fund managers. The placement was organised by Brent Potts, who quietly bought $3 million of stock for himself through his Swiss account.

One.Tel's focus now switched to Britain where it was bidding for one of the licences for the third generation of mobile phones, known as 3G. In November 1999, News Corporation had invested another $200 million in One.Tel to back Rich's UK plans. The sums involved were staggering. On 6 April 2000, One.Tel bid £2.2 billion for one of the slices of spectrum on offer. If the bid had succeeded, the total cost for the UK licence and for building the network would have been $14 billion—and One.Tel had found backers willing to advance this enormous sum. One.Tel's shares were running hot. The share price peaked at $2.80 (the shares had been split in ten after the buyback, which made this the equivalent of $28 for the original stock) and James Packer and PBL were sitting on a $1.35 billion profit. It was Jodee Rich's best and worst moment—he had completed the transformation from social pariah to trusted entrepreneur, with arguably more money in his credit line in the UK than any Australian in history. Yet all the high hopes came to nothing.

Stiff bidding pushed the licence prices in the UK auction even higher, way beyond One.Tel's reach. Their UK strategy was a complete failure and One.Tel's fortunes turned. Tech stocks crashed in April and One.Tel's share price dropped sharply. It continued a slow decline until September, when the tougher accounting policy that the ASIC investigation had forced upon One.Tel kicked in, forcing the company to report a $173 million write-off that pushed total losses to $291 million. Shocked investors were outraged to learn that, on top of this, Rich and Keeling had helped themselves to $15 million in bonuses. These events had probably crushed any real prospect that Rich could turn the situation around. He was stuck. Within months One.Tel would run out of money. With his share price spiralling downwards Rich no longer had the credibility to ask Packer and Murdoch for more funds—or even to admit that he needed them.

'We have told the market we don't need any more funds,' Rich told Murdoch and Packer in May 2001 when he was finally admitting to them he had money problems. 'If we say we are planning a capital raising, we will be crucified.'

Across town, HIH was in its death throes with a similar tale of mismanagement and woe. It had been covering up its liquidity problems with dodgy reinsurance policies. In addition, it had discovered that FAI was worth at least $300 million less than Ray Williams had paid for it. Yet not everyone was losing.

In March 2001, the Manboom trio—Kerry Packer, Robert Whyte and John Singleton—sold some of Paul Makucha's former properties to the Ten Network for $125 million. The parcels Manboom still held were reported to be worth another $75 million. In February 1999, MCI completed its Ozemail takeover, paying out $236 million to Sean Howard, Trevor Kennedy and Malcolm Turnbull.

While Sydney loves a winner, it keeps a special place in its heart for those who keep their winnings tax-effective. So it was a magical moment in June 1999 when Kennedy, that fine Catholic boy, got involved with religion. But then, the film business has always been a leap of faith. Kennedy and Sean Howard invested $41.7 million in a biblical epic, 'Noah's Ark', a two-part mini-series filmed in Victoria that ran on the American NBC network in April 1999. This was the version of 'Noah's Ark' where Noah and his family, the last humans alive, were attacked by pirates. Noah survived—only to be attacked by critics. 'Noah's Ark an Unholy Mess' was how the *New York Daily News* began its review. Then there was 'Noah a Ship of Fools' (*New York Post*), 'Boat Don't Float' (*Chicago Sun Times*), 'The Wackiest Ship in the Bible' (*Dallas Morning News*) and the more pithy headline in the *Deseret News* in Utah, 'Just say Noah'. But the ratings were respectable. On 30 June Kennedy and Howard invested almost a quarter of their share of the Ozemail payout to buy the foreign residuals for the mini-series. It looks like Malcolm Turnbull planned to join them—on the same day the other two made their move, Turnbull acquired a company he briefly renamed Grace Productions—but he changed his mind. It was an inspired decision. Kennedy saved $4.4 million in tax from the film deal in the next two years. Howard's investment was twice as large. But the irreligious types at the Australian Tax Office challenged the claim and, in 2004, Kennedy's Golden Words group had to pay all the tax saving back. Noah never had it so tough.

On 15 March 2001, HIH went into liquidation. Two months later the Packers and the Murdochs lost patience with the miracle turn-around that Rich and Keeling had been promising and dumped them from the One.Tel board. The same day, 17 May, the two families announced an emergency $135 million share issue that News and PBL would underwrite. Eleven days later the PBL–News team pulled the plug. 'We were misled,' James Packer said after Ferrier Hodgson was appointed liquidator to One.Tel on Monday 28 May and a fuller picture of One.Tel's dire financial condition finally emerged. The following Friday morning, ASIC raided Jodee Rich's home after he had begun transferring assets into his wife's name.

Just thirteen months before, Rich had been king of the world. Now he greeted ASIC and federal police officers at the gate of his Vaucluse mansion in his bathrobe. ASIC also raided the One.Tel offices . . . again. They had been doing it on a semi-regular basis since an insider trader investigation in early 1999. Later that year there was the investigation into the One.Tel accounts. In October 2000, there had been some awkwardness over One.Tel stock-broker briefings. Now the traffic between ASIC and the One.Tel office became a shuttle service. With that sort of workload, it was a mercy that an enlightened One.Tel management had previously installed an in-house coffee bar. It helped ASIC officers restore their flagging energy levels and created a certain ambience when they were able to begin interrogations with, 'White with two sugars, thanks, and one of those nice sticky buns.'

ASIC had also begun an insider trading investigation into Rene Rivkin. Only months before, Rivkin had had another narrow escape. In September 1999, ASIC asked the Swiss Banking Commission for assistance in tracing several Zurich accounts. ASIC told the SBC that it suspected Rivkin of misleading and deceptive conduct in connection with recommendations he made in the *Rivkin Report*. Rivkin had used the secret accounts to sell shares in Holyman Ltd, FAI Insurances, Infratil Australia, Abednego Nickel and Murrin Murrin Investments at a time when he was advising clients of the *Rivkin Report* to buy.

Swiss authorities agreed in April 2000 to provide information that would have exposed Rivkin's trading to ASIC. But Rivkin secretly funded a two-stage appeal process by Bank Leumi, which saw the case end up before the Swiss Federal Court. ASIC was still in the dark about the accounts and only Rivkin knew how close the regulators were to success. The obvious step for ASIC was to interview Rivkin and ask if he was connected with the Swiss trading: why start lengthy procedures in Zurich when you haven't made direct inquiries at home? If ASIC did ask Rivkin about the accounts and he denied any knowledge, he would be liable for a perjury charge. If he admitted to owning the Laira and World accounts, then the substantial shareholder notice that Laira made in December 1998 would show that Rivkin had disguised the extent of his holdings, so he would have breached the substantial shareholder requirements and the takeover code. It is not clear whether ASIC ever put this question to Rivkin.

Rivkin realised he probably couldn't stop the Swiss authorities releasing the damning information, despite his court appeal. His best prospect was to cut a deal. On 4 October 2000, Rivkin and two associated companies signed an enforceable undertaking with ASIC. The undertaking noted that ASIC believed Rivkin had broken the law by selling shares when he was advising subscribers to buy; Rivkin continued to deny he had done anything wrong but he agreed that for the next two years he would not trade against his own recommendations, and Rivkin Discount Broking would not offer any advice to its clients. In return for Rivkin promising to behave for two years, ASIC would drop all further action against him.

Why ASIC settled for this isn't clear. Presumably it feared it would never get the bank account details from the Swiss. But it meant that, when the Swiss court rejected the Leumi appeal in April 2001 and ordered that ASIC be handed the information which linked Rivkin to the World account, ASIC already regarded the case as closed.

ASIC's director of enforcement, Jan Redfern, told the Senate Joint Committee on Corporations and Financial Services in November 2003 about receiving the Swiss information:

> [We] obtained that information in 2001 from the Swiss authorities ... We had, in October 2000, already taken an enforceable undertaking from Mr Rene Rivkin and a number of related parties. The information we received was quite consistent with what we had known and the information that had resulted in the enforceable undertaking, and was covered off by the enforceable undertaking, so we did not take any further action.

In December 2000, Rivkin had moved his money from World into Laira, but the Imfeld scandal meant his Leumi accounts were frozen. On 16 January 2001, hours after Rivkin had met with Imfeld and Grosz about his account, he began his great garage sale. It began with Norris Smith and Nigel Littlewood in Sydney announcing that the newly established Rivkin Discount Broking would be sold into a tiny mining company, Kurnalpi Gold, in exchange for shares worth $21 million. Rivkin was said to be 'unavailable overseas'. Kurnalpi was the first company that Robert Pittorino and Peter 'Talky' Smith had floated after they left County NatWest in 1994. It now became Rivkin Financial Services.

Almost everything Rivkin owned was up for sale: his Leumi shares, the luxury cars, a string of Sydney apartments, even the house in Bellevue Hill where he had lived for almost a quarter of a century. He promptly bought another house and the change of address gave him the excuse to sell his artworks, which were expected to raise $20 million.

Rivkin's worlds were colliding. He had opened a nightclub in Double Bay in 1999. Now he had to worry about the drug trade. The previous July, police had closed the club for seventy-two hours, telling the Licensing Court that 'the supply and use of prohibited drugs is frequently occurring within the Embassy Nightclub to the knowledge of the management and the staff of the premises'. Police had raided Embassy eleven times in the year since it opened. They claimed the premises were used for dealing speed and ecstasy, which patrons administered after hiring booths at the nightclub for $200. Rivkin's partner at the nightclub, Joe Elcham, appealed against the ban in the Supreme Court and Justice O'Keefe weighed the merits of the police case. He found that '. . . merely observing plastic bags containing white residue on the floor' did not by itself indicate that management was involved in or consenting to breaches of the licensing act. Neither did the arrest of a waiter for selling ecstasy, nor police reports that people were 'snorting white substances in the toilet' and that 'a member of the bar staff was seen to be continually negotiating with other males in the toilet area and to be continually sniffing in a manner consistent with the self-administration of cocaine'. That said, O'Keefe found that the material presented by police 'was sufficient to satisfy a reasonable person that there was a threat to the public health from the use of the premises and a risk of serious offences being committed on such premises.' The seventy-two-hour closure order stood.

In the early months of 2001, as Rivkin battled to contain the effects of the Imfeld scandal, the ongoing appeal case in the Swiss Federal Court and the cash needs that drove his huge sell off, what he didn't know was that he was under surveillance as part of a secret police drug inquiry. Kate McClymont later revealed in the *Sydney Morning Herald* that Strikeforce Sweetsburg, which was set up in early 2001 to investigate 'organised criminal activity in Kings Cross', had targeted eight people, including Rivkin. The investigation showed Rivkin meeting a second target of the investigation, a well-known crime figure who was later arrested over a shipment of cocaine, for coffee in Darlinghurst and Double Bay. The reason for the meetings was never revealed.

Rivkin now came up against a third target of Strikeforce Sweetsburg, John Ibrahim. Back in 1995, while Rivkin was being questioned by the ASC about the Swiss Offset Alpine shares, Ibrahim was facing his own interrogation before the Wood Royal Commission. Ibrahim was accused by John Agius QC, counsel assisting the Commission, of being 'the new lifeblood of the drug industry at Kings Cross'. Ibrahim replied: 'So it would seem, but no, I'm not.' Since then Ibrahim, who had run a Kings Cross nightclub since he was eighteen, had been no-billed on a murder charge in 1998, and no-billed again for threatening a witness who was to give evidence against one of his brothers. His only conviction had been for breaking the jaw of a student at high school. He strenuously denied any link to crime. By the late 1990s, Ibrahim owned a string of investment companies and had a bank facility, which was secured against his Dover Heights home and had a maximum liability of $30 million. He was also reported to be taking over nightclubs. In late March 2001, McClymont reported, an associate of Ibrahim walked into the Embassy armed with a handgun and told staff they were taking over the club.

The only outside sign of the turmoil that this caused were press reports of Rivkin saying he had sold the Embassy, then again that he hadn't, and finally by 20 April that he had. Rikvkin's defamation case against Fairfax for the 1998 articles in the *Australian Financial Review* and the *Sydney Morning Herald* were in court at the time. On Monday 23 April, the jury took two hours, including lunch, to dismiss Rivkin's case against Fairfax, ruling that none of the seventeen imputations complained of in the 1998 articles in the two papers was defamatory. Rivkin was stunned and said he would appeal.

Meanwhile, Rivkin had a potential buyer for his house, which had been turned in at auction two weeks before. On 24 April, Impulse Airlines chief Gerry McGowan was negotiating over the house when he said his offer to buy would be dependent upon the Trade Practices Commission approving the sale of Impulse to Qantas. This was market-sensitive information, he said, and Rivkin must not use it to trade in Qantas stock. However, Rivkin ordered $130 000 of Qantas shares later that day. It was booked to Rivkin Financial Services (RFS).

Why did Rivkin do it—was it just habit? His RFS shares had sagged after the float and with the failure of his house to sell, his financial pressures were growing. The next day in Lausanne, the Swiss Federal Court rejected the Rivkin/Leumi appeal and ordered the release of the ownership details of World and Laira to ASIC. Richardson's sub-account in Laira was not mentioned. It was Thursday Australian time. Swiss court judgments are posted to the parties so it's unlikely that Hafner received it before Friday. He may not have seen it until Monday 30 April. Hafner launched an appeal to the European Court of Human Rights in Strasbourg but the Swiss court order to send the information to ASIC continued regardless.

Regulators now had the first hard evidence of what they had suspected for years: that behind the anonymity of his Swiss bank accounts, Rivkin was making tax-free profits, manipulating share prices and undertaking insider trading on the Australian share market. There were clues in the Laira paperwork to link Rivkin with Offset Alpine but nothing happened. In fairness, ASIC's resources were stretched as it battled to get on top of the HIH and One.Tel investigations. Also, the deal six months before appears to have tied ASIC's hands. After chasing Rivkin all those years, now that it had him in its sights, there was little ASIC could do about it.

With nowhere to put them, Rivkin dumped the Qantas shares as their price began to lift. When he ordered the sale on 1 May he must have known that ASIC would soon be crawling all over his affairs again. The simplest way of hiding his insider trade would have been to rebook the shares to the World or Laira accounts. But those accounts were frozen. Rivkin sold the shares just hours before the Impulse sale announcement he had been waiting on. Selling too early meant his profit was a mere $3000; holding on until the afternoon would have produced a much larger windfall. As an inside trade, it was a woeful failure.

Did news from the Swiss court that ASIC would soon know of his Zurich link make Rivkin lose his nerve with the Qantas shares? Or did he just get tired of waiting? But that fateful insider trade gave ASIC a new avenue to pursue Rivkin. While he had cashed out too soon, the $130 000 that Rivkin had originally paid for the illegal investment made it the biggest insider trade to come before Australian courts.

Everyone was having their regulatory moment. Around the time the insider trading investigation team was practising its inter-rogation technique for Rivkin, Jodee Rich was playing gracious host to ASIC in his bathrobe early in the morning on 1 June, when they came to search his house. On 26 June, it was Rodney Adler's and Ray Williams's turn for the big breakfast, as ASIC and federal police hordes traipsed through their homes. In July, Gordon Wood finally had a chat with Task Force Irondale in London.

Wood hadn't been Mr Popularity when he took up his job at PressTech Controls in November 1998. 'Gordon was there to kick the shit out of us,' said one of his fellow execs. 'He was a real bastard.'

'He seemed very brash, extremely arrogant, overconfident, over familiar with people,' said another former colleague.

Wood was a shouter. 'He was expecting our big clients in Italy, France and so forth, expecting them to set up new mandates overnight because he was shouting at them,' said a third former workmate. 'We had to tell him it doesn't work like that.'

'I've seen him turn his rage off and on—I think most of what he did was premeditated,' one said. 'Gordon's use to Glyn was just that he was an absolute bastard.'

'He told us he'd been a broker,' said another former workmate. 'He'd sit on Bondi Beach with his laptop. He had used to drive company cars—Ferraris and so forth.' Driving the cars would be the only part of Wood's story that rang true.

At one point Wood was working seven days a week, though at other times it was much less. 'Gordon Wood through Glyn Harris was charging the company a quarter of a million pounds,' says one former executive. 'He was only there three or four days a week. He was off exercising, going to the gym, playing tennis.'

There was also uncertainty about how the payments were structured. 'I don't think he ever registered for VAT—I don't think he ever paid tax in this country,' said a former senior executive. 'Gordon used to claim everything. He would drive the company car to Mageve [in the French Alps] and claim it. He put it all in the bank.'

Wood claimed he had bought a chalet at Mageve for £1 million but subsequently he said he only bought a half-share with a friend at Deutsche Bank called Christian—'But I didn't really believe it,' said a former colleague.

Wood had forged a new identity and a new life. But in December 1999, he made a critical mistake. He flew home to Australia to be with his family for the millennium celebrations. Sydney newspapers reported his return and pursued him from the airport. Further reports from close to Task Force Irondale revealed Wood's new job in the UK. Wood cut short his stay to fly back to England on 29 December, several days before he was due to be interviewed by police. Within weeks, Australian journalists were contacting PressTech for comment.

'His nervousness started in 2000, after he came back from Australia,' a former colleague said. Wood developed an aversion to answering the telephone unless he knew who was calling. 'He point-blank refused to pick up the phone,' another said. Yet another colleague spoke of a 'bizarre incident' when Wood was in the general accounting office: the receptionist rang through to say that someone at the door had come to see him. 'He just simply lost it,' the colleague said. 'He went out of the offices, went into his own office and shut the door. He said later, when he came out, "Don't ever tell anybody I'm here if they don't have an appointment." He was pretty well always looking over his shoulder.'

It was in August 2000 that a detective from Irondale had finally interviewed Rivkin and Richardson about Wood's claim that he had driven them to and from lunch on the day Caroline died. Richardson had said that his diary showed he had lunch with the late Peter Moore of the Canterbury Bulldogs that day, not Rivkin. His American Express card receipts appeared to confirm this. Two weeks later, Wood resigned from the board of most of the PressTech companies. However, he continued to work at PressTech. The bank rescue had gone badly. In 2000, when NatWest wrote off £2 million and walked away, Lloyds Bank came in as the new banker to PressTech, which was now wholly owned by Harris. Wood was still there until just before Christmas 2000, when Harris fired him. 'He basically just gave him the bullet,' said one colleague. 'One day he was there, the next day he wasn't,' said another workmate.

Wood had earned nearly three quarters of a million dollars through the job Harris had given him. He moved into an apartment at the exclusive Chelsea Village in early 2001. In July that year, Inspector Kevin Jacob of Task Force Irondale flew to London to interview Wood for several hours. Wood probably already knew his story about the Rivkin–Richardson lunch was looking shaky. The month before, Rivkin had told *60 Minutes* that he thought Wood was on the clifftop that night while Richardson criticised police in the *Daily Telegraph* for the delay in contacting him, and revealed his lunch date with Moore. In the interview with the Irondale detective, Wood strenuously denied any role in Caroline Byrne's death. Jacob also spoke to Glyn Harris, who didn't say anything about Wood being a turnaround expert. He said he had a link with Wood's mother, that they were almost related. He didn't say what the relationship actually was.

Task Force Irondale returned home. In September, Wood said he was going on a world cruise. And he disappeared. He kept in touch with his old friends but would not say where he was. Once again, Gordon Wood had become just a bunch of colourful memories. But what memories they are.

There was the time he stayed with one of the PressTech senior managers. The main bathroom had a shower but Wood preferred the one in the ensuite. Wood's host and his wife woke at 5.30 in the morning to see Wood bustle past them. They lay startled in bed, the sheets pulled up to their chins, as a tall blond man—bright, cheerful and dressed only in a shower cap and bath towel—hopped straight into their shower cubicle.

Then there was the game Wood liked to play with colleagues. It had been a favourite with the crowd he had once hung out with at Joe's Cafe, a game of Would You Do Something For a Million Quid. Typically it was sexual favours. In one of the bull sessions after work, Wood disparaged one of the women in the office as being overweight, then asked what it would be worth to 'rim' her, an oral sex term more familiar among gay circles. 'He would begin by saying: would you do it for £1000? Then it was £10 000. Then it was: would you do it for £100 000? Or, would you do it for £1 million?' a former colleague said. 'Gordon was the sort of guy who would do anything for the right money.'

And there was Gordon Wood's Master-of-the-Universe moment. A former workmate remembers speaking to the Press-Tech managing director in his office, which had a glass strip down one section of the wall, when he saw Wood standing outside. 'I could see out, but the managing director couldn't,' he said:

Gordon was standing next to this glass strip waving his cock at me. He was standing there with his dick out. When he saw me he waved it at me. Then he put it back in and walked away. He did it twice. He had a sort of funny grin. He was flopping it around. It was bizarre.

William Lewis chronicled the bizarre antics of market traders and investment jocks in his 1989 book *Liar's Poker*. But this is never what Lewis meant about being a Big Swinging Dick.

TWENTY-ONE

True confessions

2001–03

As Rivkin walked out of the ABC studios in Sydney on 28 April 2003, he believed he had every reason to feel satisfied with his latest performance. The interview he had just taped with Andrew Denton would make sensational viewing when it went to air a week later. Denton's clever technique had elicited all the ingredients that stamped Rivkin as great talent for television. Rivkin was witty, engaging, candid and, when talking about his personal life, absolutely fearless in pressing the button titled, 'Way Too Much Detail'. What could you say to a man who confessed, as Rivkin did to Denton, that at seventeen his father took him to a nudist camp where he had won the New South Wales nudist table tennis championship? Or that he had been runner-up in the New South Wales nudist badminton titles? Mercifully Denton stopped him before he mentioned anything about yachting.

'I don't lie, I was taught as a child not to lie,' Rivkin said. 'I get into trouble by telling the truth. There you go. I know it's hard to believe.'

The easy repartee between Denton and Rivkin was nothing like the less pleasant exchanges he had had four months before on the opposite side of the world, at the Zurich District Attorney's office. Rivkin's appearance there had been only the latest in a string of cameos by Australian clients of Bank Leumi. The whole thing had become quite a saga. The first of the reluctant interviewees was Trevor Kennedy, and that was really a case of being in the wrong place at the wrong time.

It began in June 2001, when Trevor Kennedy slipped out of Australia, while the aftershocks of the HIH and One.Tel collapses were still reverberating, and headed for Switzerland. Many Bank Leumi clients were complaining about discrepancies in their accounts. Being an agreeable fellow, Kennedy went to the bank to see a Mr Wolman, to share his concerns over some suspicious transactions in his own account, that suggested he too was one of Imfeld's victims. It was simply bad luck that Christopher Harris, a consultant from PriceWaterhouseCoopers seconded to Leumi to unravel the Imfeld accounts, was nearby. And it was really unfortunate that at this point Mr Wolman asked the consultant to join the meeting. Kennedy's name rang a bell for Harris. He had just been looking at a peculiar transaction on 7 July 1997, where Imfeld had transferred US$500 000 from a Leumi account to an account at another Zurich bank, Maerki Baumann, in the name of Kennedy. Ordinarily there would be little hope of tracking down the mysterious Mr Kennedy. But now, quite by chance, a man by that name was sitting in their office. A man who, it turned out, said he once had an account at Maerki Baumann. So if it was all the same to Mr Kennedy, could they please have their US$500 000 back?

'At this point Mr. Wolman virtually accused me of trying to steal the bank's money,' Kennedy later wrote.

It was a truly appalling prospect. Kennedy had gone to the bank to ask for money, only to find the tables turned and the bank demanding money back from him. And until the issue was resolved, Bank Leumi had frozen his Leumi account. Not just that, now the Zurich District Attorney's office wanted a word with him. Which was how Trevor Kennedy found himself, on 11 March 2002, sitting down for a formal interrogation with Zurich Assistant District Attorney, Bruno Stochli.

The problem was, the US$500 000 that Imfeld transferred to Kennedy's Maerki Baumann account in 1997 had been paid out of an unrelated client account at Bank Leumi that wasn't supposed to exist. The client had ordered the account closed in 1990, but it had remained open as some sort of secret slush fund operated by Imfeld. Why was it paying money to Trevor Kennedy? Kennedy told the DA's office that he couldn't remember where the money was from, but was sure it was his. He made some calls overnight to Australia to ask some of his friends—Rene Rivkin, Graham Richardson and 'some of the other associates', but they didn't have any clues either. It was pretty embarrassing, he said, but the details had just slipped from his mind.

He left Zurich with the matter unresolved and went home where, ever the journalist, he began writing letters. 'I deliberately keep no records of my affairs in Switzerland,' he wrote to the DA via his lawyer. 'I visit the country only on an annual basis. I am very circumspect about using the telephone between Switzerland and Australia. I have transferred significant funds between the banks there, and have changed banks from time to time.'

After all, it wasn't really so unusual. It wasn't as if Trevor Kennedy was the only Australian investor involved in this sort of thing. This sort of thing being transfers of large sums of money and not remembering what it was for.

'I engaged in many transactions of this magnitude, mainly in Australia, with a group of my associates,' he wrote. 'It was not unusual for us to lend each other money or to have part or all of the loan and/or interest paid offshore . . . For obvious reasons I did not keep memoranda or records relating to my Swiss affairs . . . I kept absolutely no records.'

The cruellest thing of all, it seemed to Kennedy as he wrote on 26 March 2002, was that the fellow from the DA's office who had interviewed him (he thought his name was Stochli) had seemed to be sceptical about Kennedy's explanation.

'It is the truth,' Kennedy wrote indignantly. 'Furthermore, he suggested that he might take this matter up with the Australian authorities. This would be catastrophic for me and totally unjust.' He also wrote, more in sorrow than anger: 'My only crime has been to have no recollection of a five-year-old event and to have put my faith and trust in the integrity and efficiency of the Swiss banking System.'

Kennedy was in the running for the top job at the ABC at the time, so he had reason to be sensitive about a little bad Swiss press. It turned out that Kennedy was not the only disgruntled Australian making a pilgrimage to Zurich. Brent Potts dropped by the DA's office for a chat. The DA would have liked to have a natter with Graham Richardson, but Richo kindly informed them with the easy grace of an old politician that, while he was definitely looking forward immensely to chewing the fat with the DA, his appointment book was chockful for the next 7000 years. Perhaps they could pencil something in for any time after that. That, at least, was the gist of Richardson's response.

But on 10 December 2002, Kennedy's good friend Rene Rivkin fronted for a show-and-tell session in Zurich. Initially Rivkin had made no complaint about his Leumi account. Why would he? Unlike almost every other Leumi client account, which was showing losses, Rivkin had ended up more than US$2 million ahead from Imfeld's currency trading and the Manchester United payment. By 2002, Leumi had discovered these payments and was demanding repayment. At this point Rivkin also decided to file a complaint. And so he ended up being interrogated by the DA heading the Imfeld investigation, Dr Nathan Landshut. The interview lasted all day in the DA's cramped office in the grubby Weststrasse, Zurich's noisiest and most polluted street. Imfeld was present, as was Rivkin's lawyer, Benno Hafner. The session began at 9 a.m. with Landshut cautioning Rivkin that he was a suspect (*Auskunftsperson*) in the investigation. Landshut went on to express regret that Graham Richardson had not been able to attend. Then, for the next nine and a half hours, Landshut explored Rivkin's banking history with Leumi and Imfeld. It was the only time in his life that Rivkin was confronted with the evidence of his secret life—how he began banking with Leumi more than two decades before, his strained relationship with his father and his money troubles. Rivkin in the first instance recalled little of what Landshut raised with him, or denied it outright, until the DA produced the documentation.

Midway through the morning session, Hafner gave a long explanation of how Laira was set up as a Scottish partnership with proceeds from the sale of Offset Alpine shares, after a little trouble with the Australian authorities. At the end of this Landshut turned to Rivkin and asked him if this was his understanding of events as well. It was at this point, Rivkin suddenly became more talkative and made the admission which would prove so damaging:

> The shares of Offset Alpine, which this was originally all about, were for the most part, let's say 81 per cent mine, and about 7 per cent Richardson's. Twelve per cent were held by Kennedy. The numbers don't square exactly. Where I see the amount for $1.4 million, I get the impression that this was Richardson's share, because mine was much higher.

His admission came out of the blue and without pressure from Landshut. Rivkin shopped his friends so abruptly, and in such contrast to his earlier minimal responses, that it had the air of being planned. He may have believed that Imfeld was going to reveal it anyway, so moved to forestall him. He may have wanted to divert Landshut's line of questioning from other areas where it was more sensitive for him. But perhaps most likely, while he remained as rational as he ever had been, with his deteriorating bipolar condition he was losing the ability to keep secrets.

Landshut didn't pursue the Offset revelation. His focus was Imfeld, who had been present throughout the questioning, along with Benno Hafner. Rivkin would have had no fears that his admission here would ever surface in Australia. Swiss banking secrecy is legendary. Unfortunately for Rivkin, Swiss criminal investigations are not covered by the same strict laws. But there were no immediate repercussions and, in April 2003, Zurich seemed a world away while Rivkin faced a far more immediate threat, as his insider trading trial over the Qantas share trades two years before began.

Months later, when the insider case went to appeal, Rivkin's legal team revealed the suspicions they had had during the April trial that their client had gone mad. Rivkin had given not one but two interviews to Andrew Denton, which proved disastrous. Rivkin had behaved badly in court, his advisors believed. There had been the disastrous episode of the nasal inhaler . . .

When did solicitor Mark O'Brien first twig that all might not be well in the very different world and mind of his client, Rene Rivkin? Call it a sinus moment.

There was Rivkin, head back, nasal inhaler at the ready, holding nothing back as he gave his nostrils a solid workout. Courtrooms are not renowned for their acoustics, but this was a clarion call that floated right across the hall of justice and into the jury box. At least one gathers as much from O'Brien's later evidence to the NSW Court of Appeal about his client's mental state.

O'Brien, a man whom nature has not gifted with a wide range of expressions, had at times during this case seemed to the casual observer not to be completely at ease with the client–lawyer relationship. O'Brien's evidence, quoted in the judgment, spelt out just how strained the relationship was. He said bluntly that he had concerns about Rivkin's mental condition during the trial and that, while on the stand, some of Rivkin's answers had been 'very foolish'.

The trouble began early, when Rivkin's counsel, Bruce McClintock SC, asked him for his occupation. O'Brien's view was that Rivkin must have been showing the effect of his brain tumour when he answered: 'Well, primarily it's—let's rephrase that. Most of my money is made in matters primarily relating to the stock market.'

Then there was Rivkin's decision to read a dictionary during the trial, and to laugh during the cross-examination of witnesses when it wasn't clear to O'Brien what the joke was. But this wild behaviour paled when compared to the incident that began when Rivkin asked his personal assistant to pass the nasal inhaler. Unhappily, McClintock had just begun his address to the jury. And there was Rivkin, his client, imitating a vacuum cleaner behind him. Not one of the whisper-quiet ones, either.

In the universe of legal sins, there are few more heinous than upstaging your own barrister. Some QCs favour bringing back capital punishment for just such lapses.

'Don't you ever do that again,' McClintock told Rivkin afterwards. 'I was trying to make an important point to the jury for you and they were looking at you, not listening to me.'

At this point Rivkin made the only answer a reasonable person could: 'What, you want me to suffocate?'

O'Brien was not convinced. As he told the appeal judges, 'That seems to me to miss counsel's point.'

Rivkin expected to be cleared later that week of the minor embarrassment of the insider trading charge. So there was a shrewd commercial logic in Rivkin's decision to do the first interview with Denton. When the interview ran the following Monday, it would be a celebration of Prometheus Unbound, a signal that it was business as usual at Rene Rivkin Inc. Rivkin had a gift for publicity stunts whenever his affairs ended up in court. But he had moved too soon.

Rivkin was shocked on 30 April when the jury returned a guilty verdict. He claimed he had been cut down because he was a tall poppy and he directed an angry tirade at ASIC in the *Rivkin Report*. Rivkin's private network immediately began a public appeal for support, led by a subscriber to the *Report* who turned out to be George Freris's sister. The day after his trial ended Rivkin began stripping money out of his public company, Rivkin Financial Services, with a share buyback. Publicly it seemed that Rivkin's mania was drifting out of control, exacerbated by an as-yet-undiagnosed benign brain tumour. It would later be claimed that his IQ had fallen to around 50 at this time. However, there was nothing slow about the deals he continued to make.

Over two weeks he channelled up to $2.7 million to himself and close associates. At his sentencing hearing, friends like Ray Martin, John Boyd, Richardson and Kennedy rallied around as character witnesses. Kennedy testified that Rivkin's 'respect for both law and moral code is flawless'. The hearing ended with Justice Whealy sentencing Rivkin to nine months of weekend detention.

Rivkin now seemed clearly unbalanced. He gave another interview to Denton and a radio interview to Richardson, both of which would be disastrous for the prospects of his appeal. He was the centre of intense media coverage as he began the first weekend of detention at Silverwater prison complex, and when he collapsed the following day. Days later he was operated on to remove the brain tumour.

The bell for one of the last chapters in Rivkin's fall from grace tolled on 10 September, when the High Court handed down its decision in the defamation case against the *Australian Financial Review* and the *Sydney Morning Herald*. The year before, the Federal Court of Appeal had ruled that the jury verdict in 2001 was unreasonable, and ordered a retrial. The High Court over-ruled much of this judgment and reduced the retrial to four issues. These included two counts against the *AFR*, that my story in 1998 had suggested that the Offset Alpine affair had diminished his reputation as a 'sagacious' stockbroker; and that ASIC had suspected him of being involved in shady business.

The press reports of the High Court decision were read in Switzerland by Shraga Elam, the soft-spoken Israeli journalist in Zurich who first broke the Imfeld scandal in 2001. Among a string of international scoops, in 1998 Elam had revealed that MI6 and Mossad had helped smuggle into Iran ingredients and know-how that could be used to make chemical weapons of mass destruction. In January 1999, after he had interviewed one of two MI6 agents involved in the operation, Shraga was detained at Heathrow airport by twelve customs officers, questioned for hours and had his laptop and documents confiscated. Elam has written extensively on links between Nazi Germany and Switzerland and in 2002 published a controversial book, *Hitler's Forgers*, which revealed how the Israeli government and Mossad had protected an important Nazi agent. Shraga is a man of considerable personal convictions, who after fighting in three wars as an Israeli now works as a peace activist, promoting reconciliation between Jews and Palestinians. It is work which puts him constantly under scrutiny. With many critics waiting to pull him up for any error, his research style is cautious and methodical. In early 2003, he focused once again on the Leumi embezzlement investigation, and by mid-year he had carefully won the confidence of a number of sources. They provided him with a treasure trove of documents unearthed in the course of the Swiss investigation. These included bank account details and witness statements for several Australian clients of Leumi, including Rivkin and Kennedy. By the time Shraga read reports of the 10 September High Court ruling on the Internet, he had spent several months confirming the authenticity of the documents he held. A friend of his, Swiss journalist Gian Trepp, knew me and recommended that Shraga make contact. Shraga emailed me on Saturday morning, 13 September, and I replied an hour later. In the days that followed, *AFR* journalists

Andrew Main, Colleen Ryan and Rosemary Graffagnini joined the investigation. Rivkin's defamation case had provided the link that would lead to his unmasking.

Trevor Kennedy picked up the *Financial Review*, on 30 October 2003, to see that his old paper had put his letters to the Zurich District Attorney on the front page. The *Financial Review* had obtained from Elam copies of signed transcripts of Rivkin's and Kennedy's interviews. Actually, Kennedy's embarrassing correspondence with the Zurich DA was the minor, colour story. The lead story was that the Offset Alpine mystery was solved. Rivkin, Richardson and Kennedy—the stockbroker, the political power-broker and the media executive—were the mystery figures behind Offset Alpine.

A month later, Kennedy told ASIC investigators that he remembered almost nothing of the hours that followed:

> This was an absolutely chaotic day and the—from the moment that I first learnt about this thing to the next two or three days are just a blur in my mind. There is recollections of weeping wives, of dozens of people ringing up, of all of that sort of stuff, and I think it's totally unreasonable to expect me to remember the details of conversations that occurred on that day.

ASIC put the events together as best it could. 'Mr Kennedy reads the *Financial Review* and sees the activity attributed to Messrs Rivkin and Richardson and in part what was attributed to Mr Kennedy regarding an interest in Offset Alpine,' ASIC's counsel, Geoff Lindsay SC, later told the Federal Court, with marvellous restraint. 'Mr Kennedy is surprised to be named.'

It was a complete disaster, Kennedy told the ASIC investigators. The newspaper report was the first he had heard that
Rivkin had named him in Zurich as one of the Offset Alpine shareholders. Photographers and reporters were already arriving to
stake out Kennedy's home, along with the Rivkin and Richardson
houses. Kennedy had not got where he was by being slow off the
mark, and now he acted with decisiveness. He slipped past the
press cordon around his house at Kirribilli and smuggled himself
in to see Rivkin at Double Bay.

'Mr Kennedy goes to the home of Mr Rivkin and endeavours to
ascertain if he said those things, and if so, why,' Lindsay said.
'He gets no satisfactory response.'

By this time, Richardson had shown up at Rivkin's house as
well. Eight years after he retired from parliament, Richardson's
legendary power as a backroom fixer for the NSW Right was
diminished, but the former Minister for Kneecaps remained a
major lobbyist for Kerry Packer's media group and other clients.
Politically, Richardson knew where the bodies were buried. But he
wasn't getting much joy out of Rivkin. The three of them rang
Benno Hafner, the Swiss lawyer each of them used in Zurich. How
had the press got access to these documents? Hafner too had been
taken by surprise and could say little on the telephone.

There they were then—Rivkin, Kennedy and Richardson,
three of the biggest and toughest corporate and political players
of the 1990s—reduced in the confusion to a scene reminiscent of
the Three Stooges: the Man Who Talked Too Much, the Man
Who Wrote Too Much, and the Man Who Knew Too Much. Any
moment now and they would break into an Abbott and Costello
routine: Who's on first; What's on second; Hafner's in Zurich.

Benno Hafner. Now there was a man who would have all the
answers. Kennedy went home, but the phone calls to Rivkin continued. 'He phoned Rivkin about it, on more than one occasion,
without satisfaction,' Justice Gyles would later note in the Federal
Court. That was when Kennedy decided to go to Zurich to see

Hafner. There wasn't much choice. Someone had to go, and Rene wasn't a starter. Rivkin had pleaded a dazzling variety of medical afflictions in the past five months to delay carrying out his weekend detention sentence. The justice system had managed to live with regular newspaper photographs of Rivkin dining out in expensive restaurants. But even the malleable minds at the Department of Correction would probably have some difficulty with their star prisoner skipping out on detention for a jaunt in the Alps. Richardson, meanwhile, ran the risk in Switzerland of being nabbed for that little heart to heart the Zurich DA had been so tiresomely insistent about. That left Kennedy to go to see their old friend Benno Hafner. As the man who kept their records and looked after their business, Benno could surely clear things up.

If Rivkin's testimony in Zurich were true, both Rivkin and Kennedy had breached Section 135 of the *Crimes Act* with false testimony in their evidence to the ASC in 1995. It was an offence that carried a maximum gaol term of five years. Both men knew that it was only a matter of time before the Australian Securities and Investments Commission examined them again about the *Financial Review* story. That wasn't hard to work out Justice Gyles would later comment in the Federal Court. '[Kennedy] might have felt a certain urgency on the need to protect himself.'

Kennedy flew out late on the Friday. On his way to Zurich he would go via London, where he thought he would put up at the Ritz.

TWENTY-TWO

Under the boardwalk

2004–05

Sydney's many tribes share the same spaces but they operate under different rules. There is no place where this contrast is clearer than that little triangle of land caught between the abrasive commerce of the city to the west, and the pervasive criminality of Kings Cross to the east, known as Woolloomooloo. In April 2004, three separate stories of Sydney would briefly intersect, brought together by networks and a coincidence of geography. Yet while the stories would overlap, the players themselves would remain worlds apart. It began on a fine autumn day in 2004, when the networkers dining at Otto Ristorante realised with a start that they were not alone. The Department of Immigration and Multi-cultural and Indigenous Affairs had descended on the Finger Wharf. It was an awkward luncheon moment.

Ros Reines reported the raid in the *Sunday Telegraph* several days later, on April 27. Two Otto staff from Sri Lanka, both long-term members of the celebrity kitchen team under chef James Kidman, had overstayed their visas and were carted off to Villawood detention centre. A whiff of intrigue hung about the tale. Reines said authorities had mounted the raid on the basis of 'information received'. It came just days after Lang Walker and Mr Golden Tonsils, John Laws, had completed buying Terzini and his original backers out of Otto, pumping in another $1.4 million of capital. Was this trouble in paradise? Or did DIMIA just have a thing about Woolloomooloo?

The raiders were a DIMIA team that specialised in restaurants and brothels. In February, the target had been massage parlours in Newtown. In early April, it was restaurants in Marrickville. Three weeks after the Finger Wharf affair, Immigration Minister Amanda Vanstone's finest were rousting out the Doyles seafood restaurants at Watsons Bay and Pyrmont, with a couple of keen minds from the *Daily Telegraph* in tow to watch as eleven staff were rounded up and escorted to Villawood. A day later, it was a massage parlour in Bondi, where four young women were soon helping DIMIA with their inquiries. The 'Daily Terror' boys, who tagged along on that expedition as well, held nothing back when it came to writing up their scoop. Under the headline, 'Exposing Sydney's sex slave traders', the Terror told a poignant story about Jade, a young Korean woman caught in the Bondi raid, weeping in the bare DIMIA holding room.

'I have never worked in a place like that before,' Jade sobbed. 'My family will kill me if they find out I was working in a brothel. Please don't print my picture in the paper because I'm scared they might find out what I have been doing here. They will be ashamed of me.'

Getting these quotes was no mean achievement. It emerged later in the Migration Review Tribunal, where the affair ended up, that the four Korean women spoke little to no English and no interpreter had been present. The truth was that the massage parlour wasn't a brothel and the young women weren't prostitutes—just very frightened young tourists who mistakenly thought the immigration officers guiding the journalists were threatening them with guns. In fact, it looked as if someone with an overactive imagination had invented the entire *Daily Telegraph* story. The *Australian* was the only paper sufficiently interested in the women's fate to reveal their total innocence. For people at that end of town, did it really matter?

Thankfully, back at the Finger Wharf, sanity quickly returned. By 23 April, the Friday lunch crowd was tying on their bibs at Sydney's favourite restaurant for another round of *nuova cucina*, and all seemed as before. When Terzini opened Otto in 1999, he had looked at the outside view of naval dockyards and the clutter of boats and wisely decided to make this an inside restaurant. As a little joke, he made the mood lighting so dim that, unless you bag a table on the balcony, the only place to be seen in Sydney can require a torch to find your table. Lesser restaurateurs might have written the menu in braille. Yet, even as service resumed as normal at Otto, it was hard not to feel the faintest twinge of doubt. A good kitchen team is a tight operation and it relies on four or five experienced sous chefs. Could you really remove two key players—say, by arresting and deporting them— without affecting the fine timing required for searing the herbed loin of tuna, the mix of flavours required for quail saltimbocca with poached pear, or the *guancia di vitello*, the slow braised veal cheeks? Had the immigration minister really thought this issue through before she despatched her hearties on to the Finger Wharf, the A-list asked itself seethingly. Indeed, what was Amanda Vanstone's position on veal cheeks?

Lang Walker, the proud new co-owner of Otto, had more pressing matters to attend to. On 23 April, as the two Sri Lankan sous chefs in Villawood were confronting the inevitability of their compulsory homeward flights, Lang Walker was contemplating a little offshore travel of his own. It began with a board meeting at ten minutes past two in the Walker group boardroom on Level 10, 1 O'Connell Street. Walker Corporation was finalising a $28 million loan from the ANZ Bank to fund part of its giant Rhodes development in Sydney's inner west. But there were other matters for consideration.

Four days earlier, the Supreme Court had ruled that Walker Corporation was entitled to compensation for land the state govern- ment had compulsorily acquired at Ballast Point on the Balmain

Peninsula. While the court hadn't yet decided quite how big the payout should be, nine-figure sums were being bandied about. So it was interesting timing that one of the matters that the board discussed on 23 April was a proposal to send a $100 million payment to a company in the British Virgin Islands. Walker does not comment on his private business affairs and international financing arrangements are notoriously difficult to follow. However, from an outsider's standpoint (and whether or not this was what he actually intended), it looked like Walker had the perfect mechanism, when the cheque for Ballast Point eventually came in from the state government, to ship money offshore to a tax haven. There is no suggestion that any of this was improper. It merely reflected the way the Walker Corporation had set up its finances, which showed a paper trail of half a billion dollars in funding from Monaco and the British Virgin Islands.

Walker Corp's share structure seemed quite straightforward. There were twenty-four ordinary shares, all of them owned by Lang and Suzanne Walker, and fifty redeemable preference shares, which were owned by a related company called Bay Street Finance (BSF). But behind this it was more complicated. Corporate filings from 2004 show that BSF had borrowed $340 million from Athenaeum Investments Ltd, a company that was said to be based in Monaco. In addition, another company with a similar name, Athenaeum Investments Pty Ltd—based in the British Virgin Islands—owned $169 million in redeemable preference shares in BSF. The upshot of this was that the Walker group owed $509 million to whoever owned the Athenaeum companies. Repayments of loans and preference shares do not attract tax.

There's nothing necessarily wrong with any of this. It's smart tax accounting. The arrangement appears to have been set up several years before, when Walker was bidding for a development project in Paris. In fact, it was while Walker was focused on his French plans in 2001 that trouble arose back home over his plan to buy the old ICI chemical plant at Ballast Point and turn the site into townhouses. The proposal proved hugely unpopular, triggering a wave of public indignation about the loss of public access to this foreshore. Paul Keating was scathing about Walker's development record. 'The Finger Wharf is the most cynical and undemocratic development of its kind that Sydney has seen,' he wrote in 2000. 'It represents a new low in the processes of planning and consent . . . If we were after a symbol we missed it; instead we got a memorial to Lang Walker.' The furore prompted Premier Bob Carr to announce that the state government would compulsorily acquire the Ballast Point land. Of course Walker did the decent Sydney thing, which was to sue for damages.

The case had gone very well. Walker Corporation had only ever paid a 10 per cent deposit on the site, a matter of $1.5 million. On 19 April 2003, Justice Palmer ruled in the NSW Supreme Court that Walker had won and the company was entitled to compensation for all the profits it would have made if it had been able to buy the land and then develop it. The legal argument that followed that week was directed solely to how big Walker Corporation's compensation cheque from the state government would be. Its lawyers were asking for $100 million.

Big money was in the wind when the Walker Corp board met on 23 April. The new loan from ANZ Bank was complex and involved shuffling money across the group. One of the changes agreed that day was to authorise Bay Street Finance to pay $100 million to Athenaeum in the British Virgin Islands, to redeem some of its preference shares. It may well have been linked to the other changes flowing from the ANZ loan. But the effect was that Walker Corp was preparing to send money offshore just when it had learned about its little windfall from the government.

That was the advantage of working from the business end of the Finger Wharf. While the two sous chefs from Otto glumly awaited deportation, Lang Walker from his penthouse could despatch huge sums of money halfway round the world, before Villawood opened for visiting hours. Three months later Justice

Palmer set Walker Corp's damages payment at a more modest $60 million, less the cost of buying the land. But these were not the only travel stories in Sydney on 23 April. A happier tale was unfolding at a restaurant across town. After six months of self-imposed exile, former Senator Graham Richardson was back, and heading for the meal table.

The scurrilous media reports of that lunch, Richardson would later complain, were completely erroneous. 'Mate, I'm supposed to have been taken out a back door that I've never seen, guided past the Peking ducks by a proprietor I've never met, and made my escape up a back alley that doesn't exist,' an aggrieved Richardson later claimed. To be clear here, Richardson did have lunch at the Golden Century on Sussex Street in Sydney's Chinatown with five or six people, and it might indeed have gone on for some time—he was still ensconced well after Lang Walker's board meeting at 1 O'Connell Street was finished. But Richo certainly did not leg it out the back entrance when he was spotted at about 3 p.m., and he was not assisted in his getaway by Labor Party fundraiser Robert Ho, as was reported by the gutter press. As he made it clear to Sydney's newspaper editors, Graham Richardson is not a back door kind of guy.

It was a welcome return to form by one of Sydney's legendary lunchers, who in recent years had been spotted ordering white meat and mineral water. Not that the menu mattered. The critical issue was the choice of restaurant. The Golden Century is the watering hole for the power players at Labor House and the Trades and Labour Council, just around the corner. To have lunch there meant that Richo was working his Labor contacts again. He was once more a player.

'This is the quote you want. I never owned the shares, I never owned the bank account,' Richardson told me in June 2003; his first public comment since the Offset Alpine/Bank Leumi scandal broke in the *Australian Financial Review* eight months before. Richardson stopped short of denying he withdrew money from

Laira Investment Company's account at Bank Leumi. He declined to elaborate on his connection with Laira. But the implication was clear. Whatever Rivkin had been up to in Zurich—and Richardson was not saying Rivkin had done anything wrong—it had nothing to do with him. If Rivkin, for convenience, had loaned him some money out of his account, what did that prove? He had not heard from ASIC for months.

'I was interviewed by them in November or December some time,' he said. 'I've had no communication with them since then. And I've had no communication from Swiss authorities. As you know they searched my house and took away nothing. Nothing. I did an interview with them. I was, as they say, full and frank.'

How had the last six months been?

'Unpleasant would do. Bad would suffice. Any of the above. But one keeps going.'

Richardson had dropped out of sight late in 2003 after the Rivkin/Leumi story broke. He cancelled his role as master of ceremonies at Labor Party fundraisers, and he no longer used his office in the Packer building in Park Street. He was said to be taking a vacation, spending time at his five-hectare property near Bowral in the NSW Southern Highlands. But by April, he had quietly resumed his activities as a lobbyist; he said he was working for all his former clients.

'The only change in my life is I'm no longer on television,' he said. 'I'm still representing the same clients.' The only exception was Packer's Consolidated Press, where he was on extended leave.

This was where the lunch at Golden Century became significant. Six days later, just before 10.30 a.m. on 29 April, Richardson climbed aboard Lang Walker's new Falcon 900 jet. He and Walker were running an hour late. They had an appointment in Hobart to see Richardson's old union friend, Paul Lennon, who had become Premier of Tasmania after the death of Jim Bacon. Walker had a plan for a $400 million marina at Ralphs Bay on the eastern side of Hobart but it had run into some environmental problems. They had finished their Hobart meeting and were back in the Falcon 900 taking off again by 3.35 p.m. Some things don't take long.

Richardson soldiered on. He stayed off the television (mostly) but kept working as a lobbyist behind the scenes. ASIC had requested assistance from Switzerland on the grounds that it suspected that Rivkin and Kennedy had committed perjury in the 1995 Offset Alpine inquiry. Richardson had not been questioned in 1995, so the issue of perjury did not arise for him. According to Rivkin's Swiss evidence, Richardson had been party to a breach of the substantial shareholder disclosure laws, but that wasn't a crime in Switzerland. So ASIC was not able to ask for information about his bank account from the Swiss. However, Zurich District Attorney Ivo Hoppler, who handled ASIC's request, had wide discretion over what documents he judged were relevant for ASIC's investigation.

Just before Christmas 2004, Hoppler ruled that twelve folders of bank documents and witness transcripts, which included material about Richardson, be supplied to ASIC. It also contained details for two general accounts of Bank Leumi's at Credit Suisse. Five parties lodged appeals in the Zurich High Court against Hoppler's ruling. These included Rivkin, Kennedy, Richardson, Bank Leumi and another unknown party. Leumi complained that it had operated the Credit Suisse accounts to channel money from all of its Australian clients; releasing account records could help identify new names. Richo said he didn't know what was going on or what was in the documents but he had hired a Swiss lawyer 'to get to the bottom of things'. In fact, Richardson faced a problem if the documents that ASIC eventually received from the Swiss linked him to the Cheshire and Laira accounts—he had told ASIC in late 2003 that he did not own any Swiss accounts.

In June 2005, the Zurich High Court delivered a fifty-page judgment that confirmed the release of all Hoppler's documents. The case now went to the second stage of appeal, before the Swiss Federal Court. A decision was expected by late 2005. However,

ASIC had also asked to question key figures in the Imfeld saga in Switzerland, including Ernst Imfeld himself. It is not expected to do this until 2006, and the transcripts of these interviews could also be subject to appeals. Meanwhile, the Australian Tax Office was investigating the three amigos.

Trevor Kennedy resigned from all his public boards four days after the federal police raid on his house on 13 November 2003. Life now had a new rhythm for him. Bank Leumi had dropped its claims on the US$500 000 mystery transfer. However, in December 2003, after Swiss reports of the Offset Alpine case, Bank Vontobel froze two accounts operated by Kennedy and Rivkin; they held $4.2 million and $300 000 respectively. Kennedy brought a series of legal actions against ASIC and the federal police, challenging the search of his house, the search of his office, and finally the legality of ASIC's investigation. By early 2005, he had lost on all counts.

Rivkin resumed his sentence of weekend detention in January 2004, but remained too ill to answer questions from ASIC about Offset Alpine, or from his friends about what he had said in Switzerland. In mid-2004, a long-term associate of Rivkin's made a brutal assessment of his old friend: 'Rene is completely buggered. He's totally broken down. He's completely not a person. And you can't have a relationship with someone who is not a person.' On 2 September, Rivkin's family found him unconscious from a drug overdose. Eight months later, on 1 May 2005, Rivkin took another drug overdose and put a plastic bag over his head. In mid-April Rene and Gayle had filed for divorce and Rene moved in with his mother. It was Rachel Rivkin who found her son dead late on the Sunday afternoon.

In April 2005, Rodney Adler was sentenced to a minimum two-and-a-half years' gaol and Ray Williams for a minimum two years and nine months, after both men pleaded guilty to charges arising from the HIH crash. Brad Keeling cut a deal with ASIC over One.Tel and by mid-2005 was working with another telecommunications company. Jodee Rich's civil trial over whether he had misled the One.Tel board was continuing.

Tony Byrne continues his lonely quest to discover what happened to his daughter. On Saturday 7 June 2003, while a procession of media vehicles followed Rivkin to Silverwater gaol, where he spent a night before collapsing, Byrne was on the clifftop at The Gap. It was the eighth anniversary of Caroline's death and Task Force Irondale was staging a reconstruction of the fatal night in the hope of coaxing out some last clue.

In February 2004, Inspector Jacobs forwarded the Byrne file to the Director of Public Prosecutions with a recommendation that Gordon Wood be charged with Caroline's murder. The DPP asked for further tests. Meanwhile, the *Australian* tracked Wood down to the French ski resort of Mageve, where he once claimed to co-own a chalet. He disappeared once more, though his friends said he still kept in touch.

'He used to phone me quite frequently,' said one former fellow-worker in Britain. 'He'd say, "I can't tell you where I am, but I'm sitting in a cafe in the sun."'

Paul Makucha had fallen on hard times once more. 'I give up,' he told me in a stricken telephone call in late 2004, when creditors were threatening him with bankruptcy. 'I don't drink and I don't smoke and I'm not prepared to do the things you have to do to get by in this town.' He contemplated bankruptcy. But by the next morning he was back up again, vowing to fight on. In January 2005, he left The Toaster and moved back into the 'Shithouse Hotel', the shipping container at the airport in which he had lived for five years during the 1990s.

After his attempt to mount a private prosecution of Westpac had been taken over by the Director of Public Prosecutions and no-billed, Makucha was now in trouble with a $12 million loan he had raised for a new billboard site. He had borrowed this money from Brian Merritt, a former printer who had sold his business to Helena Carr in 1993, the year after she missed out on buying Offset Alpine. Merritt had retired to Bowral and now styled himself and his wife Lord and Lady Merritt of Caynham Garden, an English title which the *Sydney Morning Herald* reported was unfamiliar to the folk at Debrett's Peerage. Makucha claimed in a court case that Merritt had paid $100 000 for the title. Merritt's lawyer said his client did not wish to comment on his private life.

After Makucha had obtained a $50 million valuation for his proposed development, his refinancing fell through and Merritt appointed a receiver to Makucha's companies in late 2004, just as Makucha was hit by a series of court orders obtained by trade creditors. It was while representing himself in one of these cases that he had his run-in with magistrate Pat O'Shane and found himself in the holding cells. This was probably his lowest point, though he later rallied. It would take more than this to knock out Paul Makucha. By late 2005 he was slowly pulling his affairs back into shape. In December the Court of Appeal ruled that O'Shane's behaviour had been 'quite inappropriate', that she had denied Makucha procedural fairness and had conducted the hearing in an 'inappropriately adversarial way'. 'The exercise by the magistrate of a little tact would have gone a long way', Justice Hunt found. The judgment that O'Shane awarded against Makucha while he was in the cells was overturned and the contempt charge was dismissed.

Sydney buzzed a little with the news of the great reversals for its favourite sons—for Rivkin, Kennedy, Richardson, Adler, Williams and Rich. The networks that had created and nurtured them were in disarray and for a time the seamy underside of the city's power structure was laid bare. The rivers of influence and power had taken new turnings. Yet not so much had changed. In the end the city shrugged its shoulders and went on with its business, as blasé as ever. The tragedy of Rivkin was that he feared that there was no way back for him, that the shame of his disgrace was overwhelming. But Sydney has never been quite so definitive in its judgments.

In mid-2005, in a year already scored by calumny and grief, the unthinkable finally happened. The blow fell just after two o'clock on Tuesday 5 July as across the nation's business districts the lunch crowd finished their mains, eased back on their napkins and turned their minds to dessert and coffee. In Sydney, Machiavelli had the reassuring buzz of a kitchen at full stretch when James Packer, PBL chief John Alexander and Crown Casino head Rowan Craigie dropped by for a late bite. No fewer than three newspapers reported the next morning on the unhappiness that followed. Machiavelli's front room was full. Every seat was taken and even Giovanna Toppi could not instantaneously conjure a table out of thin air. As her best client kicked his heels, staff were reduced to hustling an unused table along the corridor from the Queensland room at the back and hurriedly setting three new places. The table that the waiters finally produced was entirely serviceable, indistinguishable from any of the other settings in the power circle. But at Machiavelli, Queensland is a state of mind. The unpalatable truth was that Packer's table, that sure bedrock of social certainty for the 1990s, was no more; its patron transformed into a mere diner. It was a triumph for the suits. As if these were not indignities enough, in the hiatus while the maitre d' was whistling up cutlery James wandered across the room to chat idly with a familiar face: a more fortunate diner who had managed to snare his regular table, underneath his own photograph. It was a genial Graham Richardson, tucking into the prawn cutlets.

Something more than a botched lunch date seemed to be at stake here, judging by the speed with which diners gleefully recounted the incident to journalists at the *Australian Financial Review*, the *Sydney Morning Herald* and the *Daily Telegraph*. The seating crisis seemed to signal how much Australia had changed. The last remnants of the Establishment of the 1950s and 1960s based upon Australia's institutions and inherited wealth had slipped away unnoticed some time in the 1990s. The network which had taken its place in the 1970s and 1980s was also failing, the system of social ranking and power which had evolved during those decades slowly unravelling. Something more than bad luck had caught up with our heroes. These men who rode the wave of the deregulation money boom in the 1980s had survived the 1990 recession and were remarkably successful in building new fortunes, but their hold on power was slipping. Even the Packer name, while it continued to hold enormous weight, was not quite the unassailable colossus it once was. The future belonged to the Macquarie Bankers, the Babcock and Browns, the Colonial First Staters and the endless legion of fund managers, McKinsey consultants and financial neo-cons. Their ranks are filled with younger analysts and executives who know nothing of the 1970s and 1980s, for whom the turbulence of those decades was an anachronism, a blip which preceded the second coming of the institutions, along with all of the social and ideological baggage which such a change carries.

This is not merely a change in stakeholders at the big end of town. It is a change again in the way we live. A universe of technological advances and personal diversity is producing, paradoxically, a new conformity. For all its promises, in some respects economic deregulation has delivered a leaner, meaner version of the 1950s. What it shares with the earlier era, along with the new prosperity, is an underlying sense of disquiet. So we return to nervous policing of our borders and fretful subservience to our allies; to a paternalistic government with a natural right to rule which makes comfortable decisions behind closed doors with those whom it favours. How else could a prime minister say, to universal acceptance, that he was only willing to change media ownership laws when the existing power players had decided how to carve up the spoils? How did the aspirations of government come to correspond so overtly with the demands of special interest? But the current era has fewer certainties and less generosity; it is more demanding—and far less forgiving—than the 1950s ever were. How sustainable the new institutions will be remains to be seen. Meanwhile the rearguard action continues.

In May 2005, Sam Chisholm was brought back to pull the strings at Channel Nine for the Packers, fifteen years after his celebrated departure. The wheel had turned full circle. But what did it mean? Is this really the last hurrah for the generation born in the shadow of World War II? Age, if nothing else, has winnowed the ranks of this cohort, as the Baby Boomers thrust impatiently for power. Yet the group which has played such a dominant role in Australia for a quarter of a century is resilient. They are used to the limelight, and frankly they're good at working in it—far better than the new institutional culture that has grown to supplant them. Their passing will leave Australia a drabber place.

Not all is lost. For Sydney loves a show, it craves display and adores a wayward son who has managed to come back into a little money. Rodney Adler judged the town right when he protested that with all his experience he should be going not to gaol but on to the speaking circuit. Richardson always knew that no matter how high the barriers seem for wealth and privilege, there was always room for an ambitious boy from Kogarah with a sense of humour, who knew how to winkle a table out of the most reluctant maitre d'. Thus for a little while longer the pre-Boomers linger at the controls. And so to the ambitious thrusters and earnest aspirers, the consultants, rising stars and brilliant money managers—let all those would-be heirs to the kingdom kick their heels in the anteroom a moment longer, along with the merit-holders and the irredeemably worthy, captains in the company of the great unwashed. Your time is not quite come. Ask not for whom the dinner bell tolls. It does not yet toll for thee.

Postscript

MABEL: Sergeant, approach! Young Frederic was to have led you to death and glory.
POLICE: That is not a pleasant way of putting it.

It's been fifteen months since the publication of *Packer's Lunch* in hardback and some home truths need to be faced . . . beginning with the title. Let's be frank. There's nowhere near enough lunching in the book. Allen & Unwin, in all other matters an excellent publisher, resisted my suggestions to print 'CSIRO' somewhere on the cover. Ditto for any references to 'Health-Giving Sure-Fire Diet for Eternal Youth and Really Excellent Stain Removal'. That was the demographic I was reaching for with the lunch thing, and the text didn't deliver. After that, what chance did the book have? The minimum requirement, it seems to me, for a truly commercial publication would have been to include some notes on food. Perhaps some handy recipes. Kerry Packer liked his food simple, particularly in the high-rollers' room when he was taking some poor hapless casino operator to the cleaners. But the food itself is an untold story. So just how did he like his hot dogs? To a culinary neophyte all tomato sauces may look the same. They probably did for Packer as well. He wasn't one of your namby pamby fellows, slave to delicate nuances. But how did the Big Fella like to apply the red stuff? Did he get the chef to drown the saveloy *in situ* on the bun, or did he prefer holding the sausage under the surface in the sauce bowl until it stopped kicking?

The book answered none of these critical questions. Instead, most of the attention before publication was on how Kerry Packer would feel about being portrayed on the cover as a fish. The decision was made early on that he needed to be a very big fish. And as fish go, seen in a certain light, a rather attractive fish. Admittedly that may be in the eye of the beholder. Perhaps it's a marine organism thing. But at the end of the day a fish is a fish, and not everyone fancies themselves cast in the life aquatic. So it was not without trepidation that the final proofs for *Packer's Lunch* were dispatched to the printers on 22 December 2005. No further changes would be made.

It was a surprise and a grief when, four days later on the evening of 26 December, Kerry Packer died. His timing as always managed to snooker everybody. He had flown back to Sydney from Buenos Aires only days before, still with enough ticker to push through a $780 million bid on Christmas Eve for AFL rights for the Nine Network. It would create an impossible headache for the Seven and Ten networks over the New Year break, as they agonised whether to match it.

James Packer was holidaying in the Maldives on Christmas Day when he received an urgent summons home. 'I called him and he couldn't talk, and then I spoke to Mum and Dad's doctor and it became apparent that he was in real trouble,' James said later. Fifteen years before, James had been the first to gallop over when his father fell unconscious on the polo field. The dash now was far longer, and to no avail. He was there with his sister Gretel and mother Ros when Kerry Packer died on the Monday night.

Cardiologist Ian Bailey suggested the final decision on the timing of his death was made by Packer himself. 'He knew his body better than the doctors did and made his own decisions about treatment,' Bailey told journalists in the days that followed. 'He said he was running out of petrol. He was ready to die . . . he had diabetes, the kidney was rejecting and his heart had gone into failure. He knew he was on borrowed time. He could have opted for more dialysis, but he chose to go quickly and with dignity.'

In the wave of public tributes that followed, Prime Minister John Howard announced a state service at the Opera House for the man he described as 'a generous, very philanthropic person' who was 'always concerned about what was right for Australia'. Rupert Murdoch called Kerry 'a life-long friend, fierce competitor and the most successful businessman of our generation', though he didn't make it to the funeral. It was an early sign that James Packer had better not be looking for any special favours.

The Packers closed ranks to do their grieving in private, leaving Sydney society to do the thing it does best when sensitivity and compassion are called for. It drew up a seat and settled down for some hard gossiping about its late hero. There were so many scurrilous stories to revive, revisit, project, recast, amplify and generally carry on about—in a caring way, intermixed with oblig-atory protestations of grief and regret. It's what Kerry would have wanted them to do.

There were so many Packer stories. But the one the Packers themselves always came back to, the single slur that rankled deeply two decades later, was the Goanna story—those unsubstantiated allegations of money laundering and links to crime that emerged in the Costigan Royal Commission on which Packer was later cleared. It was the single issue that could still cause the family pain. So it was perhaps not so unusual that the most salacious report that emerged in the days that followed put Packer in the centre of another dirty money story. The report became the Great Packer Scam and you had to admire the timing. The story was in cir-culation complete with supporting documentation within three weeks of Packer's death. And so Kerry Packer began his last, and strangest, journey.

A bundle of documents that surfaced in Sydney in mid-January 2006 suggested that Packer had been involved in an international money laundering deal with the Russian mafia. Not just any deal, either. It was the biggest money laundering case that US authorities had ever uncovered, a fabulous money trail that stretched out of Russia and around the world. And it had gone terribly wrong.

The public story began in late August 1998, when the Republic National Bank of New York contacted US authorities with a tip-off. Unusually large amounts of money were being transferred by Russian corporations via Russian banks to an account at the Bank of New York (BNY) in the name of Benex International Company. But when Republic's investigators visited the Benex office address in Queens, New York, there was no one there. The US Treasury alerted the FBI. By October 1998, BNY was cooperating in an FBI surveillance operation that lasted eight months, tracking money flows.

Benex was set up by a Russian émigré, Peter Berlin, but was said to be linked indirectly with Semion Mogilevitch, who was suspected of being a powerful figure in Russian organised crime. Berlin's wife, another émigré called Lucy Edwards (born Ludmila Pritska), was a senior vice president of the Bank of New York based in London, heading the bank's move into Russia. Edwards set up a corporate account for Benex at BNY which allowed her husband to move funds directly from overseas accounts through the bank to other destinations. The money never really made landfall in New York—it was immediately forwarded on to offshore accounts elsewhere around the world, with minimal risk of bank supervision or intervention.

The final destination could be anywhere from Cyprus to Switzerland to the Bahamas. Edwards later testified that Nauru was a favourite spot in the itinerary because the money launderers could tell northern hemisphere regulators that the island was part of Australia (the Russian Central Bank has claimed that 70 billion US dollars was processed through Nauru). At least $US7 billion was sucked out of Russia through three BNY accounts including Benex, and more elsewhere. Edwards and Berlin were convicted of money laundering but were not sentenced. Seven years after it came to light in 2005, Bank of New York paid a $US38 million fine to settle two criminal investigations which included the Benex transfers. Republic National's owner, Lebanese-born billionaire Edmond Safra, died in mysterious circumstances in Monaco in late 1999, several months after Republic National's role in instigating the FBI investigation came to light.

That was the public story—and a thoroughly smelly one it was too. Now someone was trying to put Kerry Packer in the middle of it. Packer, it was claimed, had been one of the steps along the international money trail that the Russian money followed after it passed through Benex. With each step the money transfers had gained more legitimacy until finally the money could be pronounced 'clean'. But in late 1998, as the FBI monitored the suspect money trail, US authorities froze one of the money transfers. It was in an account said to be controlled by Packer, who was now asked to reveal details of where the money had come from. The details provided to US authorities had not been accepted, and the money had never been released. Which meant that Packer owed Russian Mafia figures a quarter of a billion dollars, plus seven years of interest. Now they wanted it back.

It was a fantastic story that would have been dismissed out of hand but for the documents that came with it. They appeared to be copies of Bank of New York files. They began with a letter of confirmation dated 12 November 1988 and signed by Lucy Edwards, addressed to a Mr Vladimir Vinogradov, regarding an international bank transfer #194.58.226.0 of $A248 million. Vinogradov was the head of IncomBank, the beleaguered Russian bank tied to much of the money laundering claims. The Edwards confirmation letter said that the $248 million had been transferred from a Russian entity, Golden Corporation, care of Vinogradov, through InkomBank. It transited through an offshore Benex account 51191055 which appeared to be in Argentina. The ultimate receiver was listed as Crown Group International, care of Kerry Packer, through Bank of New York account 93328295, SWIFT code BONYUN1U and PRT number 843GSG511.

Edwards concluded: 'Please note the transaction was executed according to the regulations of the Bank of New York. If you have any further questions please do not hesitate to contact us.'

A second three-page document dated 17 November 1998 on Bank of New York notepaper was also signed by Edwards and headed, Summary of the Transactions by Golden Corporation: 'Here please find the details of the companies belonging to Golden Group International for the period form 01.01.1998 till 11.17.1998 ... As a matter of privacy of the receiving part we are not able to provide you with any information related to further bank operations done by the receiver.' There followed two pages of names, addresses, transfers numbers and account details for 40 transfers of amounts ranging upwards from $US12 000. The total came to $154.3 million in US dollars plus $287.3 million in Australian dollars (which included the transfer noted in the earlier document). A typical entry read: '194.58.103.0 – 194.58.103.255 (ITC) St Petersburg State Technical University; 28, Grazhdansky pr.; 195220 St Petersburg; RU – USD 59,000.00'.

Another document, dated 11 March 1999, appeared to be a clear forgery. It was addressed to Vinogradov and signed A. Gore, on letterhead for the Russian–US Joint Commission on Economic and Technological Co-Operation, apparently a reference to former US president Al Gore. The letter said, in broken English, under the subtitle 'Bank of New York Accounts':

> We are looking into the recently raised threat from the part of the banking institutions around the world with our big concern. As we have previously discussed this matter we are forwarding our official enquiry into the Federal Bureau of Investigation. We hope that all funds transferred into the 'Crown Group International' will be returned into the primary holder's dispose ...

Finally there was a letter of demand from Inkom Bank, signed Vladimir Vinogradov, addressed to the Bank of New York, attention Lucy Edwards, which threatened legal action if funds transferred from Golden Corporation to the Bank of New York were not returned: 'We express our concern that we no longer having control over the above mentioned account.'

It was worth reading the memos just to savour the atrocious English. Whoever came up with those sentences needed some serious linguistic counselling. But the level of detail was troubling. The timing in mid-1999 coincided with Kerry Packer's abrupt decision to put his English polo fields up for sale, followed by the announcement that they had been bought by the saviour of Chelsea Football Club, Roman Abramovich. A friend I consulted, *Rolling Stone* contributing editor Matt Taibbi, was impressed with the addresses cited in the bank documents. In the mid-1990s he had been living with six penniless foreign students in the nondescript Grazhdansky building at St Petersburg State Technical University, which was cited in the Bank of New York correspondence. He believed only a handful of people would know of the little-used telegraph office in the building.

In the end a simple computer search resolved the mystery. A Ninemsn search on one of the telex codes cited in the documents hit pay dirt. It showed that the transfer numbers cited on the bank documents were actually internet addresses. The list of Golden Corporation companies was simply a cut and paste of a 1999 listing of internet registrations in Russia. That was why the list was so detailed with names, street addresses and telex codes. All the forger had done was insert currency amounts next to each entry and attach some letterhead. The whole series of documents was a fabrication. There was no real evidence of any Packer involvement in money laundering. It was all an elaborate scam, released just at the moment when the Packer family was most vulnerable.

It is perhaps comforting that if someone was going to scam the Packers, they would not do it in anything less than grand style. But why had they gone to such trouble, just to blacken Packer's name? It looked like an offshore production, most likely by someone with knowledge of the Russian émigré scene in New York, but not so much knowledge of English. The appearance of the forgeries coincided with moves by the Packers to become involved in a Russian casino. It seems reasonable to suspect they were related, though sources close to Packer could shed no light on it. There was a suggestion that James Packer had run into problems with his Moscow plans, and he didn't proceed with them. But the problems were unrelated, and it hasn't stopped him fearlessly chasing casino projects around the world, from Macau to New Jersey. That's what appointing a few solid merchant banker types on the board of the family company will do for you.

By June 2007 James had sold 75 per cent of the Nine Network, surrendering management control to private equity—suits with money. After just eighteen months James had given up the role of media mogul. Now he was just another rich guy.

As James assumed the reins of the empire, other characters from *Packer's Lunch* were getting on with their lives, some better than others. In the week of Kerry Packer's death, lawyers in Zurich acting for Trevor Kennedy, Graham Richardson and Rene Rivkin's estates made a tactical mistake. On 9 December 2005 the Swiss Federal Court had confirmed the decision by Zurich District Attorney Ivo Hoppler and the Zurich High Court to release twelve folders of bank records and witness statements to the Australian Securities & Investments Commission. The judgment with the Federal Court's reasons was not published until Wednesday 21 December. It was the final court of appeal for the one-time Offset shareholders. Their lawyers had run out of legal cards to play in Switzerland. But that did not mean that the game was over. According to Shraga Elam, they now made an urgent appeal to the European Court of Human Rights at Strasbourg to stop the release of the documents to Australia.

As Hoppler prepared to dispatch the folders to the Justice Department in Berne, in accordance with the Federal Court's instructions, the lawyers contacted the District Attorney's office in Zurich to raise issues connected with the Federal Court ruling. They made the approach either on the Thursday or Friday before Christmas, or on the next working day, Tuesday 27 December. But whether by carelessness or design, the lawyers did not ask to speak to Hoppler. With no formal contact made, Hoppler proceeded to send the twelve folders to Berne on the 28th with a covering letter. From there they were sent directly on to ASIC in Australia. The Swiss lawyers were still manoeuvring, but the horse had bolted.

'We've got the documents—and they're in German,' ASIC's deputy head of enforcement, Alan Turton, told me in mid-January 2006, with a nice mixture of relief and frustration. ASIC had already put in requests for formal interviews with witnesses in Switzerland. By the end of January, working under the tight time schedule that governs requests for Swiss government assistance, they had forwarded a request for further information. ASIC also filed requests for assistance from the Isle of Man, Jersey and the Bahamas, as they traced the entities behind the Leumi accounts. In early 2007 court challenges were still proceeding. Meanwhile the Australian Tax Office was taking an interest.

ATO officers had interviewed Shraga Elam and me in December 2004 and requested (under threat of a subpoena) copies of the documents I had supplied to ASIC thirteen months before. Three months later on 17 March 2005, the ATO used its powers under the *Tax Administration Act* to question Graham Richardson about the $1.442 million cheque that was paid into Laira's Bank Leumi account as his share of the Offset Alpine payout in September 1997. Rivkin was clearly too ill to be questioned. The following month he and Gayle began divorce proceedings, before his suicide on 1 May. It's not known whether Kennedy was questioned, but it seems likely. The general gist of Richardson's interrogation under oath emerged later in court proceedings. It seems when Richo packed for overseas trips his luggage of choice wasn't Louis Vuitton. At any rate it wasn't his first choice. That was reserved for his briefcase, which was the roomy sort of travelling companion into which you can stuff essential travelling gear—say $50 000 in banknotes—without too much unsightly bulging.

The ATO claimed that Richardson 'intentionally gave false evidence' that day 'by denying any interest in the amount of $1 442 000'. The most damaging issue was his alleged cover-up. In court documents later obtained by Susanna Moran of the *Australian*, the ATO stated:

> Following his failure to disclose the income of $1 442 000 he took extraordinary precautions to prevent the [Taxation] Commissioner from becoming aware of the undisclosed income. These precautions included keeping no records in Australia, maintaining a Swiss bank account under another's name, withdrawing amounts of up to $50 000 at a time, carrying the cash around in a briefcase and spending it while overseas.

It seems Richardson accepted the validity of Bank Leumi records that the ATO had obtained from the *AFR*, which showed him taking money out of the Laira account, but denied Rivkin's claim in his Swiss record of interview that the money belonged to him. 'I don't think that Rene was in full possession of all his faculties back then and that's why he said that,' Richardson told Ros Reines. In his court filings Richardson's lawyers admitted that between November 1997 and April 2001 he had 'obtained from Bank Leumi various amounts of money, and that Bank Leumi provided these amounts, in whole or in part, out of funds that were in the [Laira] bank account, but he denies that [he] made withdrawals from the bank account'. He had obtained up to $288 000 from the account in this way, all of which he had spent overseas. But this was all gifts from his friend Rivkin, 'in appreciation of the close friendship that existed between them'. Richardson had spent seventy-two days on overseas holidays over five years and received gifts of money from Rivkin about six times, he later told Brad Norington at the *Australian*. 'Most people do not have a friend like Rene Rivkin,' he said. 'This is a person who gave away Ferraris and watches. He was different to the rest of the people in the world. Giving mattered to him—it was part of his make-up. He gave the impression he had an awful lot more money than he actually had.' Richardson's lawyers argued the money 'does not represent income of the taxpayer according to ordinary concepts' and did not represent a capital gain for the 1998 tax year. There was no reference in the court documents to Bank Leumi records which showed that his wife Cheryl and his daughter Kate had withdrawn funds from Laira.

Richardson continued to exchange pleasantries with the tax man through 2005. In late October Graham and Cheryl paid $681 000 for a two-bedroom apartment on the Gold Coast. Less than a week later, on 1 November, the ATO hit him with an amended tax bill for $2.3 million. The tax demand related directly to the $1.44 million cheque that was paid into Laira. The ATO had assessed him for $700 000 in back tax from this transaction, then added $1.6 million in penalty taxes for fraud and evasion in covering up the 1997 payment. Richardson stoutly denied any cover-up and lodged an appeal which the ATO disallowed on 23 May 2006. Up to this point there had been no public sign of any problem. That was about to change. In August 2006 Fiona Buffini of the *Australian Financial Review* broke the news that Graham Richardson had launched a Federal Court appeal against a Tax Office decision to amend his tax assessment for his 1998 return.

Richardson had previously told me that he had hired a lawyer in Switzerland 'to get to the bottom of things', in the court appeal against the release of the Leumi records. 'The Swiss courts have not found that I owned a Swiss bank account,' Richardson told me in September 2006. 'What they found was that I had no standing to participate in the proceedings about an account, because I didn't own an account.' The Swiss Federal Court and Zurich High Court judgments were actually a little stronger than this, finding that Richardson was the beneficial owner of the Laira account, but ruling that since he had chosen to hide behind a corporate veil he could not expect to appeal against the release of account records. According to Shraga Elam the EBC files sent to ASIC clearly showed Richardson's and Kennedy's links to Offset Alpine and the Zurich High Court believed the files would prove a range of other crimes by various parties, including market manipulation.

Three days after we spoke, Richardson called briefly once more, in no mood for chit chat. 'Is that your photographer outside my garage?' he asked brusquely. It wasn't, but the obvious suspects were the *Australian* or the *Daily Telegraph*. 'Right, I'll sort them out,' he said, and rang off. The following day the *Australian* ran Richo's picture with a story quoting unnamed sources criticising the basis of the ATO's case. The ATO was relying on the documents it had obtained from the *AFR*, which were largely inadmissible in Australian courts, the source said. The ATO's position was that under the *Tax Administration Act*, the burden of proving that the assessment was excessive fell on the person appealing against the decision. In early 2007 ATO officers working with the Australian Government Solicitor interviewed me again as well as Rosemarie Graffagnini about our trip to Zurich in October 2003 and the steps we took to verify the documents that Shraga had obtained. A government lawyer subsequently flew to Switzerland for interviews. Richardson had also appealed against an alternative assessment for the 1995–96 year, that found he had earned the $1.44 million profit on sale of shares when the Australian Federal Court sold the unidentified Leumi and EBC Zurich shareholding into a takeover bid. For Richardson, the sting in this case was that it might not end just with a tax penalty. Where tax fraud or evasion is proven, the Taxation Commissioner can refer the matter to the Director of Public Prosecutions.

Life went on. In March 2007 Richardson picked up a $50 000 defamation settlement from Fairfax Media over an article that linked him with the bashing of state Labor member Peter Baldwin a quarter of a century before. No doubt the ATO was delighted to see him come into a little money. The lobbying work was still lucrative and he had retained most of his friends. In the NSW state election in April 2007 Liberal Opposition Leader Peter Debnam called Richardson one of 'six people who essentially run NSW', a claim that Richardson called bizarre. His former staffer, Premier Morris Iemma, concurred. What was he thinking? Victorian Premier Steve Bracks was forced to take a principled stand after some unfortunate criticism directed at meetings that one of his ministers had held with Richardson ahead of a favourable planning decision for the Mirvac property group. Bracks was having none of this sort of witchhunt, which he called 'the new McCarthyism'.

In the confused world of Richardson's affairs, at least some clarity was emerging to dispel his confusion about his lunching partner, back on that fateful day of 7 June 1995 when Caroline Byrne died. When Richardson spoke to detectives from Taskforce Irondale in 2000, he said his diary showed he had lunch that day with the head of Canterbury Bulldogs, Peter Moore, at the Hilton Hotel's San Francisco Grill, but he himself couldn't recall whether he was there, or being driven to lunch with Rene Rivkin by his driver Gordon Wood. Soon after *Packer's Lunch* was published I was contacted by a reader in a North Sydney nursing home who recalled being at the San Francisco Grill with her husband that day. She remembered the date because the lunch was a celebration for her birthday, and both she and her husband had noticed the odd pairing at a nearby table. There was Peter Moore, whose club had spearheaded the Super League breakaway from the

Australian Rugby League, talking to one of the ARL's chief negotiators, Graham Richardson. They were both so struck by this that they called a *Sunday Telegraph* journalist, Phil Rothfield, to tell him. Rothfield reported the lunch in his 'What's the Buzz' column the following Sunday in a story titled, 'Super deal in Moore's lunch pack'. Rothfield had called Moore to confirm the lunch and the date. 'Graham actually phoned and invited me,' Moore told Rothfield. 'We had a really good chat for a couple of hours.' The story had lain in the *Sunday Telegraph* archive for eleven years. No one at News Limited had recalled the story or looked for it after Richardson's lunch companion became an issue at Caroline's inquest in 1998, or during the repeated waves of press coverage about her death in the years that followed. Apparently even Richo had forgotten about it.

Trevor Kennedy meanwhile had dropped out of view. After all those headlines he seemed to like it that way. On the basis of Richardson's $2.3 million tax assessment, if the ATO believed that Kennedy received 12 per cent of the Offset Alpine proceeds compared to Richardson's 7 per cent, then Kennedy could be facing a $4 million tax bill. But there was no sign of any court action connected with this. Rene Rivkin's estate had been hit by a tax bill for $29 million as an amendment to his 1998 return. On 6 November 2006 his executors, Gayle and son Damien, asked the courts to appoint insolvency accountant Anthony Warner of CRS Warner as liquidator to the estate. Warner was one of the only liquidators in Sydney who didn't know Rivkin. Rene's estate had assets of $1.1 million and liabilities of $39 million. Gayle Rivkin was registered as an unpaid creditor who had loaned Rene $2.4 million.

It wasn't clear where all the money had gone. Rivkin's family had been selling property, boats and cars since 2003, raising some $27 million. This included the heavily mortgaged family home, Craig-y-mor, that went for $16.5 million. Rivkin's boat, *Dajosha-dita*, sold for $5.7 million, but the owner was a company in the

British Virgin Islands. The estate had no record of Rivkin having received any of the boat's sale proceeds. While Rivkin in the end left his heirs nothing in his bankrupt estate, the family was not exactly penniless. In June and July 2004 and February 2005, Gayle and the children bought a townhouse and five apartments for a total $6.7 million. Rivkin's wife, children and business associates were due to be questioned in a liquidator's hearing in June 2007 as Warner sought to trace the flow of funds in Rivkin's world.

The 2006 year brought some hope of resolution for Tony Byrne in his quest to discover what happened to his daughter. Just before 9 a.m. on Monday 3 April, British police knocked on the door of Gordon Wood's London apartment with an arrest warrant for Caroline Byrne's murder. After eleven years of sporadic investigations and nearly two years of toing and froing between NSW police and the Director of Public Prosecutions office, the Australian government had filed an extradition request with Britain. Wood, who was working as a consultant to a chain of gyms, was not home when the Scotland Yard detectives knocked on his door. He did not return until nearly eight hours later, after a weekend skiing in the French Alps. Wood did not oppose extradition and Inspector Paul Jacob and Constable Paul Quigg flew to London a month later to escort him home. In Sydney he was released on bail and was due to face a committal hearing in late 2007.

Rodney Adler's fortunes seemed on the mend. He was due to be released from prison on 13 October 2007 after serving two and a half years on dishonesty charges, touring the state's correctional facilities, from Long Bay to Kirkconnell state prison farm, to Bathurst Jail and finally Kempsey. He had begun a Bachelor of Arts correspondence course through Charles Sturt University. One of the first subjects he studied was ethics. Besides his family, one of his regular visitors was Jodee Rich, who no doubt had much to say about his own civil trial for $92 million in damages relating to the One.Tel collapse. A judgment on that case seemed unlikely until late 2007, with further appeals almost inevitable.

In Zurich, Shraga Elam became a little more security conscious after he received death threats in November 2006, linked to his work as a peace activist in Israel. Shraga was quite sanguine. He told me police regularly patrolled past the front of his apartment building because it was next to one of Zurich's best known spots for drug deals. Meanwhile he was pursuing some interesting new leads about Australian investors in Switzerland.

Paul Makucha was back in the pink, his financial worries once more subsiding. Pat O'Shane faced a judicial inquiry which vindicated her treatment of him. Makucha called me in late 2006 to ask if it was a good idea to move back into the Toaster, just to show them all that he was a survivor. I told him I thought life was too short. If he was getting out of the Shithouse Motel, he might as well find a place that he actually enjoyed. Perhaps with indoor plumbing. He seemed inclined to agree.

The biggest news in Lang Walker's household was that he sold the jet. By early 2007 the Falcon F20 with the VH-LAW registration was owned by a company linked to Paul Little, the head of Toll Holdings. One can only wonder at how Lang broke the news to Mrs Walker. Then again, he had just raised $1.125 billion selling off Walker Corporation so maybe he managed to cushion the blow.

In the last half of 2006 Walker unwound the British Virgin Islands financing for Walker Corporation, repaying the $509 million in loans and preference shares held by Athenaeum Investments. By the time he put Walker Corp up for sale in March 2007 there was no sign it had any connection with anything so unfashionable as tax havens. Like any major company, Walker Corporation attracted a periodic review by the Australian Taxation Office. In May 2006 eleven Walker companies filed challenges in the Administrative Appeals Tribunal to tax assessments. It's not known how large these assessments were and there is nothing to link them with the sale of the group. Regardless of the cause, Walker was not going to be having any trouble paying tax bills after the sale. Walker Corp's lobbyist, Graham Richardson made the transition seamlessly to acting for one of the buyers, Girvan Corporation. Meanwhile Walker's case for compensation for Ballast Point continued to bounce back and forth between the courts.

Walker appears to have retained some of his links to Europe, including a Luxembourg investment with Bob Cowper, the former Australian Test cricketer and Elders executive. Since 2003, Walker and his offsider Mark Wilkinson have been directors of PASE Private Equity Holdings SA, a *societe anonyme* on the Luxembourg register, together with Cowper and another former Elders exec, Bill Payne. Cowper, whose 307 runs against England in 1966 remains the highest score ever made at the Melbourne Cricket Ground, was instrumental in the 1983 Elders–Henry Jones IXL merger before he moved to Monaco. These days Cowper controls the highly respected Pyrford International Plc, which was formed in 1991 to take over the business of Elders Investment Management, which had run the super funds of the Elder group. Former Elders exec Ken Jarrett claimed in court cases in the 1990s that Cowper was one of the mystery investors who made a fortune from a line of Elders bonds that were issued in Switzerland and held through Monaco. Cowper and the others named by Jarrett denied this.

In Sydney, Caterina Tarchi at Machiavelli grew tired of a decade of boring political leaders and dumped politicians' portraits from the walls of the restaurant in favour of photographs of leading business figures, most of them close to the Packer family. The restaurant was the scene of the *Bulletin*'s Great Australian awards in June 2006, which honoured Rupert Murdoch as the greatest Australian of them all . . . only to see him launch a ferocious campaign in his newspapers. It began with scathing coverage of Nine chief Eddie McGuire's supposed threat to 'bone' Nine presenter Jessica Rowe, that quickly evolved into a fierce attack on James Packer—'Jamie in short pants', as the *Daily Telegraph* put it on its front page.

Despite the drama, it seemed a desperate gambit for a restaurant named after the author of *The Prince* to drop its links with politics. But Tarchi said she would reconsider the decision next year, if politics grew more exciting. That seemed to depend on whether Kevin Rudd managed to snatch government from John Howard. The issues were hardly unfamiliar. La Trobe University professor of politics Judith Brett writing in *The Monthly* in March 2007 put Howard on the wrong side of a shift from 'age to youth, from fear to hope and from private withdrawal to public engagement'.

She was describing the gathering pace of generational transfer, but there were more concrete examples of the new fault-lines of power. The speed of Sam Chisholm's exit from Nine after Kerry Packer's death was another, punctuated by the systematic ejection of his former protégés in the months that followed, which is how Eddie McGuire's boning fiasco began. By mid-2007 James Packer had sold 75 per cent of the Nine Network to a private equity group. But the move in power lines was being played out on a wider scale, a grander version of Life After Kerry.

I was still thinking about Packer's legacy when I attended his state service at the Sydney Opera House in February 2006. The media took the front seats of the gallery. Directly below me I could see Graham Richardson sitting in the back row of the main hall. Trevor Kennedy was further along from Richo. The right side of the hall, filled with business associates, family and friends, was packed. Every seat was filled. There was genuine grief here, but something more as well. The succession was still up in the air. The old game of Sticking Close to James was now being replayed with real money.

On the left side of the Opera House the picture was quite different. In the banks of seats reserved for politicians there were gaps. It seemed an effort had been made to bunch those attending together, but it left a solid rank of about twenty empty seats towards the rear, each of them representing a politician who had decided they didn't need to attend. They would never have dreamed of not coming to his funeral while he was alive. Packer would have dealt with such impertinence directly. The worry was that even now, he would somehow manage to show his displeasure. But they were prepared to risk it. They didn't come to his state service because they didn't have to.

It was the same issue with the forged Bank of New York documents. Somebody did it because they could. A wider value system was up for renegotiation. At the start of this story, the whole saga of Rene Rivkin and the amigos' Swiss bank accounts had come to light because someone had decided the three had become irrelevant. They were no longer players. Such casual dismissals are the covert symbols and signs that mark the passing of power.

Alan Jones, that flag-bearer for the pre-Boomers, was master of ceremonies for Packer's service. Cricketers were plentiful, extolling Kerry's largesse in saving the game. Rugby league players were in shorter supply. Much was said of Kerry Packer's generosity and secret philanthropy, which was certainly true, if a little under-explored. They might have looked a little further for examples. The tribute to Kerry which ran on Nine the night before told the story of Packer paying for a boy in a wheelchair to go to Disneyland with his family. Jones thought so much of the story that he repeated it in his valediction. And when John Howard rose to say a few words, he found himself talking about being on a plane to Los Angeles with a boy in a wheelchair. He was on his way to Disneyland.

James Packer spoke briefly and creditably. His sister Gretel took no part but asked Russell Crowe to speak for her. He made his way to the rostrum to recite Rudyard Kipling's poem 'If'. It was arguably the emotional heart of the service, somewhere between Alan Jones' glib soliloquies about Kerry Packer the battler's friend who never believed in handouts from government, and the massed private-school choirs singing 'C'mon Aussie Come On'. Crowe's measured tones stirred more authentic cadences of earlier times, older voices.

Just over a week before the Packer service in February 2006, the Melbourne business world had gathered at St John's Anglican Church in Toorak to mourn the passing of that son of the Establishment, Ossie Porter, aged seventy-two. John Barrie Porter, the legendary stockbroker who in his heyday had one of the biggest private client lists in the country, drew a crowd of more than 600 mourners from all over the world to his funeral. One had come from as far as Monaco. Bob Cowper, who worked with Porter at broking house Guest and Bells in the 1970s when Rene Rivkin was still just a passing shower, walked to the front to give his own tribute. Cowper recited 'If'.

> *If you can keep your head when all about you*
> *Are losing theirs and blaming it on you*

For moments in the crowded Opera House hall the two voices, Crowe's and Cowper's, in funeral services days apart, seemed to march together across the gulf in lock step: the deep rolling authority of the actor who won an Oscar for *Gladiator*, mixing with the older, world-weary tones of the maestro of cross-border currency flows.

> *If you can make one heap of all your winnings*
> *And risk it all on one turn of pitch-and-toss,*

They were celebrating, in their different ways, a nineteenth-century ideal of masculinity and empire. It was an ideal that had also proved serviceable in covering a wide landscape peopled by more shabby incarnations.

> *Yours is the Earth and everything that's in it,*
> *And—which is more—you'll be a Man, my son!*

It seemed, for a sentimental moment, almost touching. Thankfully Alan Jones was there to tidy things up and set the right tone. *Sic transit gloria*. Or as Horace would have put it if he had Google Translator handy, 'There goes the Parrot'. Rudyard Kipling and his ideals were a product of his time. But they were not the only product. He shared his age with another acute observer of the nouveau riche, who fomented his own peculiar ideas of propriety and honour in the guise of light opera; who admired the fabric that makes the very model of the modern chief executive, yet realised that some social divisions should not be bridged, some worlds should never meet. He lived at the heart of the Establishment and asked, who needs it? Sometimes even pirates must draw the line.

> *Pirate King: No, Frederic, it cannot be. I don't think much of our profession, but, contrasted with respectability, it is comparatively honest.*

Index